Schizophrenia

MARYELLEN WALSH

SCHIZO-PHRENIA

Straight Talk for Family and Friends

WILLIAM MORROW AND COMPANY, INC.
NEW YORK

The author gratefully acknowledges Harper & Row Publishers, Inc., for permission to quote from *Surviving Schizophrenia* by Fuller Torrey, copyright © 1983.

Library of Congress Cataloging in Publication Data

Walsh, Maryellen.
Schizophrenia: straight talk for families and friends.

Bibliography: p.
Includes index.
1. Schizophrenia. 2. Schizophrenics—Family relationships. I. Title.
RC514.W23 1985 616.89'82 84-20558
ISBN 0-688-04178-7

Printed in the United States of America

First Edition

1 2 3 4 5 6 7 8 9 10

BOOK DESIGN BY VICTORIA HARTMAN

To my mother and stepfather . . .
For over forty years of love

A portion of the proceeds from this book will be directed to schizophrenia research.

Foreword

"God must have been having a bad day," a father recently wrote me, "when He allowed schizophrenia to come into existence." It is a sentiment shared by most mothers and fathers who have faced the specter of this disease. An ordeal of greater magnitude than most people ever must face, schizophrenia challenges not only parents' equilibrium, economics, and ingenuity, as do many chronic illnesses, but their psychological and theological core as well. Schizophrenia, it may be said, is a job for Job.

Why is this so? Imagine, for a moment, that you have just spent seventeen (or fourteen or twenty-three) years raising your child. He or she is bright, attractive, engaging, and promising, an offspring to make you proud and to assuage the pains and inconveniences of child-raising. Then, in a matter of a few weeks or months, the personality of your child changes. He or she withdraws, develops strange ideas, begins responding to voices and behaving in a bizarre manner. Slowly the truth seeps out. Your child has a brain disease which will require hospitalization, perhaps for many months. Recovery may be slow or perhaps may not occur at all; chances that he or she will be at least partially dependent on you are high. Your family understands little; your friends even less. Nobody seems to know what causes it, and the doctors you turn to all give you different answers and contradictory advice. Some of them even tell you that you *caused* the disease. Your young adult, so recently independent and promising, has been changed back into a child about whom you must worry—victimization; unpredictable behavior; occasionally violence or even suicide. It is like some terrible game of Chance in which you were almost around the board, only to draw a card sending you back to the starting line again.

Maryellen Walsh has captured the feelings of being such a parent. She writes with her brain and with her heart, but also with her soul. It is a soul which has been seared with the flames of schizophrenia, and other parents similarly affected will find both familiarity and comfort in her ordeal. She has survived by mixing compassion and humor in equal parts, an effective anodyne. She has also survived by fighting back, refusing to accept the ignorance of the psychiatric profession or the public, working for better research and better treatment. It is a model worthy of emulation.

When the history of schizophrenia is finally written, after its component brain diseases have been sorted out and successfully treated, there will be a chapter on heroes. Foremost will be the patients themselves who suffered the terrible ordeal, trying to sort out thoughts and feelings amidst their incredible cerebral cacophony of dopamine dysfunction. Just behind them, however, will come the families who had to pick up shattered dreams and carry on bravely. In twentieth-century literature there will be few groups who will match the courage and perseverance of these.

—E. Fuller Torrey, M.D.
Clinical and research psychiatrist
Washington, D.C.

Acknowledgments

Deepest thanks to the following people who contributed professionally or personally to this book. All helped, one way or another, but none should be held accountable for the views expressed here.

To Gene Antisdel, who wouldn't let me not write this book; Philip Berger, M.D.; Tom and Maureen Blakeslee; Robert Capps; Charles Comfort, M.D.; Francine Cournos, M.D.; Hal Crow; Paul Ehrlich; Dick and Susan Foster; Doug, Geoff, Lucy, and Steve Hessel; Beatrice Hofman Hessel; John and Aileen Hessel; Tony and Fran Hoffman; Ted Hutchinson; Sumner Kalman, M.D.; Lorrin Koran, M.D.; Donald Lunde, M.D.; Eve Oliphant; Paul Patton; Frank Pritchard, M.D.; Louis Santoro; Bernie Smith; Allene Soshea; Karen Stone; Helen Teisher; E. Fuller Torrey, M.D.; Rick Van Rheenen, M.D.; Pat Williams; and the people coast to coast who trusted a stranger with their stories. Many thanks to my editor, Nicholas Bakalar, and my agent, Maryanne Cantrell-Colas. I am also indebted to my clients; they stuck with me while I took time off from their business to attend to my own. I am grateful also to Larry Lansburgh, who probably learned more about schizophrenia than he ever wanted to.

Thanks to Robert Taylor, M.D., consulting psychiatrist to the California Department of Mental Health and clinical faculty member at Stanford University Medical Center, who kept a sharp eye on the treatment chapter.

Contents

Introduction

I learned about families and schizophrenia the hard way. I lived it. I witnessed the mental illness of two people I love, one of them my son. That's what it takes to get the gut involved enough to write a book: loving two schizophrenics.

I hate, too. I loathe schizophrenia with every cubic inch of my being. I hate it for what it has done to people I love, for what it has done to the many people who have shared their stories with me, for what it does to me. But to hate is to go nowhere, to do nothing. And so this book. It is my way of refusing to take it lying down. As a researcher and writer I had a way to fight back.

I make my living writing scripts and articles about every subject under the sun. It could be the electromagnetic characteristics of a disk drive or the business plan of a Fortune 500 company. Not surprisingly I write on medical topics, too, everything from contraceptives to migraine medications; I've ghostwritten medical journal articles for physicians.

In the work I do, my previous experience with the subject doesn't matter. In fact, large corporations pay me for being the outsider whose mission it is to find the forest through the trees. I often must look at my subject from scratch. And that is what I've attempted to do here: to look at schizophrenia from scratch. I wanted to offer clear information and a fresh viewpoint, a view independent of the narrow professional alliances that can propel an investigator to predestined conclusions.

Much writing about schizophrenia has been dependent on which denomination of psychiatric thought the writer belonged to, which orthodoxy he or she accepted. Affiliations within the field are strong; one belongs to schools, like fish. There are psychodynamic fish, a bottom fish that mucks about in a tangle of ids. There are biochemical fish, which swim in the laboratory among neurotransmitters. And there are inquisitor fish nosing for signs of decay in the family of the schizophrenic. You'll find out about all of them in this book.

A scan of the detailed table of contents should get you to the part you're most interested in, if you're not with us for the whole trip. The notes and sources for each chapter are at the back of the book.

About confidentiality: To protect those who are uncomfortable making their lives and thoughts public, I have changed the names and hometowns of the hundred or so who talked to me or answered my questionnaire. However, the names and professional affiliation of the experts in this book are real.

It is also very important to know that this is not a book of medical advice. Though information about symptoms, for instance, is given as it is presented by the American Psychiatric Association, the reader should not use the text to try and diagnose schizophrenia. The disorder has many faces, can be confused with other disorders, and should be diagnosed only by highly qualified professionals.

Similarly the reader should not attempt to treat the disease. Medical help is needed. Call the nearest medical school, or ask the family doctor. Call the closest affiliate of the National Alliance for the Mentally Ill. Their members have had much experience with the psychiatrists in the area. (See the Appendix for addresses.)

I hope this book will help you with your own situation. The information here comes from many families that provided me with insights, tips, and suggestions which I pass on.

Chapters One through Four cover the basics about the disorder, what it is and who gets it. Chapters Five, Six, and Seven cover things every family needs to know about treatment and obstacles to treatment, about sensible living arrangements, rehabilitation, emotional survival, and practical solutions to living with "crazy" behavior. Chapter Eight focuses on the startling story of how the blame for schizophrenia was placed on parents. In Chapter Nine you'll find tips on how to organize for change. If you love someone mentally ill who does not have schizophrenia, but perhaps an affective disorder instead, you should still find much to help you here.

Finally, I should note that I use the noun *schizophrenic* with reluctance. It seems insensitive to label a person by the disorder he or she suffers from. I use the word only because it is less cumbersome than *person with schizophrenia.*

If you find just one memorable, or useful, or new thing here, I am the happiest of writers. By the time you finish the book, you will know you are not alone. There are millions of us, and as you will learn, there is much we can do to ensure that we will be the last generation of humans to suffer from schizophrenia.

CHAPTER

1

Schizophrenia: What It Means to the Family

A Book for and About the Families of Schizophrenics

Each person with schizophrenia has a family: a mother, a father, perhaps a spouse, brother, sister, or child. Schizophrenia ransacks their lives with a ferocity unimagined outside the family circle. Because they love someone whose illness shows itself not as a tumor, not as a heart gone bad or blood sugar gone wrong, but as bizarre and unpredictable behavior, these families are robbed of peace. They are robbed of peace and of the humblest but most necessary of pleasures: something to look forward to.

The families of the mentally ill need help, for they have had little to look forward to. First, they need understanding because the misconceptions about them are tremendous. That's one reason this book was written: to present a real picture of what it means to live with chronic, long-term schizophrenia, of what it means to try to deal sensibly, firmly, lovingly, with a situation that makes no sense, is changeable and cruel. That is some task, especially since negative myths have isolated these families from most forms of help, leaving them to trudge alone through the strange landscape of mental illness.

The most lacerating of the myths about the relatives of schizophrenics, the most isolating, is that mothers and fathers cause the disease. The parents, according to old psychiatric lore, induce psychosis in their offspring. Tens of millions of parents the world over take this charge very personally. They mind being called monsters that generate the mental illness of their own children. It's as if somebody has accused them of torturing a son or daughter not quite to death, for that's what severe, chronic schizophrenia often is: being tortured not quite to death by your own thoughts, perceptions, feelings. Parents of the mentally ill are mad, to be sure—not mad/psychotic, as some mental health professionals have charged, but mad/angry, mightily stung at being labeled the bad guys of the schizophrenia story.

That's another reason for this book: to take a look at where and why parent hating started. To my knowledge, this is the first time the origins and validity of the parent as monster theories have been examined by one of the accused. I hope readers will find that chapter illuminating. For those in the families, it may be the first time they have ever had a chance to look at the evidence on which they have been judged.

There is a third reason for this book: most relatives' utter and complete ignorance about schizophrenia. Nothing in the lives of these families has prepared them to cope with the illness. There has been almost no information—not on TV, not in the schools, not in the bookstores, and amazingly, not in the offices of mental health professionals. This vital group—doctors, nurses, social workers—has not communicated with the families. Often they will not even tell a family what the diagnosis is, much less any details about the disease, its treatment and outcome.

There is, in short, an information desert out there. I have never seen any kind of pamphlet about schizophrenia, not one, in any doctor's office, in any clinic, in any halfway house. There are no brochures in medical waiting rooms listing the warning signs of schizophrenia. (As a comparison, who of us has not seen the warning signs of cancer all neatly outlined as part of a nationwide educational program?)

Most mental health education is aimed at "wellness," at handling the normal problems of living. Most encyclopedias, the home's basic information source, are hopelessly out of date, suggesting that schizophrenia is a "functional" (learned) disorder, rather than a biological one. The media put forth stereotypes instead of truth.

So the families of the mentally ill are desperate for facts. Some relatives, despairing of help from any outside source, have become schizophrenia scholars, homegrown students of psychiatry. The richness of knowledge among certain parents is astounding. One mother told me, "I have my Ph.D. in schizophrenia."

Still, most families live in ignorance about the disease. For instance, many do not know even these basic facts:

- Schizophrenia is a disorder of the brain, perhaps a malfunction of chemicals known as neurotransmitters.
- The malfunction results in brain activity that is quite simply out of kilter. Perceptions, feelings, thoughts, the brain's main line of work, are off base. The result? Weird ideas, emotions, behaviors.
- Roughly one third of schizophrenics recover, one third are sick off and on, and one third stay chronically ill. Nobody knows why.
- A tendency to schizophrenia is inherited, but it is only a predisposition. Something has to happen to kick it off. Nobody knows what.
- Chronic schizophrenia is not now curable, but like diabetes, it can be controlled by medication in some people.

To get these simple basic facts in the past would have taken an industrious family months of detective work. This is no exaggeration; the information desert was that complete. Not having access to information, families had to feel their way, cross their fingers, and, as many told me, "just do the best we could." Often "the best they could" didn't seem to be enough, at least not for families dealing with the most puzzling, upsetting, and unpredictable of illnesses. All these families had as a guide were the myths our culture had handed them: Schizophrenia means a split personality; schizophrenics are murderous maniacs; families cause schizophrenia. To send families out to deal with the everyday intricacies of mental health care armed only with these notions was like sending a flight crew on a moon mission armed with the knowledge that the moon is made of green cheese.

To understand what the information gap has meant to families, imagine trying to deal with a mentally ill son when all you know about mental illness is what you learned from the movie *Psycho*. The Alfred Hitchcock School of Psychiatry is all most of us had, and there we learned to be afraid of the mentally ill and never, never to take showers alone.

Families deserve better education than what's given out by Hollywood. They need to know how to navigate through schizophrenia, what to do, how to hold up, and how to hold out. They need excellent and up-to-date information because millions of them, more than ever before, now care for their sick sons and daughters.

Families also need to know about each other. Amazingly they don't, for each family has lived imprisoned in house-size cubes of silence. Information about others' trials with schizophrenia didn't flow in, and information about their own predicament didn't flow out. All people in the same boat and none of them even knew the passenger list, let alone where they were going or why they were on the trip.

It's time now for the families to meet each other and for the world to meet them—to meet *us*.

> People don't know diddly-squat about the families of schizophrenics.
>
> —Arizona mother

> I feel uncomfortable talking about my daughter's illness with anybody outside the family. The only ones who understand us are other families with someone mentally ill.
>
> —California father

> After I get to know people a little, I tell them I have a son who is mentally ill. If they can't accept this, they can't accept me, I think.
>
> —Oregon mother

I never discuss our family situation with anyone.
—Tennessee mother

We were closet parents for years.
—New York father

I tell people he's a traveling musician.
—Illinois mother

I lie if I have to.
—South Carolina sister

The Big Secret

Forty million families around the world know what it means to love a relative with schizophrenia.

That's 40 million families, not people. If each family consists of 4 members, a conservative guess, there are 160 million people caught up in the biological disaster known as schizophrenia. That's as many people as live in Great Britain, Canada, Australia, Israel, Norway, Sweden, Denmark, Ireland, Greece, Laos, Ecuador, Ghana, and Angola. That many people, thirteen countries' worth, must struggle with the most widespread brain disorder on the face of the planet.

So where are they? Where are the 160 million? One would expect to run into them everywhere.

They are hidden . . . hidden in the world's largest closet.

Few know their stories. As relatives of the mentally ill they have learned the self-protective value of secrecy. The world has taught them not to tell because the world has judged them severely. For these families to disclose what is happening to them, to hint at the drama of mental illness, to touch on the stale responsibilities of caring for a chronically ill relative is dangerous, very dangerous.

Like the relatives above, families often don't tell anybody. They try to "pass" in the outside world. Telling the truth, they think, will earn them scorn, blame, even retaliation. One mother told me she wouldn't dream of saying anything to anyone about her schizophrenic son; she was sure anyone who found out wouldn't hire her. Most of the hundred families I heard from for this book told me they never mention the illness unless they were pressed, unless someone "had to know." They were afraid of losing friends, afraid of increasing their social isolation, afraid of making an already difficult life worse.

Because the silent millions have not spoken out, saying who they are and what they feel, a stereotype has crept in, a nasty cartoon that masquerades as reality. Like all stereotypes, this one is viciously simple. It runs this way:

> "Crazy people are weird. They are weird because they come from weird families. Do not hang around with any of them because the weirdness might rub off."

So, believing this stereotype, thinking schizophrenia is catching, people judge, condemn, and avoid the families of the mentally ill. Reacting in turn to the social censure, families of the mentally ill protect themselves by secrecy, and the cycle goes on and on. Silence, stereotype, misconception. Silence, stereotype, misconception.

It is now time to stop the cycle. It is now time to say who these families are and what their lives are like, for the negative image of the stereotype undermines public support of schizophrenia research and treatment projects. The cartoon of "weird" families needs to be replaced by the truth—by 160 million truths.

Everyfamily's Story

The best way to begin is to tell what it is like to live with schizophrenia. Though there are millions of people, each with a personal story, it's possible to see a pattern in their lives. The pattern is not the one of the stereotype. It is Everyfamily's story, and though it has been a grim story, there is, for the first time, substantial hope that we may be the last generation to live out stories like this.

* * *

Once upon a time there was a family with a mother, father, two boys, and a girl. They had a pretty good life, not perfect, mind you, for they were human and as full of glitches and goofs as anybody else on the planet. But they had what most people would recognize as a pretty nice time together. The mother and father got on well and fought only about the joint checking account and whose family they would visit over the holidays. The kids' work at school ranged from OK to very good, depending on the kid, the grade, and who had been up too late watching sitcoms the night before.

Then things began to change, but what happened was so subtle, so much the passing of a silent shadow that the family did not know their lives would never again be the same.

One of the sons was named Mike. Mike did just fine until he was around fifteen years old, a fact which made him like most young people starting a midteen crisis. Mike began staying in his room. His marks went down. The family figured he needed some "space" and was doing some adolescent rebelling. They gave him more privacy, a talking-to about his marks and decided not to worry, at least not very much.

Then Mike began not sleeping at night. He roamed the house instead. He began saying that he thought his algebra teacher had a grudge against him. Mike's mother and father asked if anything was wrong. He said no. They said maybe he would like to talk with them or with a counselor. Mike said no and went to his room. He went to his room a lot in those years.

Mike left for college. His parents sensed something was still wrong but hoped he would grow out of it, get over it, do whatever it is that helps most of us overcome the troubles of growing up. But Mike acted strangely when he came home for Thanksgiving of his freshman year. He hardly left his room. He avoided his family. He avoided his old high school buddies. He didn't smile. His mother wondered if he was on drugs and thought he should see the college psychologist. His father thought he needed a man-to-man talk. His brother and sister thought he acted like a jerk.

Mike *was* acting like a jerk, and for good reason. He was on the long, slow glide path into an illness known as chronic schizophrenia. The family was to learn later that this long, slow glide path is known as insidious onset, one of several ways that schizophrenia can strike.

Mike's onset didn't remain slow. By Christmas vacation his life had really hit the fan. He wasn't on the plane when his family went to meet him at the airport. His phone was disconnected. After two days of silence Mike called. He told his mother he was fine . . . great, really. He couldn't wait to show the family his new powers. He could throw his thoughts for miles around. He had absolute ESP. A witch was hexing him, to be sure, but with his new powers he could handle witches.

At the other end of the phone his mother knew without a doubt that Mike had flipped. No one else in the family believed her. They didn't believe her until they heard for themselves about the witches when Mike got home. The witches convinced them.

The father and mother sat and stared at each other. They could not believe that this was happening to Mike, to them. Their kid was acting really—the word did not come easily—really . . . crazy. Craziness was something that happened to other people, to awful people, to families that were abnormal, to families that treated their kids badly. It couldn't happen to them. Except that it was happening to them, in a nightmare they couldn't wake up from.

Maybe they had made a mistake in thinking he was mentally ill. After all, who among them knew anything at all about such things? They reconsidered the evidence. Was Mike really crazy? There was no getting around it. He was.

The next day he showed them card tricks to prove his great new powers of ESP. "See," he said, "I can tell what card you have in your hand." He called every single card wrong. Still, he insisted his ESP was invincible.

The family told Mike gently that he needed help. He said he didn't. They said he did. It was a horrible Christmas. His brother and sister wouldn't let their friends come to the house.

During the holiday vacation Mike stayed up all night rattling dishes in the kitchen, running the water in the bathroom while he talked and laughed to himself. He piled big stacks of pots and pans on his windowsills so if some unnamed awfulness tried to get into his room, he would hear. He didn't want to listen to TV because the witches sent poison rays into the house that way.

Everyfamily was frantic. They couldn't sleep. They were scared. They were worried. Nothing in their lives had prepared them for this. They didn't even know the name of the problem. They just knew they had one.

The mother called a psychiatrist, and he told her to have Mike come in right away. At the table the father once again told Mike he needed to get help. Mike said he didn't.

Mike's brother, hearing the conversation, said, "Yes, you do, you're crazy."

Mike ran up the stairs to his room. His brother ran after him. His brother shouted, "Mike, you're nuts. You've got to go to the hospital."

Mike yelled that nobody or nothing was going to take him to a hospital. Then, feeling scared, acting cornered, Mike threw a lamp at his brother. He missed, but the mother called the police because she too was scared and because she sensed this might be the only way to get Mike to the hospital.

Two very polite policemen came and took Mike away. They put handcuffs on him, though he was as quiet and subdued as a prisoner of war. That bothered the young sister more than anything else—the handcuffs.

And so Everyfamily met schizophrenia. And that was just the beginning, for Mike was destined to be ill on and off for decades. He would get to know the county hospital and the halfway house, though he could never figure out what the house was halfway to. He would get to know the voices inside his head. The strange perceptions caused by disordered brain chemistry would become a part of his life. For instance, to Mike, things sometimes looked funny: too big, too small. His hands seemed distant, almost disconnected. Often he couldn't make sense of what people said. Their language was scrambled. He himself had trouble speaking, so he talked mostly in monosyllables. It was easier that way.

He was often terrified of a nameless thing, and sometimes, when he took medication, he felt a little better, and sometimes he didn't. It depended on the pills he took. Once when he took new pills, his jaw froze. He couldn't open his mouth. He got really scared, but someone took him to the hospital, he got a shot, and his jaw unfroze. The people at the hospital said it had been a side effect.

He hated the hospital. He hated the pills. He hated his voices. Once he tried to kill himself by running a car into a tree. He hurt the tree, and he "killed" the car, but not himself.

In fact, Mike was having a very ordinary life for a chronically ill schizophrenic. It was an odd kind of career that had reached out and claimed him. His degree was one he never wanted: CMI . . . chronically mentally ill.

That, in brief, is the story of how Everyfamily met schizophrenia. Of course, with 40 million Everyfamilies, there are variations, nuances, differences in timing, symptoms, outcome, but one thing, in most cases, remains the same: Everyfamily continues to love the stricken one. Hell or high water, in sickness or in more sickness, love continues to rise in the family like springwater in a well. If it didn't, if the sources of feeling ran dry, the families of a chronic schizophrenic couldn't possibly endure what they had to endure, for long-term mental illness is a sentence, a "stretch" that must be served, as well as a medical condition.

The Psych Ward Called Home: The Disruption of Family Life

Just what does Everyfamily have to endure?

Put simply, a profound disruption of life, a severe laceration of the spirit, and suffering so great that only those who have been through it will know what I am talking about. Others, those on the outside looking in, can only guess at the feelings of the family by imagining themselves living in a psych ward called home.

If you want to understand, begin by thinking of home, the most trusted and beloved of human places. What it means to most of us is sweet beyond expression. A place to hang our hats, yes, but more than that, a place to relax, to be ourselves, to become restored, refreshed, and ready once again to tackle the cruel world.

For families who shelter a schizophrenic, the cruel world is *inside* the front door.

For instance, like all families with a sick member, they must deal with symptoms. Here, though, the symptoms are not shortness of breath or pains in the chest, but the bizarre behavior that comes from a human brain not working right. These families must deal with a strange assortment of unpredictables: perhaps a person who is hearing voices that no others can hear, maybe midnight shouts for help as the sick one is swept by terrors, probably calls from the police ("We found her wandering on the freeway"), and often, frightening rides to the emergency room.

Here are just a few of the "ordinary" concerns voiced to me by parents:

> "I wonder if he will get killed. He's been lying down in the road, right in the middle of the road. So far he's done it in the daytime, when people could see him and stop. Will he do it at night? Lord!"

> "She ran away and has been hospitalized ten times in fourteen months in several different states. Last time she got out, the people at the mental hospital bought her a Greyhound ticket to Los Angeles. The bus dumped her there right in the middle of skid row."

> "We're worried about him. He keeps eyeing his father's home computer. Says the screen is blinking and sending him bad messages. We try to distract him, but we're afraid he'll damage the machine because he's scared of it. We use the computer a lot in our home business, so we can't hide it."

> "I'm afraid to come home since he tried to commit suicide. I never know if I will find him electrocuted in the tub or hanging in the garage. Finding him barely alive last time was more than I can take. I dream about it all the time. He stands on the edge of a cliff and pleads with me to help him. I'm helpless, so he jumps. I wake up just before he hits bottom."

> "He burned everything that belonged to him."

> ". . . insisted he had glass in his veins."

> ". . . buried his wallet."

Similar events are reality for 40 million families. Coping with them is difficult and disruptive. Deciding what to do, what to say, where to draw the line—these are draining decisions, but just as difficult is the interior task of changing one's mindset about bizarre behavior.

We grow up, all of us, learning to be threatened by bizarre behavior. We learn to turn our heads away when we see it on the streets. We learn to judge it. We learn to discourage it in our own children. "Don't act that way. What will people think?" we say. But one thing we do not learn is to look at bizarre behavior as a *symptom* instead of as a *character defect.*

This is an extremely hard lesson for families to learn. It sometimes takes years for the lesson to sink in: Disordered behavior comes from a disordered brain and is a symptom, a way the disease of schizophrenia expresses itself in the body. Some families never learn this lesson. Even worse, one member of the family may learn it while the others do not. For instance, a mother may have figured out in a gut way that her mentally ill son leaves restaurants without paying because he is ill and disorganized. She perceives the behavior as a symptom of the illness. The father may still have the mindset he grew up with: The kid is bizarre—bad, not mad. If he leaves without paying the check, he should be punished, not treated.

These differing mindsets can and do cause tremendous problems within the family, for each parent will have a different way of handling unusual behavior. The father may think the restaurant owner should press charges. The mother may think the family should quietly pay the bill for the son and keep him out of restaurants. These disagreements can add to the disruption of family life and can polarize the family into camps just when the members of that family most need to be united as good friends and allies.

The disruption of family life is not all high drama. It is important to remember that. Sometimes, when the disease strips the victim of all life, humor, and energy, the story is relentlessly, mind-numbingly dull. Day after day a zombie sits on the couch. To families who have near-catatonic relatives, it seems as though they are dealing with a presence, not a person. So deep is the mental disability with this kind of schizophrenia that relatives are delighted if the ill one can concentrate enough to watch images flicker on a TV screen. The shell of the person sits day after sad day, but it seems nobody is home inside.

Schizophrenia disrupts family life in many ways, some visible, like the behaviors above, some invisible. The feelings of these families are invisible, unseen, but they are often the biggest burden of schizophrenia. Fear, guilt, anger, frustration—these and more have been suppressed as the families kept their pain to themselves. It is time to hear them now as they speak from the heart.

How Families Feel

From Eagle Grove, Iowa, from Red Wing, Minnesota, from all over the country, relatives wrote to tell me what it means to live life on the schizophrenia front. Their stories arrived, written in pencil, typed crookedly on a page, scrawled in ball-point. One letter looked as if it had been crumpled, then smoothed out, folded, and mailed. It had. The writer had thrown it in her wastebasket because she "just couldn't bear to think about schizophrenia anymore." Later she retrieved it and mailed it to me.

Not being able to think about it anymore is business as usual for the families of schizophrenics, for life with schizophrenia is emotionally arduous. Here is a brief sampling of the storms that can sweep even the most stable of families when schizophrenia strikes. I present the words of the relatives without comment or editing except to group their remarks under general subject headings.

Sorrow

"It is our biggest problem . . . to look at this handsome, intelligent, formerly kind and good person and see him suffering so much."

"We feel like we lost a child."

"Our mental anguish and grief have been formidable."

"He just gave up and lived with his mixed-up head."

". . . sadness over his lost life."

"I don't know how my other children feel about it. We can't talk without crying."

"It's as though he had a terminal illness, except he never dies."

Fear

"He's suicidal. My other kids are afraid to leave him alone or hurt his feelings, for they're afraid they'll find him dead."

"My son told me he thought of killing himself and also me because he knew I would find his death so painful."

Disruption of Family Relationships

"All our lives were bent 'round the problem."

"My relationship with my husband became cold. I seemed dead inside and couldn't respond to his attentions."

"It tears a family apart. Each has his own idea as to how schizophrenia should be handled, which causes severe friction, even between husband and wife."

"We don't get together at family get-togethers."

Disruption of Family Health

"My husband had to be treated for depression."

"I aged double time in the last seven years."

"We have been through the mill, and it shows in our health."

Despair

"Our problem is this: knowing this is forever and it won't improve."

"God help the family."

". . . unspeakably sad. Seemingly hopeless."

"Happiness is a word in the dictionary."

Anxiety About Treatment

"He just won't stay on his pills, and then gets worse, and doesn't see he's getting worse, until he has to be dragged off to the hospital again."

"Runaway, breakout, take a walk, elope—whatever you call it, we can't keep him in a treatment center."

"The side effects of the drugs scare us silly. We worry all the time if he would be better off with nothing."

Exhaustion of Spirit and Resources

"My son took a great deal of time and energy. I could have reared three others and expended less energy."

"I have no desire to remarry. My problem is too big to allow enough energy for that." (A widow)

"Our costs were $40,000. Might as well have flushed it down the drain for all the good it did."

"I spent $15,000 for treatment. My income is $13,000 a year."

"Medicine payments and private hospitalization have added up to about $75,000."

Shame

"He entered a track meet stark naked."

"It's like hiding out at home."

"We are prisoners in our own house."

Anxiety About Work

"I have to miss work for the court appearances."

"I had to quit to take care of him."

". . . sometimes unable to concentrate, as when he's in jail."

"My son is constantly calling me at work, hassling me about money. I have to hang up on him. I'm afraid my boss will hear and can me."

Feelings of Isolation

"We are an island. We can't invite people in. We can't go away without a relative staying with her."

"We feel our friends have abandoned us."

"Our grown kids don't come back much. They can't stand being around their brother."

"Too many of the so-called professionals have not lived with mental illness and do not really understand the strain of living with it. So they can't help."

Guilt

"I worry that I'm not doing enough, but what else is there to do?"

"I tell myself not to worry, even professionals can't handle this disease. I feel guilty anyhow."

"Sometimes I wonder if I'm fiddling while Rome burns, but I don't know what else to do for him except what I'm doing."

"Was it something we did to him?"

"I wanted to die for a long time."

Hurt from the Criticism of Relatives

"They blame us. Think he just needs discipline."

"They hate him. They can't see he's mad, not bad."

"We understand that they don't understand."

Anger

"Social workers told us we caused it."

"The hospital told us we couldn't visit for three months. It was clear they thought we would contaminate him."

"An M.D. told me that my entire family would probably end up in the hospital because of the way I had used Dr. Spock as a guide."

"I can't answer your questions about mental health professionals. It is too hard . . . thinking of how they treated us."

Confusion

"We tried to treat him the same after he was ill as before. Utter confusion. There was so much we didn't know or understand."

"We didn't know what it was, what to do, where to go, how to act, what to think."

Frustration

"There is no mental health system. It is a mental illness system and hasn't helped us at all. I would advise people to steer clear of it."

"No help at all from our state system. Everybody's hands are tied."

"The system is interested only in the nonchronic patient. It does nothing for the severely mentally ill."

"Professionals are too rigid and bound up in theory and jargon to be of any help."

"It is a system all right! A system of dumping. Aftercare is nonexistent in this state. Once discharged, you are on your own for worse . . . or much worse."

Difficulty Accepting the Illness

"My son has been the one who had to convince me. I just couldn't accept the fact that he had an above average IQ, was good-looking, had a good personality, and was ill."

"I loathe his being taken to the hospital. I loathe the locked wards. I didn't want to give up his becoming a capable person."

"This has been by far our biggest problem: accepting the fact that he is chronically ill, that he will be that way his whole life, and that we must deal with it for the rest of ours."

Apprehension About the Future

"It haunts us every day—what will happen to him after we're gone?"

"We are afraid. We can see him on skid row. He has no brothers or sisters."

"This is one of the biggest concerns we have. What's going to happen after we're gone? Who will take care of him?"

It's not a pleasant recital, for schizophrenia is not a pleasant disease. Schizophrenia drops on families like an emotional Hiroshima. Surviving it is one of the greatest challenges any of us can face.

A Way Toward Hope

No doubt about it. This chapter, this peek into the private world of schizophrenia, has been depressing. I've cried more than once writing down the words of these families, crying for the sorrow of others, crying for my own. But if tears were the only thing at the end of the schizophrenia road, I wouldn't have bothered either myself or the reader with this book.

It's likely that we can, with the judicious application of thought, money, and action, find a cure for schizophrenia, thereby obliterating the necessity for these sad stories. While writing this book, I had the honor of talking with some of the finest researchers in the world. Those conversations convinced me that we are on the threshold of understanding how the brain works, of discovering the mystery world within our skulls, a world of chemicals and brain processes yet unknown. It gives me hope, and if we work for it and support the necessary research, we can empty the closet where so many families have hidden.

Meanwhile, we can make living with schizophrenia bearable. Relying on the experience of others, we can begin to make sensible choices about the everyday conduct of life on the schizophrenia front. (See Chapters Five, Six, and Seven.) It may not be perfect, but with effort and applied intelligence, we can reduce schizophrenia from a dread disease to the level of a disability that can be overcome.

CHAPTER

2

What Schizophrenia Is, Who Gets It, What Their Chances Are

> SCHIZ-O-PHRE-NI-A, n. Any of a group of psychotic reactions characterized by withdrawal from reality with highly variable affective, behavioral, and intellectual disturbances. Formerly called "dementia praecox."
>
> —*American Heritage Dictionary*

> What is schizophrenia? I'll tell you. The damnedest thing I ever ran into in my whole life. God must've been mad at us the day He came up with that one.
>
> —Father of a chronic schizophrenic

> It's a lifetime sentence of poor care, social stigma, unemployment, isolation, abuse, and silence.
>
> Letter from a mother

What Is Schizophrenia?

One disease occupies more hospital beds than any other. It's not cancer. It's not heart disease. In fact, it occupies more hospital beds than cancer, heart disease, diabetes, and arthritis combined. That disease is, of course, schizophrenia, a severe disorder characterized by delusions, inappropriate emotional responses, disorganized thinking, hallucinations, and deteriorated social functioning. What these terms mean in everyday language is that someone with the disorder may act strangely, have peculiar ideas, and, because of these problems, have much trouble getting along in the world. It is amazing that people manage to function at all, given the ferocity of the symptoms.

Schizophrenia might be a cluster of brain disorders, a collection of malfunctions, rather than a single disease. Current thinking at the National Institute of Mental Health suggests that as many as ten or twelve brain diseases are now lumped together as schizophrenia. They remain to be precisely differentiated and defined. What these disorders may have in common is an out-of-order switching system in the brain, but what causes the malfunction nobody knows.

One of the most widely held theories is the dopamine hypothesis. According to this theory, the culprit of schizophrenia is an excessive amount of a brain chemical called dopamine. Dopamine is a neurotransmitter, one of a group of chemicals that carry signals from one brain cell to the next on a complex and rapid-fire cerebral journey. These cell pathways in the brain are conduits for our thinking and feeling. If the pathways are out of kilter because of a chemical imbalance, then what we think and feel will be out of kilter. Chemical imbalance equals mental imbalance.

This chemical imbalance is treatable by medications that help minimize symptoms. In its chronic form schizophrenia is regarded as controllable by medication but not curable—much like diabetes. Diabetes is often used as a model for explaining chronic schizophrenia. In both disorders the medications don't cure. They control and improve instead. While the diabetes model is very useful, it is still inadequate for understanding chronic schizophrenia since schizophrenia involves bizarre behaviors that are not part of diabetes.

Another way to get a more accurate perspective on schizophrenia is to focus on the idea of the brain as a complex switchboard. In most people the brain's switching system works well. Incoming perceptions are sent along appropriate signal paths, the switching process goes off without a hitch, and appropriate feelings, thoughts, and actions go back out again to the world. For instance, if we hear our spouse got a raise, our brain processes the information and links it with an appropriate emotion. We feel happiness, and we say, "Congratulations." If we hear the family dog was run over by a car, our brain processes the information and again links it with appropriate emotions and behaviors. We cry; we ask how it happened; we plan for a new puppy.

People with schizophrenia may react in dozens of different and inappropriate ways to the same two bits of news. They may ignore what's said, or misunderstand it, or immediately launch into a story of their own without acknowledging the other person's statement about a promotion or the death of a dog.

Why? The brain afflicted with schizophrenia is simply not working well. Perceptions come in but get routed along the wrong paths or get jammed or end up at the wrong destination. We still don't know exactly how the switchboard goes astray, but anybody who has met schizophrenia is sure of one thing: The brain is badly in need of repair.

Right now, we can do no more than patch it with medications that sometimes work and sometimes don't. Prevention of breakdown; determination of causes; reliable cures—these essentials are still not known because schizophrenia has been the black sheep of the medical world. Pitiful funding and a profile so low it recedes into invisibility—that's been the story of schizophrenia research.

We should all ask why. Why has one of the most serious diseases in the country been ignored, its research programs half-starved, its victims left to vegetate in shabby halfway houses that some say are halfway to nowhere but hell? Look to myths and misconceptions—polite names for lies that are universally accepted.

Myths and Misconceptions

Schizophrenia is one of the most misunderstood diseases on the planet. Most people think that it means having a split personality. Most people are wrong. Schizophrenia is not a splitting of the personality into multiple parts, not a Jekyll/Hyde phenomenon, despite the popular hold of the Robert Louis Stevenson story. Most chronic schizophrenics are much too disordered to carry off double lives. Split personalities are rare and are a form of hysteria, not schizophrenia. Nevertheless, the equation "Schizophrenia equals split personality" is pervasive. When people in everyday life describe something as schizophrenic, they mean "split into two disparate parts." How did the confusion get started?

In 1911 the psychiatrist Eugen Bleuler invented the term *schizophrenia* to describe the disorder. (*Schizophrenia* comes from the Greek *schizo* meaning "split" and *phrenia* which means "mind.") What Bleuler was trying to convey by the term was the split between perception and reality. Today many psychiatrists regret the existence of the term because it is misunderstood.

But the split mind myth is not the worst to warp the perceptions of the public. That honor must be given to the myth of the violent madman. This misconception is so much a part of our culture that it is hard to perceive. It's like trying to see the air in front of our eyes. In films and print, schizophrenics are shown as menacing figures, ax murderers, chain saw specialists with rage in their eyes and blood on their hands. Because of these off-base depictions, millions of people have the erroneous idea that schizophrenics must be violent.

For instance, no paper reports that a murder was committed by a raging sane man, even though in fact, the great majority of murders are committed by sane men. However, when a murder is committed by someone mentally ill, we read about it: EX-MENTAL PATIENT SLAYS HOUSEWIFE—never SANE MAN SLAYS HOUSEWIFE. So ingrained is the myth of schizophrenic violence in our culture that most of us don't even recognize media prejudices against the mentally ill.

Here are the facts about violence and schizophrenia: Mental patients are slightly less violent than nonmental patients. Psychiatrist Donald T. Lunde, in his book *Murder and Madness,* says the percentage of murderers among people who have been mental patients is slightly *lower* than that in a general population. What seems to be true is that violent people will be violent whether they are sane or insane. The great murderers of history—those who organized the carnage of the Jews, those who plot mass political or religious exterminations—are lamentably sane. We may label them "insane" because we don't understand them, but it's doubtful that the people on trial at Nuremberg were anything but ordinary people committing extraordinary acts of violence. It's psychologically comforting to label all violent acts as "crazy" since it gets us "normals" off the hook. We think we couldn't do anything violent since we're "normal," but the fact is we could and do, every day. Ninety-five percent of the murders committed every year in the United States are committed by people who are sane.

Harvard psychiatrist Patrick O'Brien notes that many schizophrenics are exactly the *opposite* of the aggressive madmen of the myth—that is, they are timid, afraid of being further hurt in their vulnerable state. O'Brien puts the matter succinctly: "If one is prone to violence to begin with, then a disorganizing process like schizophrenia, and especially like paranoid schizophrenia, may exacerbate those tendencies, but if you are a calm, meek soul, such a process will result in a disorganized lamb and not a disorganized lion. . . . The important point to remember . . . is that the violence and the schizophrenia are quite independent of each other."

Even mental health professionals misperceive the mentally ill. S. A. Shah, in the Task Panel Report of the President's Commission on Mental Health, said that "available studies indicate quite clearly and consistently that psychiatrists and other professionals over-predict dangerousness to an extraordinary degree . . . [and] the overwhelming majority of mentally ill persons who are committed to mental institutions or are denied release from such facilities because of their presumed dangerousness do not engage in dangerous behavior following their release."

Why do professionals overpredict dangerousness? Is it because they are pressured by a misinformed public? Frightened by the rare cases that grab headlines, the public accuses psychiatrists of being softheaded do-gooders who become do-wrongers when they let the "loonies" out. But to talk with doctors in state hospitals is to learn that there is concern about dangerousness, the same concern that Shah has noted. After all, psychiatrists are the public, too. Said one to me: "I feel we get it in the ear from people when it comes to the subject of releasing patients. What people don't understand is that we, the psychiatrists and our families, we're in the community, too, and are just as concerned about our safety as anyone else."

It is a far different story, however, if someone, sane or insane, has a history of violence. Then it's necessary to take appropriate precautions. The point is, though, not to automatically be afraid in the presence of the mentally ill. It's not fair, and both suffer, the feared and the fearing.

Now, having cleared away some of the popular misunderstandings about schizophrenia, let's return to our main task: finding out more specifics about the disease. Diagnosis and symptoms are the next steps in understanding.

Diagnosis: A Little Background

How do doctors know schizophrenia when they see it? Exactly what leads to a diagnosis of schizophrenia anyway?

First thing to learn: There is no "exactly" when discussing the disorder. As noted earlier, the term *schizophrenia* has been used to describe what is most likely a variety of different brain diseases. Schizophrenia, to mince no words, has been a diagnostic wastebasket. What wasn't clearly a known organic disease, or depression, or mania, psychiatrists labeled "schizophrenia." Many different types of people, with many different kinds of mental illness, were lumped under the label of "schizophrenia."

Then, too, diagnostic practice varied from physician to physician, some using the label selectively, others using it to describe a wide range of behaviors. To complicate matters on a global level, diagnostic practice has differed significantly from country to country, with U.S. doctors using the diagnosis of schizophrenia much more frequently, for instance, than doctors in Great Britain. (British doctors are more likely to use "manic-depression" as a label.) As the reader may have guessed, this confusion about labels, this mixing of apples and oranges, has led to more confusion, especially in research. Some investigators were studying apples that they called schizophrenics, while others studied oranges that they called schizophrenics. It is one of the main reasons why so much schizophrenia research contradicts itself. Investigators were not studying the same medical entity.

The most widely used diagnostic guide in the United States is the *Diagnostic and Statistical Manual of Mental Disorders* of the American Psychiatric Association. The third edition (1980), known as *DSM-III,* sets forth a precise menu of symptoms, bringing greater order to past diagnostic chaos. In the section on schizophrenia the manual outlines characteristic symptoms, including disturbances in the following areas: "content and form of thought, perception, affect, sense of self, volition, relationship to the external world, and psychomotor behavior." Let's look at these disturbances, one at a time, using nontechnical language and examples of each.

Symptoms and Signs

Content of Thought

Thoughts are often bizarre, with certain common beliefs forming patterns. For instance, there might be ideas of persecution ("The FBI is after me"); delusions of being controlled ("The man next door puts thoughts into my mind"); notions of broadcasting one's thoughts ("I can throw my thoughts for twenty miles around"); delusions of reference in which other people or things are given great significance ("The number of the first license plate I see tells me what to do for the rest of the day").

Form of Thought

Called a thought disorder by doctors, this disturbance means that logical connections and associations are often absent. Though words are spoken, little information is conveyed by the person with the disorder. What is stated is often incomprehensible. For instance, one day in a park a street person said to me, "Let me tell you about pigeons. They are the perfect circles of the universe." Over my lunchtime tuna sandwich, I spent fifteen minutes listening to him. I never "got" why pigeons were the perfect circles of the universe.

Perception

Auditory hallucinations are a common disorder of perception in schizophrenia. The person hears a voice or voices that seem to come from outside his or her head. The voices often comment on the sick person's behavior. When a person with schizophrenia is in a room alone, loudly telling someone to go away, that someone is probably a voice. Mind you, no lie is being told here, no story made up. The disordered person *is* hearing those voices.

There are other disorders of perception, too—for example, thinking that food tastes strange ("You're poisoning me!), feeling unusual sensations in the body ("My heart keeps stopping!"), and hearing one's thoughts spoken aloud within one's head.

Affect

Blunted affect is a term lay people may run into, and it means "acting like a zombie." There's little or no emotion to be glimpsed. (It took me years to figure out that blunted affect is deceptive and that despite outward appearances to the contrary, much may be going on inside the schizophrenic that is highly emotional.)

Sometimes there's inappropriate affect. That means the person isn't registering the "correct" emotion. For instance, a young man may laugh when hearing of a death in the family.

Sense of Self

Here we have a disturbance of what makes most of us know that we are unique individuals. Doctors call this loss of ego boundaries. It is a vagueness about the sense of self, who one is and where one is going. When a person with schizophrenia tells you that he or she is going to grow up to be a blue grasshopper, he or she may really think that's possible. (My son actually told me he was going to be a blue grasshopper. At the time I thought it was a charming extravagance of the imagination.)

Volition

Parents whose schizophrenic sons and daughters can't get or keep jobs are familiar with problems of volition. There seems to be a lack of interest in the world and their own courses in it. People often see volition problems as a defect in motivation, as a lapse of character, rather than as a symptom of illness. Disturbance of volition is one of the most misunderstood symptoms in that it is rarely recognized as a medical problem by families. Instead, already overwhelmed schizophrenics are called to task for their lack of motivation. We may as well criticize them for having hallucinations.

Relationship to the External World

Often there isn't any. Withdrawn and preoccupied, the person with schizophrenia may sit on the edge of his bed all day, seeking out no one, indifferent to human contact. Detached to the point of autism, the schizophrenic may rarely look for companionship. Again, this is a misunderstood symptom in that families sometimes interpret the hermit tendency as a personal rebuff, a rejection rather than a symptom.

Psychomotor Behavior

Movements can be unusual (grimacing) or greatly reduced (catatonia). The person who sits for hours, unmoving, in one place, is experiencing disturbed psychomotor behavior. Involuntary facial movements are also disturbed psychomotor behavior. (Twitching of the mouth is usually thought of as a side effect of antipsychotic drugs, but it can exist in unmedicated patients. In fact, Eugen Bleuler noted back in 1911, before the era of antipsychotic drugs, that schizophrenics sometimes suffered from tremors.)

All the symptoms discussed above result in a much noticed phenomenon: deterioration from a previous level of functioning. The deterioration may be social, work-related, and connected to grooming. Friends may be avoided, work neglected, showers not taken. All add up to the person's "not being the same." No wonder, given the severity of what we have just described.

Think, for a moment, how you would feel if you heard voices that seemed to come from an invisible source, thought that the TV set was out to get you, lost your job because of lack of motivation, lost your friends because you couldn't "relate," and alienated your family so that they disowned you. To round off this perfection of disaster, imagine that you were confused and frightened not only because of the above symptoms but also because *you couldn't tell where you left off and the world began.* What's amazing is that people with schizophrenia function at all with these handicaps. We should pay tribute to their spirit and courage.

Diagnosis is an important matter. Though still imprecise (there are no lab tests, for instance), it determines what will be done to treat the patient—what labels and medications will be given. As in any uncertain human enterprise, errors occur.

For instance, when people are mistakenly diagnosed as schizophrenic, they may be unnecessarily subjected to the risks of the major tranquilizers. Such tranquilizers can do neurological damage in the form of tardive dyskinesia (TD). Tardive dyskinesia is a much publicized side effect of the antischizophrenic drugs, affecting some people on long-term medication. It reveals itself in persistent movements of the neck and face, particularly of the tongue and mouth. (More on TD and on the risks and benefits of antipsychotic medication in a later chapter.)

That diagnosis is difficult should be easy for the families of schizophrenics to understand. Living over a long period of time with a schizophrenic means being amazed at the variety of emotions, behaviors, symptoms, and lack of symptoms that stream along over time. In fact, the changes can be so chameleonlike that one wonders if several people have taken up residence inside the familiar skin. Perhaps these changes are what reinforce the Jekyll/Hyde myth.

There are also strong social reasons for using great care in diagnosing schizophrenia. Schizophrenia is still a fearsome label. Once the label has been attached, it's difficult to remove. Stigmas stick like fishhooks.

It is important to remember that there is not one clear disease named schizophrenia. There are at least several medically defined forms of the disorder: subchronic, chronic, subchronic with acute exacerbation, and so forth. (Some doctors still use the old classification systems like "hebephrenic" and "catatonic," but these terms are disappearing.) Most of the families interviewed for this book have been contending with the long-term or chronic form of the disorder. Some of their relatives have been ill for several decades, so the bulk of experience related here is about the chronic, long-term disorder and may not apply to the many people who have had one or two "psychotic breaks" or who have been told they have a schizophreniform disorder.

Note, too, that most of this book does not apply to the millions of borderline schizophrenics who manage to function in the world. (Readers who are interested in finding out more about the different forms of schizophrenia would do well to consult *The Disordered Mind: What We Now Know About Schizophrenia.* The book is by Patrick O'Brien, M.D., of the Harvard Medical School, and covers diagnosis and treatment in a way that the nonmedical reader can understand.)

Shirt-sleeve Symptoms

Yes, families notice all the official symptoms listed in the psychiatric manuals like *DSM-III.* I call them white-coat symptoms because they have been codified by doctors. But there are unofficial symptoms, a cluster of observations by people who have lived with chronic schizophrenia over decades and who have seen how the disease changes the personalities of the afflicted. I think of these symptoms as shirt-sleeve symptoms. They have been identified on the front lines by people sweating out the experience of living with a psychotic.

There is one profound change in personality, for instance, that medical books acknowledge but pay little attention to. It is one of the saddest hallmarks of schizophrenia: the loss of pleasure. *Anhedonia* is the official word for it, a bland term for a devastating happening. Scientists think the brain's neural reward mechanisms may be damaged. Whatever the biology, severe anhedonia may affect some chronic schizophrenics. What it means to their lives and the lives of their families is profound. It means that joy, affection, desire, pride, humor are all drained away. What makes life worth living disappears slowly, relentlessly until nothing seems to be left of the schizophrenic but a shell, a staring robot.

If this sounds terrible, it is. Nothing I can say will express the sheer horror of watching anhedonia creep in and claim the person who once laughed with you, who once hugged you, who once loved to be first on the hill to catch the new powder snow. The lights go out one by one. It is the death of the spirit.

Other shirt-sleeve symptoms families notice are social clumsiness and ineptitude; lack of interest in people, hobbies, even TV; withdrawal from family life; and weight fluctuations.

The Big Question: Outcome

Being diagnosed as schizophrenic leads to the big question. What will the future bring? Will the disorder disappear? Will it continue as is? Will it get worse?

Early in the century anyone who asked these questions would have gotten a pessimistic answer, for schizophrenia was thought of as a disease with a predetermined and depressing outcome. A diagnosis of schizophrenia, or dementia praecox, as it was called then, was considered a lifelong sentence to an ever-worsening illness.

Our present view of schizophrenia is more optimistic. There is hope—substantial hope—for anyone with schizophrenia. Manfred Bleuler, son of Eugen Bleuler, is a world-recognized authority on schizophrenia. He studied the life courses of 1,158 schizophrenic patients and reached the following conclusions:

1. At least 25 percent of all schizophrenics recover entirely and remain recovered. They have no symptoms, go back to work, have normal social lives.
2. About 10 percent remain severely psychotic.
3. The rest fluctuate between periods of psychoses and phases of recovery.

4. After five years' duration, the psychosis does not progress any further. It tends, rather, to improve.

This last piece of good news is startling because it is little known. It has been confirmed by other investigators. Even so-called chronic schizophrenics can get better over the course of time. After years of being ill, some schizophrenics begin to improve, to "mature" out of their illness in midlife. There has been almost no research to track down the cause of this improvement.

Many other researchers have looked at the outcome of schizophrenia. What is known can be summarized by a rule of thumb that has become a staple of the literature: The past is the best predictor of the future. If people did well before admission to hospitals, they are likely to do well after leaving. If they got along well at work and at home before admission, they are likely to do well after leaving. Conversely, if they deteriorated slowly for years (what doctors call an insidious course), they are not as likely to pull off a full and fast recovery.

A last word about outcome: The World Health Organization (WHO) sponsored a cross-cultural study which identified the variables that might predict good or bad outcomes. The group found that being socially isolated and being unmarried or widowed are connected with a poor outcome. Being surrounded by friends and being married are associated with a good outcome. The WHO study also affirmed the predictor mentioned above—that is, a past history of psychiatric treatment, a poor psychosexual adjustment, a bad environment, and a history of behavior disorders (night terrors, tantrums) were associated with a poor outcome. Patients who had lifelong personality problems before their breakdowns just didn't do well, while a "good" history was clearly associated with a more benign course.

Last, the WHO investigators looked at the nature of the psychotic episode and found that the following characteristics were associated with a bad outcome: a slow (insidious) path to the psychotic episode, long episode, and flatness of emotion. The following characteristics were associated with a good outcome: sudden onset of the illness, short duration, illness seemingly related to life circumstance, and emotional symptoms (as opposed to blunted emotions).

The WHO group also discovered some surprises. Patients in underdeveloped countries had better outcomes than patients in developed countries, and in developed countries men had a worse outcome than women. Again, nobody knows why.

In summary, then, the outlook tends to be negative if the illness is slow in coming on, if the life history has been full of problems, if the illness is a long one, if the emotions are flat and blunted. The outlook tends to be good if the illness comes on suddenly, if the life history has been relatively free of problems, if the illness is short, if there are emotional symptoms.

Who Gets Schizophrenia? Population, Age, and Sex

The fact that schizophrenia is common surprises most people because we have done such a superb job of concealing the disorder. In fact, schizophrenia hits 1 person in every 100. Imagine 500,000 children across the nation watching *Sesame Street*. Statistically about 5,000 of those boys and girls will get schizophrenia during their lifetimes. In the United States alone there are a minimum of 2 million schizophrenics. Add to each mentally ill person a family cluster of at least 3 other people, and you have 8 million United States citizens caught by a mysterious disorder that everybody fears and nobody understands. The magnitude of the suffering is almost incomprehensible.

Some investigators, like Dr. Paul Wender, believe that 2 to 8 percent of the population have a milder form of the disorder. For the United States, that means an additional 4 to 7 million people with a schizophrenia-like affliction.

If the problem is immense in numbers of people afflicted, it is vicious in timing. For most people, young adulthood means leaving home, finishing school, starting a job, getting married. For many schizophrenics, young adulthood means first admission to a psychiatric hospital. Schizophrenia strikes most often just as the young are at the peak of their physical powers, just as they are about to embark on life in earnest. The average age at first hospital admission is about twenty for males and the mid-twenties for females.

Why men land in the hospital earlier than females is unknown, though there's been a great deal of theory spinning on the subject. Perhaps, some say, life is tougher for young men, and because of greater stress, they break down sooner. Maybe women are somewhat protected against the disease by female sex hormones. Or is it that society tolerates bizarre behavior in women more than in men? Perhaps women, since they can stay home in the accepted role of housewife, are less often identified as schizophrenic.

These questions stimulate more: Are men more affected than women by the disease—that is, not in numbers, but in severity? Can women, when afflicted, hold out longer against the symptoms? I started thinking about the severity question when I put two pieces of evidence together. The first is that schizophrenia may well be a disease of the left brain. The second is that certain brain studies, none of which I have ever seen discussed in connection with schizophrenia, suggest that women have less lateralization—less specialization—of the two hemispheres of their brains. They may not be as "left-brained" or as "right-brained" as men, as restricted in hemisphere function.

For instance, one researcher set up tests for men and women who had been brain-damaged on either the right or the left side. Both sexes had representatives with left- or right-side damage. The tests were for verbal IQ, supposedly a left-brain function. Women scored about the same on the IQ test whether they had been damaged on the left or right side (99.1 versus 98.9). They seemed to have "generalist" hemispheres. Men with left-brain damage, on the other hand, did much worse on the tests than men with right-brain damage (a mean score of 83.1 versus 106.8 respectively). If the left hemisphere of the male was damaged, the right hemisphere didn't seem to "jump in" to make up for the deficiency of the left as often as it seemed to in women.

Are males less able to function with left-brain injury? We need to find out more. We also need to find out if schizophrenia is definitely a left-brain disease. Right now, though, nobody yet knows what accounts for the five-year average discrepancy between men's and women's initiation into the world of schizophrenia.

Do both sexes get schizophrenia at the same rate? Most textbooks say yes, schizophrenia is an equal opportunity disease. Maybe, but is something new happening? I've been struck by the high number of males with schizophrenia in the family groups that I heard from. About 75 percent of these families had a male that was afflicted. So, too, with a California survey done by another family member. Most of the afflicted were male. The National Institute of Mental Health is currently sponsoring a multicenter epidemiological study that should tell us more about what is happening.

Winter-Born Babies at Highest Risk

When it comes to risk factors in schizophrenia, there's a strange winter's tale to be told. Babies born in the late winter or early spring have a higher risk for schizophrenia than those born at other times of the year.

As long ago as 1929 it was noticed that schizophrenia patients were born disproportionately in the winter and early spring. The world yawned at this fact for forty years. The late 1960s, though, saw the growth of studies that continued through the next decade. They were done in various Northern Hemisphere countries—for instance, Japan, the United States, Denmark, Ireland, Germany, and Norway. Altogether the studies looked at the birth records of more than 125,000 people, a hefty sample. The findings were similar. It was clear that people with schizophrenia tended to be born in the winter and early spring.

What to make of this fact was the next dilemma. Again, nothing is sure, but much has been suggested. For instance, since a seasonal pattern is common in virus diseases, it could be that some kinds of schizophrenia are due to a virus's attacking the fetus and remaining latent until young adulthood and the onset of schizophrenia. Viruses that take twenty years to cause symptoms are not unknown. Infectious agents, then, are a guess that fits fairly well with the seasonal pattern.

Nutrition or, rather, the lack of optimal nutrition is another theory thrown into the ring. (Any number can play the schizophrenia guessing game.) Some think mothers are protein-deficient during the summer months, adversely affecting fetal development. Others wonder if the villain could be a nutritional disaster like lead, which unknowing children evidently ingest at a higher rate during the summertime.

There are even X-rated theories about winter and spring births, one being that male and female patients in mental hospitals get a chance to make love only during the summer months, when they are allowed out on the grounds, away from the watchful eyes of the wardens. The results of summer dalliance arrive nine months later, populating the world with a group of winter or spring schizotots. This theory, though farfetched, has a certain visual appeal. One imagines a scene of group romance that is a cross between *King of Hearts* and *Gidget Goes to Fort Lauderdale.*

What families should remember about winter and spring births is that season of birth cannot be used to predict whether or not a particular individual will become schizophrenic, so do not waste time hovering anxiously over the February-born young people in your family, scanning them for signs of schizophrenia.

Schizophrenia: The Bottom of the Social Ladder

Who else is vulnerable to schizophrenia? When asking this question, researchers have also looked at social class. Some say schizophrenics are concentrated in the lower classes. Critics of this view counter that the disorder hits all classes equally but that the rich protect and hide their relatives, keeping them out of public facilities and therefore out of statistical samplings. Others assert that if the lower classes do get more schizophrenia, it's because life is stressful for people with few advantages. Still others argue that the disorder hits all classes equally, but because of vocational disruption, the schizophrenic ends up down-and-out.

Nobody really knows the answer, but the issue is inflammatory. People don't like to be dismissed as "lower-class."

And what about the worldwide picture? Do people in certain countries get more schizophrenia than people in other countries? Not if we believe the traditional answer outlined earlier in this chapter, which is that schizophrenia occurs in all populations at an equal rate: about 1 percent of the population. But here again, we have a majority report (1 percent across the board) and a minority report (the distribution varies tremendously from country to country, with some countries, like Ireland, experiencing an epidemic of the disease). While I apologize for adding to the complexities here, the whole tale wouldn't be told if we ignored the minority reports about Ireland.

Shamrocks and Schizophrenia: The Irish Epidemic

What is the story in Ireland? Did St. Patrick drive out the snakes but overlook a worse plague, schizophrenia? Yes, says psychiatrist E. Fuller Torrey, who has spent time living and working in Ireland, tracking down the phenomenon of a high schizophrenia rate. And he means *high,* asserting that one Irishman out of twenty-five will have schizophrenia.

Torrey traced a striking rise in the number of schizophrenics in the Irish population from the eighteenth century until the present. From the middle of the nineteenth century until the beginning of the twentieth, the rise continued despite the fact the total population decreased in that same period. (The decrease followed the great potato blight and the resulting emigration.) The high rates continue even now. Why, again, nobody knows.

What would be needed to solve the Irish puzzle is investigation on many fronts. Are viruses implicated? Some very good investigators think so. Is the epidemic related to metabolic and dietary factors? We can only guess.

If it were your problem, where would you start looking? Those intrigued by dietary influences on human behavior might start with the lowly potato, which produces, when exposed to light, an alkaloid called solanine. Though most people don't know it, solanine can induce gastrointestinal disturbances and psychotic symptoms, including hallucinations. Your mother, by storing potatoes in a dark place, was following a cultural custom that kept you from getting solanine poisoning. So are the potato packagers who put their product in opaque bags.

Are some forms of Irish madness an unrecognized result of diet? A result of sun-kissed potatoes that produce solanine? It sounds farfetched, but so did the idea of the American diet causing insanity in the southern states. Then it was proved beyond a doubt that southerners were spending lifetimes in mental institutions because of the lack of a vitamin. The disease was pellagra, the vitamin niacin, and the time was the twentieth century. It leaves one humble before the number of possibilities that we could be overlooking in Ireland.

As an example, let's stick with the mundane potato and run through just some of the possibilities that could be studied by schizophrenia researchers. Besides examining how solanine interferes with normal body chemistry, investigators might look at the effect of the organic phosphorus insecticides that are applied at planting time. These highly toxic materials are carried to all parts of the potato. Insects that eat any part of the plant are, in the words of the plant biologists, "easily killed." According to agricultural scientists who have studied the potato to a fare-thee-well, the toxic action here is "related to the ability of these chemicals to interfere in the normal functioning of the nervous system by upsetting the transmission of nerve impulses. The specific action is believed to affect the cholinesterase-acetylcholine system, so essential to proper nerve function." What, we may well ask, do these toxins do to humans, especially to pregnant women?

Sticking to the same humble tuber, investigators might look at the studies that show what happens when blighted or discolored potatoes are fed to pregnant mammals. For instance, when these potatoes are fed to pregnant marmosets, the ensuing offspring behave strangely. They display no anatomical defects, but they have abnormal play patterns and are unable to be weaned. Their behavior is downright peculiar, but no gross physical abnormalities can be seen. The parallel to schizophrenia is striking.

Let me throw another possibility into the ring. As we noted earlier, it has been theorized that schizophrenia is related to an excess amount of dopamine. Dopachrome, chemically modified dopamine, is present in potatoes and increases during the life of the potato. New potatoes have less dopachrome than old potatoes. Could the amount of potato ingested and the age of that potato have any bearing on the eater's biochemistry—for instance, aggravating an existing case of schizophrenia? Who knows, and isn't it time somebody found out? I dwell on the Irish spud, not because of a galloping potato fetish, but to show how much work can be done in just one small humble area, that of a single diet staple.

The same efforts might be focused on foods with high methionine, an amino acid acknowledged to aggravate schizophrenia. The Food and Agriculture Organization (FAO) of the UN found that of the many hundreds of foodstuffs tested, cured fish was highest by far in methionine. Can dietary methionine intake aggravate the disorder? Again, we don't know.

Multiply dietary studies by thousands of other possibilities, and you have a new growth industry: a broad-based, multidisciplinary schizophrenia research effort. (More on this later.)

Ireland is just one of several countries haunted by a high schizophrenia rate. Other blighted areas, according to Torrey, are Croatia, a part of Yugoslavia, and some of the Scandinavian countries. That's the bad news.

The good news is that in some countries schizophrenia is hard to find. Dr. Torrey went to New Guinea in search of schizophrenia and found not one case in the 150,000 people surveyed. Readers who want to know more should consult his *Schizophrenia and Civilization.*

So there are many stories to be told when looking at schizophrenia on a global level. A dry-as-dust subject, epidemiology, turns out to be fascinating, puzzling. If we believe the minority reports, some countries are open-air insane asylums, while others are left practically untouched. Over all floats the gigantic mystery of why.

CHAPTER 3

Running in the Family: Fact or Fiction?

> Will I be sentenced by a lousy strand of DNA to a life of schizophrenia?
>
> —Son of a schizophrenic

"Is schizophrenia in the blood?" people ask. "Does it run in families? Is it in the genes?"

"Uncle Charlie is nuts. Will I be, too?"

There is always the fear: Can it happen to me? Will it happen to me? Will I have schizophrenic kids? Schizophrenic grandchildren? "Will I be sentenced," asks the relative above, "to a lifetime of schizophrenia?"

And so it goes.

Is there an answer?

Scientists have tried hard to find one. The story of their search for facts is enough to restore a belief in the intelligence of humankind.

Detectives in Denmark

The controversy raged: Nature or nurture? Heredity or environment? Are we what we are because of genes or because of how we were brought up? Are people schizophrenic because of something in the blood or something in the environment?

Until twenty years ago little was known about the nature or

nurture question as it related to schizophrenia. In the 1950s and 1960s it was a popular indoor sport to blame the family for schizophrenia. Toxic parents produced crazy kids—that was the chic psychiatric view of the era. Needless to say, some of the not-so-chic disagree with that view.

The less that was known, the more the subject was argued. Walsh's Law was in full operation. Useful for judging debates and arguments of all kinds, this is Walsh's Law: The hotter the argument, the fewer the facts. In other words, the number of agreed-on truths about a subject is in inverse proportion to the heat of the controversy, for people are at their most vehement when they least know what they are talking about.

True to Walsh's Law, the nature or nurture controversy in schizophrenia was simmering along when a small group of scientists entered the scene in the 1960s. The scene was never the same again, for these men decided to substitute facts for fury, a thoroughly refreshing and sometimes radical notion in the field of schizophrenia. Their names were Seymour Kety, Paul Wender, David Rosenthal, Fini Shulsinger, and Bjorn Jacobsen, and their problem was this: how to set up a test to find out if schizophrenia had a genetic component. The question of inheritance loomed—important, immense, and unanswered. How to ferret out the truth was a logistical problem in search of an elegant solution.

What choices did these men have? What detective work would have to be carried out to approach an answer? How would one begin to tease the longed-for facts about heredity versus environment from the helter-skelter called real life? The first move of the group was to reduce the helter-skelter by conducting research in a country that keeps extremely orderly records—Denmark. The Danes have countrywide registers of who lives where, who has been adopted by whom, and who has been treated for mental illness. In Denmark it is difficult to lose people in the demographic shuffle, a dream situation for anyone trying to track mental illness in a large population.

So the stage was set: Denmark. What then was going to be the main action of the drama? The pressing need was for a research design that separated the two disputed variables: heredity and environment. The group decided to focus on adopted children; what better way to separate heredity from environment? Tracking more than 5,000 adopted children, the medical detectives asked and answered questions like: What happened to the children of schizophrenics who were adopted by mentally healthy parents? When an adopted child became mentally ill, what kinds of things could be said about the mental health of his or her biological parents? About his or her foster parents?

Rosenthal (first in 1968 and then in 1971) compared the mental health of the adopted-away offspring of one or more schizophrenic parents with that of control adoptees whose biological parents were not mentally ill. Kety (in 1968 and 1971) compared the prevalence of mental illness in the biological relatives of two groups of adoptees—one group diagnosed as schizophrenic and the other free of mental illness. What emerged from these studies is the fact that being biologically related to a person with the disorder increases the risk of schizophrenia. This risk is present whatever the bringing up—whether the child lived with the biological parents or the adopted parents.

Since being biologically related means that some genetic material is shared, the Danish studies have been accepted by the scientific community as suggesting very strongly that there is a genetic component to at least some forms of schizophrenia. If you think the scientists are being awfully cautious here, with words like *suggest* and *some,* you're right, and they're right, too, because nobody has yet seen a schizophrenia gene. Scientists don't like to go out on a limb without seeing what they call somatic evidence, real stuff that can be seen under the electron microscope. Despite that, though, there has been wide acceptance of the detective work in Denmark.

A few people have been reluctant to go along with the genetic-basis group, but they are mostly old-fashioned psychiatrists who spend their professional lives ignoring biology and claiming that family environment caused schizophrenia. Their opposition is not surprising. They've established reputations by writing papers and getting grants to "show" that families are the villains of the schizophrenia story. It's hard to do a public turnaround without losing face—or grant money. As Upton Sinclair noted, "It is difficult to get a man to understand something when his salary depends upon his not understanding it."

Those who say genes aren't part of the picture have some explaining to do. For instance, how can we account for the fact that when children of schizophrenics are adopted at young ages by normal foster parents, they still have an increased risk for schizophrenia? Or the fact that when children of normal parents are adopted into a home where one parent is schizophrenic, they do not have a raised rate of schizophrenia? The life experiences of the more than 5,000 adopted Danish children have put a very large dent in the theories of psychiatrists who worked solely out of the family environment camp.

A Lot More Than Peas

Things have changed in genetics since we struggled with the subject of dominant and recessive genes in high school. To put it simply, there's been a revolution in our understanding of what goes on in geneland. Remember the stories in Biology 101 about Mendel the monk and his garden peas? Little did he know that his experiments were one day going to develop into a DNA Disneyland that would end up on Wall Street as Genentech.

Today scientists think the genetic principles operating in schizophrenia are a lot more complex than good old Mendelian genetics with its brown eyes and its blue eyes. Currently there are at least two additional theories about the transmission of schizophrenia: Besides riding along on one common gene, schizophrenia may arise from various rare genes or a combination of relatively common genes. Families of schizophrenics, however, don't care so much about the mode of transmission as they do about their risks for the disorder. A risk table, compiled on the basis of what is known up to now, appears later in this chapter.

While it's important to know that genetics has gone far beyond the monastery garden, families of the mentally ill don't have to know the difference between a garden pea and a double helix to be able to contribute to genetic research. In fact, some of the family groups in the San Francisco Bay Area, all affiliates of the National Alliance for the Mentally Ill (NAMI), have sponsored what are fondly called Dracula Parties. A Dracula Party is a mental health advocate's version of a Tupperware event. A group of family members meets at one home. Instead of buying, though, each gives, and what each gives is a small sample of blood to a researcher, in this case from the Stanford Medical Center. The blood is then taken to that hospital to be used to study human genes and their relation to mental illness.

Dracula Parties might be a cooperative vehicle for family groups and researchers the world over. Interested families may well want to get in touch with the genetics department of the nearest university or medical school to see if they can be of service. Someday, by cooperating with the DNA detectives, we might even catch sight of that somatic evidence, those villain genes whose presence we have felt but not seen.

The Mystery of X

The team in Denmark made history by being the first to separate heredity from environment in schizophrenia research. In doing so, it provided the first solid clues to genetic involvement in schizophrenia. This group and other investigators have also opened more doors to more mysteries. For instance, it is very clear from studies of identical twins that genes are not the whole story. Identical twins have identical genes, yet in about 50 percent of the cases in which one twin gets schizophrenia, *the other will not.*

Genes, then, are not a modern form of predestination. One may inherit a predisposition to schizophrenia, a vulnerability to the disorder, but something else has to happen to kick off the process. That something else is one of the key mysteries in the schizophrenia puzzle. If it isn't genes alone, what is it? What is the mysterious X factor that causes schizophrenia?

"Stress" is the answer that comes trippingly to the tongue, but the evidence for stress precipitating schizophrenia is ambiguous and conflicting.

For instance, on one hand, psychiatrist Eugen Bleuler, one of the first greats in the field, said that "strain . . . is also very often mentioned even by prudent psychiatrists as [a] cause of schizophrenia. I have never yet seen any indications which would suggest this relationship."

Supporting Bleuler is Professor Ming Tsuang, who has reviewed the British and American studies on precipitating factors and concludes that "no specific type of life event has been found to precipitate the onset of symptoms."

On the other hand, Professor Tsuang adds, ". . . an abrupt change in environment tends to trigger off schizophrenia in a vulnerable person." As examples, he cites the fact that soldiers during their early months of service and immigrants after their arrival have higher rates of schizophrenia than their more settled-in counterparts.

Nevertheless, we would be on shaky ground to say that a connection between two factors (schizophrenia and immigration, for instance) is equal to causation. Someone who believed that schizophrenia was caused by a virus, for instance, could take the same connections and make a case for the soldiers' and immigrants' getting schizophrenia because they were in new, crowded environments that fostered the spread of a transmissible virus.

What is amazing here is that despite the ambiguity of results and even though there is no clear evidence that specific life events cause the disorder, stress is still accorded an important position in the hierarchy of causes. Perhaps it is a bromide that fits in well with current cultural beliefs and concerns. For instance, at different times in history people's ideas about the causes of schizophrenia were tied to whatever notions were "hot" in their particular cultures. In the Middle Ages, for example, when people couldn't think of what to say about the cause of schizophrenia, they blamed it on the devil. To a culture focused on theology, the devil made sense as an explanation. In the 1950s and 1960s, when people couldn't think of what to say about cause, they blamed schizophrenia on parents. As you will see in a later chapter, blaming parents at a time when the cultural focus was on hearth and home made sense. Now people blame schizophrenia on stress. To each age its own scapegoat.

What unites us, though, with all ages past, is the desire to say *something,* for our ignorance about schizophrenia is almost as hard to bear as the disorder itself. Have you not felt uncomfortable every time you have read in this book that something is unknown, or disputed, or needed more research before we can know what is really going on? Certainty is comforting, especially in rough times, and one thing people do agree on, no matter who they are or what they do, is that schizophrenia is one rough time. Saying something to comfort others during a rough time, even if it's lore rather than fact, is easier than tolerating ignorance. Saying, "I don't know," is scary, both to the professional, who wants to be reassuring, and to the patient, who wants to be reassured. Stress is a culturally acceptable way out of these dilemmas.

If stress isn't *the* answer to the mystery of X, the missing factor that generates schizophrenia, what is? The field of candidates is as wide as the human imagination. And remember, there may well be more than one X. There may be several X's or many X's. Here is a partial listing of X candidates, made without any attempt to judge their validity. Only research and time will sort out the mirages from the real answers.

Candidates for X

- Viruses, especially slow-acting viruses that infect the embryo. Some viruses can take years to manifest themselves. Some may be activated by hormones, which, if viruses are implicated in schizophrenia, would explain the appearance of the disorder in adolescence and its frequent alleviation in late middle age.

Others interested in viral theories suggest looking into prions, peculiar and newly discovered viruslike entities.

- Yeasts, like *Candida albicans.* Some orthomolecular psychiatrists wonder if this common yeast is implicated in schizophrenia. Mainstream medicine hasn't yet been interested in pursuing the question.
- Industrial chemicals. Remember the mad hatters, who were victims of the mercury used in the manufacture of hats? Every year new chemicals are introduced into the environment, in in-

dustry, home use, and farming. What effect do they have on brain function? Not much is known, yet more chemicals are invented, manufactured, and released into our environment each year. What is especially interesting here is that many of the insecticides work by disrupting neurotransmitters, which most investigators believe are the key to some forms of schizophrenia.

• Metals, perhaps lead, perhaps others. Some say the copper from water pipes may be a culprit. Others doubt it.

• Dietary deficiencies. Niacin has been much suggested and much disputed. Certainly a B vitamin deficiency was clearly a major cause of insanity in the American South (pellagra), as mentioned earlier.

• Plant sources. Alkaloids, such as solanine, in potatoes exposed to the sun (discussed earlier), and ergot, from fungus-infected rye wheat, have been known to cause psychotic disorders. (People find this possibility easy to believe because they know that other alkaloids, like magic mushrooms, cause the self-induced acute psychosis known as a psychedelic experience.)

• Legal drugs—among them, dopa, carbidopa, amantadine, atropine, cimetidine, disulfiram, ephedrine, phenelzine, glucocorticoids, isoniazid, and digitalis. These drugs are used to treat a wide variety of common ailments, among them asthma, bronchitis, allergies, ulcers, tuberculosis, alcoholism, depression, viral respiratory tract infections, urinary tract infections, and Parkinson's.

• Illegal drugs. Man-made craziness to order, overdoses of amphetamines provide an experience that is the closest mimic of schizophrenia now known. PCP (angel dust) can also cause schizophrenia-like symptoms.

• Allergies. A perennial candidate for X, allergies as a cause of psychosis are still being debated. The allergy most often mentioned: an allergy to wheat.

• Psychosocial factors. This category is broad and could include stress, or the fact that you lost your job, or live on the wrong side of the tracks or in a developed country, or that your father yelled at you a lot.

* * *

These are just some of the candidates for X. The choice is rich, and the possibilities for detective work are almost endless. What is astonishing is that we have focused on such a small and narrow part of the possible spectrum. Historically psychiatrists have been handed the responsibility for schizophrenia. They weren't virologists, or plant pathologists, or chemists, or epidemiologists, or pharmacologists, or allergists, or biochemically skilled nutritionists. They were doctors of the psyche, who, given their interests and professional training, focused mainly on the psychological possibilities.

What is being said here is extremely important: *Because the spectrum of possible causes is so broad, the mystery of schizophrenia needs all kinds of detective work to be unraveled. It needs virologists, chemists, epidemiologists, nutritionists, all the people and skills mentioned above and then some. This has not been happening. We have been digging in only one corner, and with very limited and frail tools like psychotherapy. We need to expand our efforts, using a truly multidisciplinary approach.*

Are multidisciplinary efforts possible? Certainly they have been used with great success in other fields, notably space exploration. But can they work with schizophrenia? Some may not think so, especially in a world where traditional psychiatrists who treat psychosis with drugs won't even talk to orthomolecular psychiatrists who treat psychosis with vitamins and minerals. Will psychiatrists talk to anyone else if they won't even talk to each other?

Some will. What I see among the psychiatrists I know is that they are leaving traditional psychiatry to labor in fields like genetics and allergy; cross-fertilization is already taking place. Also, pioneering multidisciplinary efforts are now getting off the ground. For instance, consider the program of Lorrin Koran, M.D., of Stanford Medical Center. It brings psychiatrists together with other medical specialists to treat hospitalized patients with the full effectiveness of a multidisciplinary approach. That's good. Now we may simply need to broaden and extend our idea of multidisciplinary investigations to include specialists whose labels are not strictly medical.

Meanwhile, we have little chance of effective prevention until we solve the mystery of X. If we don't know the enemy, we can't wage war. As we search, millions of people vulnerable to the disorder remain at risk.

Genetic Counseling: Better Than Nothing

Once families of the mentally ill have become aware of the schizophrenia/gene connection, they ask this question: What are the chances of its happening again? Will anyone else in the family get schizophrenia? With their worry factories in high gear, relatives scan the newborn for signs of abnormality. During the adolescence of offspring in families of the mentally ill, parents wonder if they are dealing with normal teen rebellion or a preschizophrenia countdown. Brothers and sisters of the mentally ill ask themselves what later life may bring. They wonder what to tell prospective mates. Sometimes they wonder enough to look up a genetic counselor and ask about their risks.

What kind of help can they find? Well, genetic counseling for schizophrenia is still in an inexact stage. As you may remember, nobody has seen a gene for schizophrenia, so somatic guidance isn't available to evaluate risks. Nobody can yet take a blood sample, look at your genes, and tell you yes or no—yes, you're at risk or no, you're not.

Another drawback is the difference in risk for the families of chronic patients and the families of one-time only or rare-occasion patients. The chronic disorder may carry the greatest risk. Relatives of nonchronic patients probably shouldn't set too much store by tables based on chronic patient statistics.

Then, too, no table and no risk statement from a counselor can accurately evaluate individual cases. My risk for auto accidents, for instance, as a midlife female may be low, but if I drink a quart of gin a day, drive a car with no brakes, don't use a seat belt, and drive on the wrong side of the road, those low-risk estimates will not apply very accurately to me. So, too, with schizophrenia risk statistics. They can't be used to accurately predict the course of individual lives.

They can be used, though, as a kind of ball park risk guide. Charts aren't perfect, but it's better to be guided through a dark room by feeling the way than to use no guide and bump into the furniture.

Risks to Relatives: Charting the Chances

Readers who flipped directly to this page would do well to read the short section before this. It outlines the drawbacks of using a chart or table as a literal guide to your individual life. On the positive side, readers who worry deeply and often about getting or transmitting schizophrenia may be relieved by the following risk table.

The Relationship to Schizophrenic	*The Risk of Schizophrenia**
Parent	4%
Brother or sister	8%
Brother or sister (1 parent schizophrenic)	14%
Child	12%
Child (both parents schizophrenic)	37%
Half brother or half sisters	3%
Aunt or uncle	2%
Nephew or niece	2%
Grandchild	3%
Risk to general population	1%

*This table is based on James Shields's work. See bibliography.

To use it, look in the left-hand column and find your relationship to the person with schizophrenia. Then read to the right to determine your approximate risk for the disorder. As an example, if you are the parent of a schizophrenic (first entry in left-hand column), your lifetime risk would be 4 percent, one chance in twenty-five. If you are the brother or sister of a schizophrenic, your lifetime risk would be 8 percent.

If you are worried that your schizophrenic offspring might have a schizophrenic child, please note that the child of a schizophrenic has an approximate 12 percent risk for the disorder, a little more than a one in ten chance for schizophrenia. However, if one schizophrenic marries another and they have a child, it is at high risk for the disorder: 37 percent. Compare that to the 1 percent risk for the general population, and you will see why many believe it unwise for two people with schizophrenia to marry and have children.

CHAPTER

4

It's Not All in the Head: Physical Clues

> The best thing that happened to us in the last ten years is that people no longer think schizophrenia is "all in your head"—just psychological, you know. That's a heck or a step toward getting at solutions.
>
> —Virginia father

Body and Mind: Not Either/Or

The notion that schizophrenia is all in the mind is a result of either/or thinking. I call it computer thinking. Computers work by discriminating between two possibilities: a 0 and a 1. Those are the only choices. The scheme works fine for computers, but the either/or mode is not appropriate for dealing with real-life complexities.

Such narrow, two-sided thinking has choked our perceptions of schizophrenia. According to our culture, schizophrenia has to be either "all in the mind" or physical. The first alternative (it's in the mind) has won hands down over the other (it's a physical problem), at least until very recently.

This chapter was written to redress the imbalance, to present an array of evidence that suggests schizophrenia is not all in the mind. Here you will find facts suggesting the disorder is physical. That it's related to what's going on with brain cells and brain chemicals. That it's associated with certain abnormal brain structures, and connected to unusual motor movements and kinesthetic sensations.

And while the emphasis will be on the physical in this chapter for the purpose of adding balance to a picture that has been skewed toward the psychological for several decades, I do not believe that the answer is one or the other, body or mind. I believe the answer is both and that both are one, a unity.

Now how do we know schizophrenia's not all in the mind? One wondrous way is through the use of imaging machines that let us see the differences between normal and disabled brains.

The Brain Picture Machines: Giving Us the Inside Story

Think of it. There's the brain, mission control for all we do, think, and feel, the only major suspect in the crime called schizophrenia, and we haven't been able to get to it. Not very well, anyway, because it's under house arrest in a fortification called the skull. The brain cannot be reached the way the heart can, for instance. In fact, if the brain were more centrally located, say, the way the heart is, up front and center, we'd know a lot more about it.

To make things more difficult, the brain happens to be a large organ. It has billions of cells, perhaps as many as 100 billion. These cells, or neurons, form electrochemical bridges with each other, making intrabrain connections that may add up to a quadrillion. (One big circus goes on between our ears.) Moreover an area of great interest to researchers, the limbic region, which controls emotions, is buried at the bottom of those billions of neurons.

Have humans been deterred by these obstacles? Not very much. We are curious animals and want to know what makes us tick, difficulties or not. We are brained creatures who want to study brains and have devised ways to take pictures of what's inside the skull. X rays were our first success in medical imaging. X rays can pick up on densities—is that a .22 caliber bullet in the frontal lobe?—but are not useful for giving the kinds of detailed structural and functional information that we now crave. For instance, X rays aren't senstive to soft-tissue differences in inflamed or swollen areas. They don't track blood flow. They don't indicate changes in brain chemistry.

So we needed new tools to learn about brain functions. Scientists and the manufacturers of medical instruments responded. Impressive imaging techniques have come on the market: for instance, PET scans (positron emission tomography; and CT scans (computerized tomography).

National magazines now run color reproductions of these brain images, for they are newsworthy. They clearly show differences between normal brains and those that are schizophrenic or manic-depressive. Images in the press have done much to dispel the idea that mental illness is "all in the mind"—without a physical basis. If it can be captured as an image, it must be real; that's what people are beginning to comprehend. Since a picture is worth a thousand scientific articles, the brain scans are doing nothing less than changing the minds of people about the nature of the mind.

What has been done up to now, however, will seem crude in just a few years, for the new whiz kid of imaging techniques is on the horizon. It's called nuclear magnetic resonance (NMR). Nuclear magnetic resonance is being heralded as the imaging technique of the 1980s. It can pick up on densities, giving high-resolution anatomical information. It can give information about blood flow and body chemistry. NMR performs a flexible array of imaging tasks and does it without the radiation risks associated with other scanning devices. What's more, new NMR techniques are being developed that will allow imaging of three-dimensional volumes. (Right now medical images must be served up in two dimensions, slice by slice.)

NMR is exciting. It could be one of the keys that decipher the biochemical mysteries of mental illness. It may well occupy a pivotal point in our understanding of brain chemistry, turning out to be a Rosetta Stone that allows us to penetrate enigmas that have been incomprehensible for centuries.

Let's turn now to other physical clues.

Finding Abnormal Ventricles

For years schizophrenia was thought of as a disease that showed up in the behavior but not in the body. Nobody ever found a "schizovirus" or a "bacillus schizophrenii." Nobody saw a brain lesion, or if anyone did, it was diagnosed as something else, not as schizophrenia, for it was one of the axioms of schizophrenia that the disease has no known, visible, touchable, dissectible organic cause.

Now the pendulum swings. New biological findings appear every month. Nobody has yet put them together in a pattern that makes sense, but the base of clues is broadening. Take the ventricles of the brain, for instance. (Ventricles are small spaces in the brain through which cerebral-spinal fluid circulates.) Thanks to information provided by CT scans, it is now accepted that a number of schizophrenics, some say about one third, have enlarged ventricles.

What does that finding mean? At the most basic level it's a sign that something has happened to the brain that is not normal. What, nobody knows, but enlarged ventricles are associated with:

1. A more chronic course for the disease
2. Deviant eye-tracking movements (more on that later)
3. Poor life adjustment before the illness
4. Less favorable response to medication.

In brief, the message is that enlarged ventricles are bad guys, indications of a persistent illness that doesn't improve much with medication. Again, the associations above are just that—associations. They prove nothing about cause. They are simply another part of the puzzle. More pieces need to be put out on the board before we can understand the whole. Nevertheless, neuroscientists familiar with ventricular enlargement in schizophrenia note that a virus known as cytomegalovirus (CMV) produces ventricular enlargement. In fact, CMV as a causative agent pulls together bits and pieces of the schizophrenia puzzle better than many other theories.

Other variations from the normal have been reported within the brain, specifically variations in cell structure and placement.

Brain Cells That Are Wondrous Strange

The following event evidently happened in a region of the brain called the hippocampus, a comically named area of the brain's limbic region where some very unfunny things can happen. One very unfunny thing that can happen is a dramatic disarray of brain cells. Two UCLA researchers who studied brain tissues taken at autopsy from schizophrenic and nonschizophrenic people claimed there was a striking difference between the brain tissues of the two groups. (The tissues were rated blindly, without the researchers' knowing which tissue belonged to schizophrenics and which belonged to the normal controls.)

In a normal person the nerve cells of the hippocampus, pyramidal cells, were arranged in orderly rows. Comparable cells from schizophrenics were highly disorganized. For instance, some were rotated as much as 90 degrees from normal alignment. Furthermore, the cells' dendrites, which are threadlike structures extending from the main cell body, were also askew. It should be noted that the researchers found no evidence that the cell defects were caused by outside factors, such as electroshock treatment, brain injury, or medication. (Other researchers have not been able to replicate these findings, so the story may have more chapters.)

The strange goings-on in the hippocampus were featured on ABC-TV's "20/20," where dramatic photographs of the normal and disarrayed cells were shown and compared. These are perhaps the first cells from the limbic region to make it to national television. One hopes that they will be the first of many as public opinion begins to become informed, instead of inflamed, on the subject of schizophrenia.

The Eyes Are the Mirror of the Central Nervous System

The hippocampus and the ventricles of the brain are not the only source of clues coming in about the physical mysteries of schizophrenia. The eyes have it, too, "it" being something that isn't quite right in the ocular function of schizophrenics. In fact, two very perceptive men (A. R. Diefendorf and R. Dodge) noticed, way back in 1908, that there was something abnormal in the eye-tracking movements of schizophrenics. Again, the world yawned at the finding until the 1970s, when a man named Philip Holzman began looking at what was going on when schizophrenics were asked to follow moving pendulums with their eyes.

Before you yawn at the idea of pendulum experiments, consider that this work may provide many clues to schizophrenia. For instance, some scientists are deep into eye-tracking research to see if it could be a predictive marker of a vulnerability to schizophrenia or of the outcome of the disease once it has appeared. Others think that this research may tell us something about where to look for abnormalities within the central nervous system.

But let's back up and see what the researchers discovered. When asked to track moving objects (often a pendulum), schizophrenics displayed abnormalities in the smooth pursuit eye movements that most people use in such a task. Specifically, they tended to use jerky eye movements called saccades. Right now, as you read this, you are using a series of progressive saccades, or small movements, as your eye jumps from word to word. Schizophrenics disrupted their smooth eye pursuit tasks with saccadic movements far more than any other group. For instance, in Holzman's 1974 study, 86 percent of chronic schizophrenics had eye-tracking dysfunction (ETD), as evidenced by saccadic movements. Compare that to the 8.3 percent ETD rate for normal controls—a significant difference. What was also striking was that nonschizophrenic first-degree relatives of schizophrenics had a 44 percent rate of ETD. That figure suggests a genetic component to the dysfunction.

Now it would be nice and neat if schizophrenics were the only folks with ETD, but as noted above, relatives have it, normals have it, and other people with other kinds of psychosis have it (but at a rate below that for schizophrenics). What to make of it all is still up in the air, but ETD may be a way of identifying a selective subgroup of schizophrenics. (Please remember what most people keep forgetting: that schizophrenia is likely to be several illnesses, not one; that it is likely to be a cluster of diseases that need to be differentiated from each other before specific, effective action can be taken to remedy each.)

ETD may be a clue to a subgroup, a kind of trait marker. In a fuzzy field like schizophrenia, in which even diagnosis is hotly debated, we need all the clear markers we can get. Good luck to the pendulum people.

Minimysteries: Touchings That Don't Take

The hunt for clues about schizophrenia has turned up some intriguing minimysteries, as medical detectives track down the glitches in the nerve functioning of schizophrenics. What they have discovered is that schizophrenics sometimes can't accurately tell where and exactly how they have been touched. If you draw numbers on the palms of their hands with the cap of a ball-point pen, some can't tell what has been drawn—for instance, if it was a 1, 3, or 7 that was outlined on the palm.

Before you try this on a friend, remember that this feel-the-drawing test is positive (that is, the subjects can't tell what's been drawn) for other neurological conditions, such as minor brain dysfunction. The procedure is not a kitchen-table diagnostic tool for schizophrenia.

Here's how this test has been run in a scientific setting. The patients, who had been diagnosed as schizophrenic, were seated with their eyes closed. The numbers 1, 3, and 7 were drawn in large letters on each palm with the cap of a ball-point pen. If any of the numbers was missed, the test proceeded, using 2, 4, 6, and 8. The test was scored positive if more than half the numbers were missed on either palm.

The palm test was run along with a face and hand touch test.

Here the patient was seated, eyes closed, and told that the investigator would touch him or her on either the cheek or the hand, or both. According to the investigator, "simultaneous touching was then done in the following order: right cheek-left hand; left cheek-right hand; right cheek-right hand; left cheek-left hand; both hands-both cheeks. If the patient named just one touch, he . . . was asked 'anywhere else' the first time this happened and thus given a chance to correct himself. The test was scored positive if the patient missed two or more of the dual touches."

So what were the conclusions? Some touches just don't "take" with some schizophrenics, especially with the chronic patients. They can't accurately tell where they have been touched or, in the case of number drawing, how.

The investigator found something else that fits in with clues from other research. Several patients could feel accurately with one hand but not with the other. The dysfunctional hand was almost always the right, and if you remember the peculiar crossover construction of our brains and bodies, the left hemisphere of the brain controls the right side of the body. What's being suggested here is that schizophrenia might be a left-brain dysfunction, a possibility mentioned in the last chapter. Again, more clues are needed to fill out the neurological part of the puzzle.

Families that wish to help investigators concerned with physical findings should consider supporting the Brain Tissue Resource Center near Boston. This group, led by Edward Bird, M.D., serves as a nationwide collection depot for brain tissue, which is then dispersed to investigators throughout the country. The center is very much in need of brain tissue from deceased schizophrenic patients. Relatives of the mentally ill can arrange for the collection of such tissue, just as relatives now arrange for other organ donations. Prompt action after a death is necessary to preserve the quality of the organ donation.

Such contributions are priceless, and we, the families, are in a unique position to help. A twenty-four-hour answering service provides a mechanism for collecting brains from anywhere in the country. The emergency number for this service is (617) 855-2400.

For more information, write Dr. Edward Bird, Brain Tissue Resource Center, McLean Hospital, 115 Mill Street, Belmont, Massachusetts 02178.

Over the next decade we can expect to find an array of new physical findings, along with more information about the ones discussed in this chapter: differences in brain physiology and structure, in eye movements, in body sensation. NMR will provide us with entirely new clusters of physical information. The idea of schizophrenia's being "all in the head" will probably diminish as the mass of physical evidence grows.

Perhaps the greatest leap in understanding will come when people realize that the distinction between body and mind is out of date, inaccurate, and damaging to our understanding of schizophrenia in particular and human behavior in general.

CHAPTER

5

Treatment: Benefits, Risks, Limits

Every schizophrenic needs intensive study—physically, chemically, socially. A very meticulous physician is necessary, one who can treat the whole patient instead of a case. If possible, get the patient into a research hospital where he will be treated by a multidisciplinary team.

—Tennessee mother

Look for a doctor who is up on things, who knows what's new in research. Professional, of course, in that he knows his stuff, but somebody who takes a personal interest.

—California mother

Good doctors are hard to find. Select one who believes the disease is biological in origin. Don't waste money on traditional analysis or family therapy.

—Virginia father

I wish I knew when he got sick how difficult it was going to be. We have tried everything . . . nine different doctors. My son won't try another. I just wish I had known, had been prepared for the difficulties.

—Missouri mother

A Rocky Road

In the best of all possible worlds medical treatment would be straightforward: accurate and swift diagnosis; appropriate medication; and good results—that is, a patient relieved of his or her complaint. Schizophrenia is the worst of all possible worlds, and its treatment is difficult. There is no cure, only control of the more florid symptoms by drugs called neuroleptics or antipsychotics. The drugs do little to change the negative symptoms of the disorder, such as social withdrawal and lack of motivation.

That's the bad news.

The good news is that antipsychotic medications can help people who are having acute attacks of schizophrenia. Patients who are hallucinating, agitated, and delusional can get dramatic relief from the drugs. Furthermore, there is strong scientific evidence that antipsychotics can and do keep many schizophrenics from relapsing and being rehospitalized. Families themselves confirm the benefits. One survey showed that 85 percent of families with relatives on antipsychotics reported that drugs to be very or somewhat helpful to the ill person.

The medications, of course, have drawbacks and some side effects, but they are the chemical life raft we cling to until something else comes along. Not ideal, to be sure, but that's how it is for now.

As a participant in the great drama of schizophrenia you should be aware of the difficulties in treatment so that you do not end up disappointed, blaming your relative, the doctor, or yourself when things don't go well. I will give you the straight story, nothing held back, because many parents of chronic schizophrenics have said they wished someone had told them at the beginning of the treatment journey that it could be rough. So I tell you, it could be rough.

I also think it greatly helps the family and physician relationship to have families understand just what a difficult task the psychiatrist has. The psychiatrist probably won't say this, professional pride and all, but let me briefly outline what he or she faces.

It boils down to this. We're asking the doctor to diagnose something for which there is no accurate diagnostic lab test, cure something that has no real "cure," use medications that must be watched carefully for side effects, and decide by the only means available, trial and error, if your relative is one who needs drugs for a short time only, for a long time, or forever. Meanwhile, we expect the doctor to project confidence and relieve our worries. That, in a nutshell, is what we ask.

Well, knowing the problems of the physician is going to help you understand treatment so that you can be an informed ally during this sometimes uncertain process. Here are some of the difficulties the doctor and you face:

1. Schizophrenia can be difficult to recognize. Its onset may be very slow. This is especially true of people who become chronically ill. Because the illness may be subtle in its early stages, it may go undiagnosed. The person may be perceived as difficult and weird, rather than ill. Even families living day to day with schizophrenic patients misperceive the illness as waywardness. It's easy for a physician to do the same. Remember how John Hinckley's psychiatrist allegedly told his parents that what he really needed was to be kicked out on his own?

2. There are no lab tests for schizophrenia, no infallible physical markers. (See Chapter Four.) It's difficult to practice good medicine without solid scientific ground on which to base your recommendations. The doctor must work with primitive tools.

3. Schizophrenia can be confused with other things, such as bipolar disorder, amphetamine psychosis, and temporal lobe epilepsy, so the road to diagnosis may be treacherous.

4. The fourth obstacle to treatment is that there is no way of knowing which of the many antipsychotic drugs will work at what doses with which patient except by trial and error. The trial-and-error phase of drug selection and dosage adjustment may be nerve-racking for patient, doctor, and family.

Families with more than one schizophrenic can try to shortcut the trial-and-error process. For instance, if one schizophrenic relative has responded favorably to drug X at Y dosage, you should mention it to the doctor treating the next relative who has become ill. The doctor may decide to start the second relative on drug X at Y dosage, too, figuring that if the relatives share some biochemical similarities, they may both respond well to the same treatment. This realization has saved families with more than one ill person a lot of time and trouble.

5. Another obstacle to treatment is that antipsychotic drugs can have side effects, among them tardive dykinesia. (More on this drawback later.)

6. The sixth barrier to treatment is immense. Many patients—some say as many as 50 percent—refuse to take the drugs prescribed. This is enormously frustrating to physicians, for there is currently little else that psychiatrists can do. You may have been frustrated by this situation yourself, especially when your relative has been doing well on medication, stops taking it, and regresses.

7. Physicians' hands are increasingly tied by the growing focus on the patients' legal right to refuse treatment. There are two compelling sides to this story, with some physicians and families believing that a seriously delusional patient can't make a reasoned choice. They think patients should be given medication to relieve their symptoms whether or not they think they need it. On the other side, one finds patients and lawyers asserting that nobody has the right to make a person take drugs against his or her will. This battle does not make treatment easy for anybody.

8. Another obstacle faced by the doctor is the brevity of the hospital hold on the patient when he or she is committed. Increasingly state laws limit the time a patient may be held. Often this time is too short to make therapeutic headway.

9. No list of obstacles is complete without mentioning that which holds the mental health care delivery system together: red tape. Medical care is hard to deliver when the hands of mental health professionals are tangled up by bits and pieces of bureaucratic laws, rules, procedures, customs, eligibility requirements, turf concerns, record-keeping obligations, and a thousand and one other considerations.

10. We families sometimes make treatment difficult because of our own attitudes. Some of us fear having our relatives become

"dependent" on drugs. When we see improvement after medication, we think, *Well, they're all right now,* and we go along with their wanting to stop. We tend to treat antipsychotic medications like penicillin: Take it for a little while, and the problem will go away. That may be true for a single acute psychotic episode, but antipsychotics for the long-term patient aren't like penicillin. For a certain subgroup of the chronically ill, they're more like drugs for diabetes, which must be taken regularly to treat an underlying medical condition that is a continuous fact of life for the patient.

11. There are several drug treatment strategies available to physicians when it comes to schizophrenia: short-term medication; long-term continuous; long-term with drug "holidays"; intermittent (as needed). A conscientious physician will want to determine which is best for your relative. The only way the doctor can do this, given the present state of medical knowledge, is by trial and error. If you get angry with your doctor, thinking he or she is experimenting with your relative, the fact is that trying things out is the *only* way to find out what works.

12. The last obstacle to treatment is invisible. It is our expectation that the doctor can and will make it all better. Often a physician may try everything in the book, plus much from outside the book, yet our loved one will not get well. Yes, you can try another class of drugs, another doctor, but keep your expectations within bounds, so you won't be disappointed.

This, then, is the twelve-point obstacle course to treatment. Readers who have run the course many times may have examples to add. Whatever the total impediment count, the fact is that it's difficult to treat chronic schizophrenia.

Nobody likes this state of affairs: not the physician, not the families, and most of all, not the patients. The long-term answer is research. New knowledge is our main hope. Only then can we clear the treatment course of the obstacles and barriers that the hard-pressed physician must navigate.

The Doctor: Mission Control

Difficult navigation calls for a good navigator, a good doctor. How do you find one?

We all had a glorified wish list when searching for a mate, and we seem to do the same for our doctors. Please, Lord, send me someone who is intelligent, kind, decisive, caring, involved, professionally competent, etc., etc. To find such a paragon, books of advice suggest calling your local medical society for a referral. To me, that has always seemed a hit-or-miss way of identifying excellence, somewhat like calling a computer dating service for Prince Charming. I don't know of a single family that has found a doctor this way.

What does one do? Sometimes the family GP, depending on his or her experience and interests, will take the case. Often he or she will have a name to suggest. You might try friends in the health field who are clued in to professionals with good reputations. Do you have a friend who is a psychiatric nurse or psychiatric social worker? If you do, ask for a referral.

Do you have a teaching hospital nearby? You might call the psychiatry department and ask for a referral.

Perhaps the best way, though, is to ask the families in your local Alliance for the Mentally Ill (AMI). They are likely to be up-to-date on who is tops in your town. They are looking for the same things that you are in a doctor and have learned who is good and who isn't and who knows and treats chronic mental illness. (Not every psychiatrist does this. Some are much more at home treating the worried well who need help with the predictable crises of life.) AMI groups are also in touch with orthomolecular and holistic doctors, who offer treatments that are often ignored by mainstream medical people.

What, specifically, should you look for when you talk with a physician? (I know we don't always have this nice choice and that after waiting with an agitated relative for an hour in the emergency waiting room, you take what you get.) There are times, though, when you can choose. Look for a doctor who:

- Believes that schizophrenia is biologically based
- Takes a detailed history
- Screens for the many overt organic problems that can mimic schizophrenia
- Uses antipsychotic drugs judiciously
- Follows up thoroughly
- Corrects course if necessary
- Reviews medication periodically
- Is interested in the patient's entire welfare and can make appropriate references for help with aftercare, housing, social support, and financial aid.

Affiliation with a first-rate hospital is desirable. The physician should also communicate clearly and simply and be approachable. Some doctors are inaccessible; they give out the message that you shouldn't take up their time with questions. And some doctors aren't accessible because they literally can't speak your language well, so whatever your native language is, find someone who can communicate in it.

Excellence is important in a doctor. He or she is mission control, calling the shots in the treatment of your relative. Find the best you can. And when you do, make sure that you get a first-rate physical exam.

The Physical Exam: One New Program

Several things called schizophrenia turn out to be something else: a brain tumor; epilepsy; trouble with the thyroid gland. These diseases can hoodwink the most experienced diagnostician. Seen from a distance, unexamined by tests or physical probings, these mimics look like schizophrenia but are not. The problem is to root these masqueraders out so that they may be treated appropriately. (For more information on mimics, read *Mind or Body: Distinguishing Psychological from Organic Disorders,* by Robert Taylor, M.D.)

You can see why it's important to distinguish one disease from another, for not only is it inappropriate to give antipsychotic drugs to a person with a brain tumor, but it's dangerous. The treatment does nothing for the growing tumor, which is taking over brain tissue, and it subjects the patient to all the side effects of a drug he or she doesn't need. Never mind the fact that the patient is by this time in a mental hospital instead of a surgical ward.

But the mimics are being exposed, and California is one state with a pilot program especially geared to identify them. Knowing a little about the program can give you a clearer idea of the kind of physical screening that may benefit your relative.

Here's how it's being done near San Francisco. Medical teams are examining 500 people in the California state mental health system to ferret out undetected illnesses—illnesses that may have an impact on mental as well as physical health. To do this, Stanford Medical Center has assembled a team consisting of an internist, a neurologist, two specially trained physician's assistants, and a diagnostically programmed microcomputer. The group is led by psychiatrist Lorrin Koran. Exams and tests are conducted in a mobile van, which covers a four-county area. Besides a complete history and physical exam, each patient who volunteers gets a neurological exam and a battery of laboratory tests. The results are reviewed by the internist and the physician's assistant. Together they decide whether to refer the client to another internist or a neurologist for definitive diagnosis and treatment. (The project's physicians do not treat the clients. Their role here is that of medical detective.)

Some 300 people have been examined at this writing. Previously undetected disease has been discovered in 15 percent. What has been found? Diseases known to masquerade as mental troubles: endocrine disorders, neurological problems, and organic brain syndrome. Clearly, if your relative is in the 15 percent minority, it pays to be checked for biological disorders. Physical and neurological exams plus lab testing may uncover a problem that isn't "mental" at all.

Now, assuming that you have found a doctor, had a good

physical screening and an accurate diagnosis, the next thing to learn about are the drugs that will almost certainly be used in treating your relative.

Drugs: A Hot Issue

One subject, more than any other, is likely to bring forth strong opinions from the families of schizophrenics. That subject is drugs, the most widely used and effective treatment for schizophrenia. You probably know some of the brand names: Thorazine, Mellaril, Prolixin, Trilafon, Haldol, Stelazine. There are now seven different classes of these drugs available in the United States, marketed under forty-seven brand names.

Some doctors call the drug antipsychotics. Some call them neuroleptics. But here's what parents call them:

"A godsend!" says a mother in Maryland.

"A boon," says another.

"Our son's lifeline."

"A necessary evil."

"Medically indefensible."

You can see that opinions are mixed as well as strong, but families worrying about the drug issue should remember what was stated earlier: Most families have found drugs helpful. In the survey mentioned before, done by the California Alliance for the Mentally Ill, only 11 percent said the drugs didn't help.

Remember, too, there is strong scientific evidence the drugs work for most people in controlling hallucinations and delusions. In the 1960s J. O. Cole did several studies that showed the effectiveness of antipsychotic drugs compared with placebo (no medication). Three fourths of the medicated patients during the six-week trial showed substantial improvement. Virtually no medicated patients got worse. Contrast those results with what happened to the unmedicated patients in the same study: There was deterioration detectable in 50 percent.

Also, it seems clear that ongoing maintenance medications protect patients against relapse. Of schizophrenics who have not been treated with antipsychotics, 84 percent will relapse within two years. Only 50 percent of those on medications will relapse. (Note, though, that not all untreated schizophrenics will relapse and that not all medicated ones will avoid relapse. The trick is to identify those who need maintenance drug therapy and those who don't. We're back to trial and error.)

What seems to be at issue here is not if the drugs work but how long to use them and how to control their side effects. In the next sections we will review some of the major concerns and fears families have about drugs and see what role the family can play in successful drug administration. Then we'll look specifically at side effects, especially at tardive dyskinsia.

Can You Get Hooked?

This seems to be the fear perennial: getting hooked. Families are afraid that antipsychotic drugs are addictive. They think that if their relatives stay on them long enough, they will never be able to stop taking them. Where families got this idea is hard to tell, but it is off base, according to E. Fuller Torrey, M.D., who writes: "There is no evidence to date that anti-psychotic drugs cause addiction. The person's body does not slowly get used to them and therefore require higher and higher doses, and the stopping of the drugs does not cause withdrawal symptoms."

So save your energy. You have enough to worry about without imagining that your relative will get hooked on Haldol. He or she may be one of those who benefit from long-term administration of the drug, just as a diabetic benefits from insulin to compensate for an innate biochemical defect.

About another fear that the drugs are "dangerous": Some families worry that a depressed relative will use the drugs to commit suicide. Physicians say that it is virtually impossible to commit suicide by overdosing on most of the antipsychotics. (One exception to this seems to be thioridazine, which is reported to cause severe cardiac effects when taken in overdose. Thioridazine is marketed under the brand names Mellaril, Novoridazine, and Thioril.)

Nevertheless, much of what you now have in your medicine

cabinet can probably do more harm in high doses than most of the antipsychotics. If you wish to know more about drugs, their actions, dosages, and general use, read *Surviving Schizophrenia* by E. Fuller Torrey, M.D. You may also want to look up the drug your relative is using in the *Physicians' Desk Reference (PDR)*, widely available in libraries and bookstores.

How the Family Can Help with Drugs

Some people with schizophrenia take their medications every day without being told, asked, cajoled, bribed, or harangued. This is great, and if it is happening in your family, count yourself lucky. Such compliance is, however, not always the case. People forget to take their medications. People resist taking their medications. People flush their medications down toilets, "cheek" them, stuff cotton in their mouths to absorb the drugs if they are given in liquid form. Why? How does this happen?

Well, for those who have received no help from medications, the answer is obvious. The drugs just don't work for them. Others resist because they have not yet found a medication they are comfortable with. Many reject drugs because they have had negative experiences with side effects.

Patients become frightened and discouraged when the drugs do surprising and unwelcome things to their bodies. So would I. So, probably, would you. One side effect in particular, akathisia, has been suggested as a deterrent to continued medication. Akathisia is motor restlessness. The person may pace, complain of feeling jittery, anxious, even doomed.

Another deterrent, though, exists, and it has nothing to do with side effects. Over and over again I heard one common reason for noncompliance from families. Luckily it's a difficulty that families can help with.

Here's a typical situation: A relative chronically ill with schizophrenia has taken an antipsychotic drug with good results over a period of months or years. Symptoms are controlled. The person can function on a higher level than he or she did unmedicated. Drug "holidays" may have indicated a clear, continuing need for medication. In other words, without the drugs, the person relapsed. Side effects may have been minimal. Nevertheless, the relative may begin to "forget" to take the medicine or decide that it is no longer for him or her. Why? Often there are two reasons:

1. The person with schizophrenia feels so good he decides he is all better and doesn't need the drug, so he stops. Again, it's like a diabetic going off insulin.
2. The person may very much want to be considered normal, restored to "real" society. He thinks continuing to take the drugs means that he is still "crazy." So, again, he stops.

When it's clear that drugs need to be continued, the doctor and family can become educators. They may point out the parallel with diabetics who live productive lives despite a continuing reliance on insulin. So, when antipsychotic drugs are in the medicine cabinet instead of in the person, try talking about the dilemma in terms of diabetes. It may do some good.

Another way families can help is simple and easy: *Learn the medications your relative is taking and in what doses. Write down what drugs were eliminated and why. Write down what drugs seemed to help and in what doses.* That way, if your relative switches doctors or hospitals, the physician doesn't have to start over from square one with the trial-and-error process we discussed before. You may want to insert this information conspicuously in your relative's wallet, especially if he or she is a wanderer or a street person who gets picked up in different towns or states and taken off to psychiatric emergency rooms where nobody knows him or her.

If the patient is living at home and is not a wanderer, families can be of service in a different way. They can help, for instance, when the doctor is changing the kind of medication or the dosage or is making a trial run of discontinuing the drug. At such times, if both patient and doctor agree to let the family work as part of the treatment team, the family can be useful. They are often the daily observers of symptoms and side effects in the patient and are alert to changes, both desirable and undesirable. They can report what they see.

One family I know made a pact with their daughter. As her medication was reduced, the family promised to tell her directly when, how, and if she began acting weirdly. All agreed this would be the time to tell the doctor that decompensation was in progress and that the medication needed to be increased to a more effective dose. The agreement worked pretty well for them. The daughter did begin to express bizarre ideas. The family said to her, "Hey, Helen, your conversation is beginning to get strange again." Helen told the doctor. The doctor upped the dose a little. All is better now because they agreed to communicate with each other to prevent a crisis.

If this seems simpleminded to you and you think that any sensible family would communicate in such a case, I can tell you that they often do not. Families sometimes will not tell their relatives when they begin getting "strange." They are afraid of provoking worse symptoms, or of offending, or of retaliation, or of getting into arguments and increasing family tensions. Often families just cross their fingers and hope the symptoms will go away. An agreement like the one Helen had with her family is much more productive.

People who live with schizophrenics who function on a very low level find it especially hard to communicate about medication. Often they don't talk; they act. These families make a daily and deliberate ritual of medication. They have to hand their relatives medications, make sure they are swallowed, and in general, act like drug-dispensing nurses.

What happens when your relative absolutely refuses all medication? If you have living with you a relative whose behavior is disruptive and uncontrollable and who refuses to take medication, you should, in my opinion, consider other alternatives. You might look up your state's commitment laws. These laws, which are in the appendix of this book, may help you out of your situation if your relative has harmed or threatened to harm you or himself or is "gravely disabled" beyond a shadow of a doubt. Such actions are common grounds for commitment.

Sometimes an unmedicated relative may be absolutely impossible to live with yet not be "committable." For instance, your brother may be hallucinating uncontrollably, pacing the hall all night talking loudly to his "voices," and still be capable of feeding and dressing himself and getting around town one way or another. In other words, he can take care of his basic needs; it would be hard to prove he was gravely disabled. This situation can be a real problem to families. Commonly such a relative is uncommittable yet unendurable. He will not take medicine and will not go voluntarily into any kind of facility. Sometimes the only alternative left in this squeeze is one that nobody is happy with.

For instance, I know one family who lived with their twenty-two-year-old son's extremely bizarre behavior for months and months. The doctor told them that medications were the way to control the delusions and hallucinations, but their son refused to take drugs, saying that he was perfectly OK. The family finally rebelled. They said to the son, "If you don't take medication, you can't stay here." They didn't like doing it, but they did it, thinking it was the only way to force their relative to get help. The son left and was picked up by the police within hours for driving dangerously. Acting "crazy" at the time he was stopped, he was taken to a hospital by the police. Later he went to a crisis house, where he began to improve.

In this case the parents had felt trapped. They couldn't commit their son to a hospital; they couldn't tough it out at home without medications. For them, the only way through was out—out of the house. For them it worked. For others it may not, but sometimes it is the only choice parents can think of when a seriously ill relative refuses medication yet doesn't meet the state's requirement for commitment. We need to develop better ways of handling such crises.

Side Effects

Antipsychotic drugs have side effects. Fears of these side effects are part of life for families of medicated schizophrenics.

Are these fears realistic? As you ponder this question, please remember that not everybody on antipsychotic drugs experiences severe side effects. Some people do get distressing side effects, some don't. Several common reactions like constipation, blurring of vision, drowsiness, and dry mouth may appear when a patient first starts taking medication. Often, though, these reactions disappear or at least diminish with time.

Sometimes movement is affected by the drugs. People become very restless—akathisia, mentioned before. Sometimes they get quite stiff. They also may get shaky, or they can get something called a dystonic reaction. During a typical dystonic reaction the neck muscles may become rigid. Turning the head becomes impossible. One patient told me it felt as if he had lockjaw. Dystonia can be a frightening thing for a patient who was not warned that such a reaction was possible.

Some doctors think it unwise to disturb patients by telling them about the possibility of dystonia. Advising patients about the risk, however, may be preferable to having an outpatient with dystonia rushed to an emergency room and diagnosed as having meningitis or tetanus. Again, it makes sense for the patient to carry a card telling what antipsychotic medication he is on.

Dystonia frightens people especially when they don't know what on earth is happening to them. In fact, dystonia can be reversed in a very short time by the injection of a class of drugs called anti-Parkinsonian. Many of you may have heard of them by brand name—for instance, Cogentin.

What other side effects are there? Sexual desire may be diminished. Menstrual cycles may be disrupted. There may be some discharge from the breasts. Weight gain may occur, but it also may occur in unmedicated schizophrenics who sit all day. Some types of drugs are connected with a supersensitivity to the sun. This can be simply addressed by the effective sunblockers on the market today.

There are times, and these times are rare, when side effects can be very serious and even fatal. As mentioned before, Thioridazine (Mellaril, Novoridazine, Thioril) can have severe cardiac effects when taken in overdose. This same class of drugs, in very high dose, can lead to damage of the eye lens or retina. Antipsychotic drugs have also been known to interfere with the formation of white blood cells, leaving the patient susceptible to infection. To repeat, though, these effects are rare.

Certain classes of drugs are thought to be linked to specific side effects, one class being more likely to cause oversensitivity to the sun, another more likely to cause impotence, and so forth. Your relative should be asking the physician what to expect.

So how can one summarize the risks of the drugs and the management of those risks?

For its physician members, the American Psychiatric Association (APA) sums up the situation like this: ". . . the currently available anti-psychotic agents virtually all carry some risk of inducing early or late neurological toxic effects. Most of them can be managed with [anti-Parkinsonian] agents or by thoughtful and conservative use of the available neuroleptics. . . ."

The message here is that there are potential risks, but they can be dealt with by using good medical judgment—yet another reason for exercising care in choosing your physician.

Another message, even simpler, comes to us from a leading psychopharmacologist, Leo Hollister, M.D. "It is wise," he says, "not to use potent drugs for small reasons."

In conclusion, then, if your son has been lying down in the middle of a busy road to test his immortality or if your daughter has tried to slice her wrists open with a can opener because her voices told her to, you may have big reasons for using the antipsychotic drugs. Just make sure that your relative is medically monitored and that you have information about the possible side effects of the particular drug being used.

Tardive Dyskinesia: Caution, Not Panic

Tardive dyskinesia. Two powerful words. Just say them, and families get nervous. What is tardive dyskinesia (TD), and how did it get such a bad press among the relatives of the mentally ill?

Tardive dyskinesia is the repeated involuntary movement of the tongue, of facial and neck muscles, sometimes of the trunk and extremities. It is thought to be caused by antipsychotic medications. It may be so mild it goes unnoticed. It may be moderate or severe.

It is hard to know how many medicated patients have TD since the symptoms may be subtle. Perhaps 10 to 20 percent of patients in mental hospitals have it. Drs. Dilip Jeste and Richard Jed Wyatt estimate that the prevalence of persistent TD attributable to antipsychotic drugs is about 13 percent.

Nevertheless, much higher rates of TD have appeared in the press and frightened families. In fact, the claim that TD is widespread is just one of a quartet of claims that scare families into thinking disaster will almost surely befall their medicated relatives. The other three popular beliefs are: TD is always irreversible, TD will always get worse, and TD can't be prevented.

Let's look at each of the four assumptions and see whether or not we should run for the exit doors of the clinic.

Assumption one: TD is very widespread.

This first assumption really puzzled me. Like other parents who read the papers, I believed TD was around every corner. Then I noticed a very peculiar fact. I had been in touch with more than 100 families, heard them tell their troubles, and not one mentioned a problem with tardive dyskinesia. They would mention oversedation or restlessness as a problem, but not TD.

As I read further, I noticed that even the most respected authorities would quote the higher TD prevalence studies and then say their own clincal experience didn't support the large estimates of people who supposedly had TD. Dr. Leo Hollister, writing about one study that estimated a 36 percent prevalence rate, says, "This estimate of prevalence is far greater than any in [my] experience."

Something just isn't jibing between what some of the TD investigators are saying and what others of us are seeing and hearing. The investigators who come up with high figures may be mistaking the involuntary movements that can be part of the disease for the involuntary movements that can be a side effect of the drugs. Epidemiological studies now in progress may give us more information.

Relatives who wish to know more may want to read "The Changing Epidemiology of Tardive Dyskinesia: An Overview," by Dilip Jeste and Richard Jed Wyatt in the March 1981 issue of the *American Journal of Psychiatry.* Meanwhile, the TD rates may begin to go down because of new emphasis on prevention by constant medical monitoring and early detection.

Assumption two: TD is always irreversible.

This was an article of faith ten years ago, but further investigations have shown that TD certainly can be reversed. The earlier it is detected, the greater the chances for its being reversed. Even TD of long duration can be reversed once the responsible drug is stopped. In the latter case TD may take several years to clear, but it can happen. Improvements in long-term TD are not uncommon. (See Dr. Frank Ayd's article in "Psychopharmacology Update," *Psychiatric Annals,* January 1984.)

Assumption three: TD will always get worse.

This one has really bothered families because it made them feel as though they were caught between two equally obnoxious alternatives. Families thought they could have one of two things: Either they could have relatives whose schizophrenic symptoms were under control but who were likely to get TD from the medication, or they could have relatives who acted "crazy" but were clear of TD because they were unmedicated.

Families got this idea, of course, because medical opinion at the time held that if you continued antipsychotic drugs after the onset of TD, the TD would only get worse. Recently, though, investigators George Gardos and Jonathan Cole reviewed more than 500 patients who were on continued antipsychotic treatment. They conclude: "Simply stated, it is not at all clear that once tardive dyskinesia had developed, continued neuroleptic therapy necessarily worsens the prognosis." They add, "The schizophrenic patient who has had chronic drug treatment and who has developed mild to moderate dyskinesia is unlikely to change markedly or to develop severe tardive dyskinesia."

So remember, current thinking is that long-term therapy does not necessarily make TD worse.

Assumption four: TD can't be prevented.

Severe TD certainly can be prevented. The key is early and repeated monitoring by the physician. Frank Ayd, M.D., gives down-to-earth advice to fellow psychiatrists: "Since the risk of tardive dyskinesia can be minimized by early detection, it is imperative that . . . we say to patients, 'Open your mouth and stick out your tongue.' If the patient has an emerging tardive dyskinesia, you will notice [wavelike] movements of the tongue or that the tongue cannot be protruded for more than a few seconds. Such warning signs should prompt immediate reduction of the dose of the neuroleptic. If the dosage is reduced or discontinued at this early stage, there will be a complete resolution of symptoms."

So the simple and time-honored act of sticking out your tongue during a medical exam is the key to early detection of TD and the prevention of its development.

In conclusion, then, families have been right to be cautious about TD, but panic is an inappropriate response. Fear adds a completely unnecessary burden to the backpack of troubles that families already carry. If you have a relative on long-term medication, think prevention. Make sure the medication plan and your relative are periodically examined by an alert physician.

Hospitalization

Hospitalization provokes different responses in different families. Some see it as a savior, a respite from turmoil at home, a time of relief when a family knows, at last, that the person it loves is getting help. Others perceive hospitalization as an admission of failure. They tried to take care of their relative themselves, and it didn't work. Now he or she is exposed to the world, diagnosed as mentally ill, and taken behind closed or locked doors to a mysterious world of pills and therapists and regimens and treatment plans.

So reactions differ, and so do hospitals and ways of getting to hospitals. Let's look first at how people get to hospitals. Either they decide to go under their own steam, voluntarily, or somebody else decides they need to be there, and they are involuntarily committed.

As a voluntary patient your relative may have determined, along with the doctor, that hospitalization was a sensible choice, especially with a first-time acute episode. In a hospital setting, diagnosis can be solidified. Medication can be administered under the watchful eyes of a trained staff. Tests can be run to rule out grossly physical causes. If your relative has been badly disturbed and frightened, the hospital may provide him or her with a sense of haven, of being helped, of not being alone on the planet with a gigantic problem.

On the other hand, if a relative is grossly disturbed, agitated, and aggressive and refuses aid, you may have to find out the commitment procedures for your state and follow them. What you also need to know, though, is how those laws are being interpreted where you live—for instance, do repeated verbal threats constitute dangerous behavior? To find out more, call the admissions unit of a hospital or your community mental health center. Your local AMI group is likely to have families that have been through this process many times. They can give information and help you navigate the legal and emotional waters. Since they have already lived through what you are experiencing, their advice is not theoretical. They can probably tell you what help to expect from the police, if there is a mobile crisis unit in the county, where you can drive your relative yourself, who at AMI is willing to receive calls from you in the middle of the night, and so forth.

If you must take the involuntary route (and most families do so only under duress), you will find that these initial commitments are usually for a short period of time—a few days. Commitments for longer periods require further legal action. Such procedures may seen burdensome to a family that has been suffering from great turmoil, but they are there to protect patients from abuses of the past, when people were committed to institutions without due process and sometimes for very long periods of time. There is little doubt redress was needed, but many now think the pendulum has swung too far the other way.

There are several kinds of hospitals: university, community, private, county, state, and federal (VA hospitals). In fact, the choice of your doctor will most likely determine where your relative will go since doctors send their patients to the hospitals they are affiliated with.

Hospitals vary. Most are accredited by the Joint Commission on the Accreditation of Hospitals. When judging quality, do not assume that because a hospital is private and very expensive, it can do a better job than a well-run public facility. Don't let old stereotypes about public versus private mislead you. Some of the finest schizophrenia researchers in the country work at VA hospitals. Some state hospitals are good. (Ask your AMI group for an evaluation of yours.) My own county hospital is putting in an emergency psychiatric facility that is first-rate.

Last, another word about stereotypes: When thinking of mental hospitals, our heads have been filled with musty images of snake pits where patients stay forever. Here reality is more comforting than myth. The length of stay at a hospital has been greatly reduced. People used to go for years. Now, with antipsychotic medications, they increasingly go for days or weeks. And often, instead of going "away," a patient may go right into the town's main hospital as a short-term resident of the "psych" ward until he or she is stabilized on medication.

If you foresee that your relative might need hospitalization, you can reassure yourself by checking out the facilities, services, and staff of the hospital ahead of time. My son's psychiatrist kindly arranged for me to visit the hospital where he was due to be admitted. (He never got there, but that's another story.) Anyhow, you will find that most facilities offer daily medication, group meetings, opportunities to talk with therapists about what's happening, some occupational therapy, someone to play cards and hang out with, and TV, of course. Some have exercise bicycles and other recreational equipment.

Yes, there are hospitals with locked wards, isolation rooms, and restraints for aggressive patients. Your relative may be asked to part with any object that can be used as a weapon. All this isn't pretty to think about until you realize that these are ways to keep everybody safe until an extremely disturbed patient quiets down.

For more about how to cope with the hospitalization of a relative, read *How You Can Help: A Guide for Families of Psychiatric Hospital Patients,* by Herbert Korpell, M.D. The book is one of a new series of APA publications meant for the nonmedical reader.

Vitamins and Orthomolecular Treatment

Families often ask about orthomolecular treatment. The word *orthomolecular* means "right molecule," and the treatment is derived from the theory that mental and physical wellness depends on having just the right balance of vitamins and minerals in the body. Fair enough.

Here, though, mainstream medicine and the orthomolecular psychiatrists part. And I do mean part, for they have been feuding and sniping at each other for years. The orthomolecular people say that most "regular" physicians know and care little about nutrition and human biochemistry. The charge is: nutritional illiteracy in the first degree.

Mainstream forces, on the other hand, led by the American Psychiatric Association, say that orthomolecular claims are unfounded and unscientific. The APA even assembled a task force to examine the claims made by the orthomolecular group for the therapeutic use of niacin. The task force could find no evidence that niacin was helpful. Since then mainstream medicine has dismissed the orthomolecular people as being unable to "prove" their claims scientifically. This disdain always amuses me when I consider the quality of some of the mainstream "research" that used to pass as science in American psychiatry. (See Chapter Eight.)

As these battles rage, we families ask ourselves what to do, whom to believe. Many families try both kinds of treatment, mainstream and orthomolecular, using antipsychotics along with vitamins and minerals. It's as though we were hedging our bets in a low-risk way, and indeed, many mainstream psychiatrists will go along with a daily vitamin and mineral program, as well as with special diets if they seem to help. Some psychiatrists have even experimented with the use of choline, a widely available nutritional supplement, as a treatment for tardive dyskinesia. At least one state hospital has adopted several orthomolecular practices on one of the wards, so it is becoming increasingly possible for a family to use the best of both worlds.

Obviously, if either group had *the* answer, we'd know about it by now. Perhaps our best strategy as relatives is to support and encourage both groups, along with any other people whose work may be related to schizophrenia. After all, who knows where the keys to the schizophrenia puzzle will come from?

Psychotherapy

The term *psychotherapy* covers a wide range of therapeutic techniques. At one end of the spectrum are the psychoanalysts and the analytically oriented psychiatrists who delve deep into the past and talk about transference and other arcane matters. At the other end are those who specialize in behavior modification, such as changing phobic reactions. In the middle are the coaches or supportive therapists.

What parents are wary of, and with good reason, are the psychoanalytically inclined physicians. During the 1950s and 1960s parents were given a very hard time by analytically oriented psychiatrists who dominated the field. According to the lore in fashion at the time, diseased family relationships produced schizophrenia. Talk therapy with the patient was supposed to produce insights into his or her tortured family connections. These insights were in turn supposed to be healing. Such was the theory and treatment.

What families thought they got from the treatment was something else. It was, in their opinion, *mis*treatment, a litany of disaster. Specifically, the families objected to:

1. Being blamed
2. The promotion of mistrust within the family group
3. The lack of medical effectiveness
4. The upsetting of their family member during "therapy"
5. The high medical bills.

One mother told me, "It took us awhile to catch on, but essentially we paid that doctor to tell our son that his father and I were bad. That's what it boiled down to: paying a shrink to undermine what good feelings were left. Our son became suspicious of us. Just what we didn't need, spreading his paranoia. And there was no improvement in his symptoms. And the doctor treated us with contempt . . . as he sent us whopper bills, which for a while we paid because we didn't know what was going on or what else to try.

"Much later our son got copies of the files this doctor sent to the next one we used. (We finally had the sense to switch doctors.) In the file was a letter the psychoanalyst wrote about our family to the next doctor. It was viciously critical of us. For instance, when our son was sick and at home, we tried to keep his interest in the world alive, to make him feel well and useful instead of sick and useless. We involved him as much as possible with the work the rest of us did around the place. The doctor criticized us for that, saying we were giving our 'infantilized' son 'make-work,' fostering 'dependency,' and giving 'mixed messages' by telling him his contribution was important when anybody could see the work we gave him was insignificant.

"With this guy, we couldn't win. And we didn't. We had much better results with a doctor who knocked down the hallucinations with drugs and gave our son some friendly coaching about how to survive the damned disease."

What happened to this family was not unusual in the decades before the widespread use of antipsychotic drugs. The influence of parent blamers and psyche probers has waned, but there are still a few in the woods. What should you do if you find one?

In a word, run. I have yet to meet a family whose advice is other than this.

Some relatives are even stronger in their aversion to old-line psychoanalysts. One father said he thought any doctor who was still using shrink talk alone as a treatment for schizophrenia should be sued for malpractice. Another said the relatives of schizophrenics should organize and influence insurance companies to refuse coverage for schizophrenia treatment that relied solely on psychoanalysis. Obviously, these parents have been burned. Their emotions are high; their wounds still raw.

Is there more to be said on the subject? What, for instance, do comparative treatment studies tell us about the efficacy of insight-oriented therapy for schizophrenia?

Several have been done. The study carried out by P. R. A. May in the 1960s provides us with 352 pages of fascinating reading. Dr. May compared five kinds of treatment: drug therapy, psychotherapy, psychotherapy with drugs, shock treatment (ECT), and milieu therapy (a rather vague treatment that consists of much patient and staff interaction and group goal setting—it's living together, respecting each other, and working for the greater good of everybody).

What were the results? The drug only and the drug plus psychotherapy yielded the best results. Psychotherapy alone and milieu did the worst, with ECT occupying a middle position. Clearly, the physical approaches were the way to go.

Judd Marmor, former president of the APA, has said that treating schizophrenia with psychotherapy alone without using drugs is malpractice. And E. Fuller Torrey says, "To do insight-oriented psychotherapy on persons with schizophrenia is analogous to directing a flood into a town already ravaged by a tornado."

Coaching: The Practical Alternative

What, then, makes sense in the treatment of schizophrenia? Do we just give the patient antipsychotics and leave it at that? No, not by a long shot, for there is a kind of help that is practical, humane, and oriented to conscious behavior instead of unconscious drives. Some people call it supportive psychotherapy. Some call it counseling or psychosocial treatment. What it is is coaching. Here's what it can be in the hands of a sympathetic and skilled mental health professional.

The professional acts as a friendly coach, helping the schizophrenic patient deal with the real-life problems that are part of the disorder. As the relationship progresses during regular meetings, the two can work together on a wide range of issues. The needs of the patient determine priorities here, but general areas might include learning about the disorder itself, learning to separate what is real from what appears to be real (voices, for instance), setting goals and limits for oneself, and making sensible living arrangements.

The two might specifically discuss such things as finding a place to live, setting a daily routine, getting Supplemental Security Income, beginning a rehabilitation program, handling delusions and "voices," becoming more effective socially (learning to make eye contact, for instance), overcoming feelings of worthlessness, recognizing drug side effects, and avoiding life situations and people that are upsetting to the patient.

Notice that the process is very different from that of psychoanalysis. No unconscious drives are being explored. The focus is on the present and future rather than on the misty past. The patient and therapist work together on a practical, down-to-earth level, trying to make life as normal as possible for the person with schizophrenia.

Professionals who are skilled coaches deserve a great deal of credit. It is not an easy task, for often they must work with a recovering person who still has many of the negative symptoms of schizophrenia—for instance, withdrawal and lack of motivation.

Most of all, though, we should recognize and praise the people with schizophrenia, for they, not we, must actually navigate the treatment course laid out in this chapter. They are the ones who live this drama at the very core of their beings. They are the ones who take the medication, who go to the hospital, who experience the side effects, and who struggle with the reconstruction of their lives.

CHAPTER 6

A Family Survival Kit

> What you discover after a period of trial and error is that you can survive as a family. You can be happy because you learn how to cut a disaster like schizophrenia down to the size of a disability.
>
> —Canadian father

From disaster to disability—that in four words is the purpose of this chapter: to give you specific information about reducing the trauma of chronic illness. It can be done, no doubt about it, for there are techniques that minimize confusion and heartbreak and maximize every family member's chance at happiness. And that is one common, but unvoiced, concern of family members: Have they lost their chance to be happy? Have they been condemned by chance to a lifetime sentence of worry, of heart-shredding sorrow?

No.

People can lead productive lives in the shadow of schizophrenia. Inevitably these lives will be influenced by the presence of mental illness, for schizophrenia exerts a strong pull on our personal fate. The point is that we can reduce the force of that gravitational pull so that it doesn't draw our lives completely out of their natural orbits.

People Without Patterns

Before we get to specific methods for surviving as a family, I would like to examine one issue affecting every household that lives with severe mental illness. I've never heard this issue mentioned, yet it permeates the home atmosphere like smog, omnipresent but unnoticed at close range. What I am talking about is social uncertainty. Social uncertainty means that most of us simply don't know how to act when we are confronted with crazy behavior. Nothing in our experience has told us how to handle a relative who says that he really is St. Francis. Our hearts seem to stop when it happens, and we don't know what to do or say.

Most of us, when faced with crazy behavior, feel as if we were walking on eggshells . . . in hiking boots.

We are taught how to behave at work, in love, in common social situations, and at clan rituals, like funerals and weddings, but our only model for how to treat the mentally ill is to ignore and shun them. Most of us have to throw out the one existing model right away, for we don't want to ignore and shun those we love no matter how incomprehensible their behavior.

Without doubt, social uncertainty wears down families because we spend so much time and energy wondering what to do. Shall we pretend we didn't hear or see the latest psychotic act? Shall we confront? Shall we try to talk our relatives out of crazy behavior? Shall we be all-tolerant, all-understanding? Shall we yell at them to knock off the noise at 3:00 A.M.? Shall we commit them or kick them out? Should we let friends know what's happening? Is it OK to be mad at Uncle Joe for inviting everybody to his wedding except you know who? The list of energy-draining decisions goes on and on.

Once you begin to notice the smog of social uncertainty, you can see the effect it has on the health of the family. It drains us of positive energy. Decisions, decisions, and we have no way of knowing if we are right or not, for there have been no rules to guide us. We live in the closet and have nothing to compare ourselves to. This navigational uncertainty takes its toll, for it is hard to take a life's journey as the caretaker of a relative with no map and no guide.

We, the relatives, are people without patterns, without traditional standards, at least in this one vital area, so we have been left to invent our own. Inventing your own culture is exhausting work. It's confusing and uncertain and one of the reasons the families of the mentally ill are tired. Working from scratch, they have to make up a whole new set of social responses, and mistakes, if they make them, can have serious consequences for all concerned.

Let's look at one example. Young John says he is going to slit his wrists with his Swiss Army knife because a voice told him a bloodletting would cleanse him of evil. What should a family do? Ignore John? (He's just trying to get attention. Let's show him such theatrics won't work.) Talk rationally to him? (Let's try to convince him there are no voices and that what he proposes is extremely dangerous.) Increase his medication? (He'll get rid of these delusions as soon as we get more Stelazine into him.) Take him to a hospital? (Let somebody else handle this. We're in over our heads.) Call the police? (This kid is clearly dangerous. We need to call in heavy artillery.) Ask his doctor? (He's the professional. Let him deal with it.)

Here we have at least six possible responses to one situation. What's the answer? Each family invents its own, depending on the personalities involved; the history of the relative making the threat; past responses to increased medication; the availability and quality of the hospital, the doctor, and the police; and last, but never least, the present strength and morale of the family making the decision.

So, too, with the less dramatic decisions that are part of everyday life. We, the people without patterns, must make our own way through the mechanics of daily existence with the severely mentally ill. This chapter is intended to make that way a little less difficult by passing on what has been learned by families making up their own special patterns for living.

The Biggest Decision

There is one decision that influences most of the others: whether or not to have the ill person live at home. A family that decides to make a go of it with its ill member at home has a different set of problems from one whose relative is living in an apartment, a halfway house, or a hospital.

Many families have experienced both situations, for real life is not a tidy matter of either/or. Some of us, early in the illness, before its chronicity became apparent, had our family members living at home. In fact, we wouldn't have had it any other way. Our idea was to provide complete and loyal support.

Some families manage to continue the at-home arrangement. Others, for a variety of reasons, look for new options. The ill person may become so disruptive that normal family life cannot continue. The marital relationship may become seriously strained. The other siblings may feel neglected, their rights to normalcy invaded by the presence of a seriously disturbed person.

The question is—which arrangement will work for you? The answer depends on the individual family and on the health and capabilities of the person with mental illness. At-home arrangements seem to work under the following circumstances:

- The ill person functions at a fairly high level, has activities outside the house, has friendships, and can "maintain" in a variety of circumstances.
- There are no younger siblings whose lives are negatively affected.
- The family is accepting and noncritical.
- The interaction among family members is relaxed, rather than intense and judgmental.
- Some outside support group is used (a day center, a school, a rehabilitative group).

My impression is that of all these, the single most important factor determining the success of at-home arrangements is the health of the person with schizophrenia. If that person can "pass" in the outside world, then he or she can probably function and do well at home.

It's another story, though, when "crazy" behavior begins to run the household. One mother I know was so frightened of her son's irrationality during a particularly bad time that she would leave the house in the morning when her husband left for work and spend most of the day sitting on a bench in the local shopping mall. For that family at that time, at-home living merely spread the suffering from one person to several.

In general, at-home arrangements are not appropriate in these instances:

- The person with schizophrenia is seriously ill and disruptive, so that there is little or no chance to lead a normal family life.
- Brothers and sisters become frightened and resentful and feel as if they were living in a mental hospital instead of a home.
- The family becomes critical, intense, judgmental.
- The strain is so great that marital relationships become frayed and disrupted.
- The lives of family members are pulled out of normal orbit. There are few or no satisfying outside interests. Everything and everybody seem to revolve around the person with mental illness.
- No outside support group is used.

Despite the drawbacks, at-home living does have some advocates among parents, though I found them to be in a minority. In fact, when I asked, in our local AMI newsletter, to hear from families managing successfully at home, only two people came forward. Later a few others wrote to me when they heard I wanted to offer examples in this book for readers who wished to make at-home arrangements for themselves and their relatives.

One mother chose at-home living because she found it difficult to endure the uncertainties of her daughter's being away in the hospital:

> She was far from here, and I never knew if she was being neglected or holding her own. I worried and was prepared to hear the worst at any moment. Then she came home to live. I resolved to do my best if she would try to do hers. It gives me great comfort to see her and to know she is all right. We have a good support group in her rehabilitation workers and in the members of a day center she attends. We don't know

> what the future holds, but for now I feel very good about my choice. Perhaps someday she will choose, or will have to consider, a group living facility, but whatever she does, we'll work on it together. She knows that we want to provide her with a life she can live to the fullest and that my needs also are to be considered.

The at-home arrangement seems to work for this family. The "sick" person is healthy enough to participate in outside activities and to discuss her life and future with her mother. The family is noncritical. Two outside support groups help carry the load, and the needs of others to live normal lives are honored and respected.

Another parent who makes it work at home was also frustrated by hospitalization:

> After years of so-called professional therapy and "know-it-alls" who espoused the classical "separate them from their parents" theme (which involved much hospitalization and institutionalization), we finally got our son home. We decided to be the therapists. Our son gets his monthly checkup from an internist who has had much experience with psychosis. He is on two milligrams of Stelazine a day and is attending school on a part-time basis. We find living with a schizoid difficult, but it can be done. We've gotten some help from a nearby parents' group. We are now looking for a school for the time when he shows a desire to move toward greater independence. We will not push this as his stress tolerance is low. We are happy finally getting him away from the hospital on which he became so dependent.

Again, this "ill" family member is well enough to participate in outside activities. The family uses a support group. The parents are positive and sensitive to the issue of pushing too hard. Interestingly the family sees its home as a kind of halfway house between the hospital and independence.

For families that choose this alternative, the reward of having relatives at home is freedom from the worry of not knowing what kind of care or treatment they are getting. These parents do not lie awake nights wondering if their sons and daughters are being abused by ward attendants or robbed of Social Security checks. They know the quality of care their family member is getting, for they are the care givers.

There's another reward, too: guilt prevention. Knowing that you are doing everything possible for your son or daughter is a powerful motivator for people who are scrupulously conscientious toward their family members.

For some people, the psychic rewards are worth the difficulties. What are the drawbacks? One is that it can be difficult to live in the same house with any adult offspring, whoever they are, whatever their health. Then there are the familiar risks of family stress and marital disruption, and at least one other exists: Mothers and fathers do not live forever, and one day the mentally ill relative will have to make it without parental support. True, surviving brothers and sisters may take some interest, but parents are wise not to count on this.

So should living at home be considered only a short-term solution, with the final goal being to live alone or in a group facility? Each family must ask itself this all-important question.

Dr. E. Fuller Torrey writes:

> As a general rule, I believe that most persons with schizophrenia do better living somewhere other than at home. I have come to this conclusion after working with many schizophrenic persons and their families for several years; but it is a fact often learned painfully and at great emotional cost, by families. The reasons for living elsewhere are complex. They include the facts that most people who are not schizophrenic do better living away from the family home once they are grown and that schizophrenic persons often function at a higher level living away from home. Most schizophrenics I have known do better, and are happier, in a half-way house or similiar setting.

He continues:

> This does not mean that NO persons with schizophrenia should live at home. A minority can, and it may work out well. This is true for females more often than it is for males. Nor does

> it mean that the schizophrenic family member who is living elsewhere should not come home to visit overnight or for weekends: this arrangement is often mutally satisfactory. Such persons may also live at home temporarily while they are waiting, for example, for an opening in a half-way house.

Despite similar advice from many professionals, families often want to try the at-home alternative. Maybe they'll be able to make it work, they think. After all, aren't they good parents or spouses? Won't affection, understanding, care, and patience find a way? Not likely with a severely ill, unmedicated, and disruptive relative, for love cannot conquer all.

At 2:00 A.M. love cannot conquer the sleeplessness as you listen to your relative pace the hall outside your bedroom door. (He and his voices are having an unpleasant conversation.) Love cannot conquer your anxiety and night terrors when screams from another room pierce your sleep. (The demons were after him.) It cannot conquer your sadness as it becomes impossible to talk with the shell your relative has become. It cannot conquer the anger as your relative does and says cruel things. ("I only live here because it's cheap.") It cannot conquer the frustration as you attempt to work at home (if you do) or attempt to play at home (and who doesn't?). It cannot conquer the shame, the fear, the unsettledness of it all. If your relative is very ill, delusional, and disruptive, you may save yourself and your family much unnecessary suffering by recognizing that love alone simply can't conquer all the problems associated with chronic schizophrenia.

I am convinced that living with someone whose emotions and behavior are bizarre and disruptive has just one result. It spreads the unhappiness from one person to several. In that sense, schizophrenia certainly is catching. Spreading unhappiness is not progress. It is not the way to turn a disaster into a disability. It is, in my opinion, a way to allow the schizophrenia monster to feed on more than one member of the family. Doesn't it make sense, instead, to protect the family from emotional battering and to make the group as strong as possible so that it can give effective and intelligent aid to the mentally ill person who desperately needs it?

Chapter Seven includes information about other possible housing alternatives. Your local AMI group should know your town's board and care homes, crisis houses, and other living facilities.

What to Do About Six Trouble Spots

No matter what is decided about living arrangements, families have basic trouble spots that they need to learn how to handle. Reducing a disaster to a disability requires certain simple information that can help minimize distress, whether family and patient interactions are daily or occasional. Here are a few positive ways to handle each of six common trouble spots.

Communications

It's difficult to communicate well. Period.

So how difficult is it to communicate with someone who has severe schizophrenia? With someone whose transmitting and receiving faculties aren't working right? It can be very hard, but there are guidelines that help.

For example, keep communications simple. If you are trying to tell what chores need doing, do not confuse things by making a long and complicated list. Do not say, "Well, first go out, would you, and check the flower beds for snails and then, if you see more than three or four snails, get the snail bait (I think it's in the garage on the workbench, or come to think of it, maybe it's on the shelf in the laundry room) . . . anyhow, if there are many snails, put out some bait, except don't put it where the dogs can get at it. Try putting it under the deck instead, and be careful not to get any on you, and for heaven's sake, remember to wash your hands after you put out the bait, and then, when that's done, you need to pile up the newspapers for recycling, except save last Sunday's because I haven't done the crossword puzzle yet."

That kind of long and involved communication is confusing. Instead, be simple. Be clear. Say, "Here is the snail bait. Please put a half box in under the back deck. Wash your hands after. Thank you." And when that chore is done, you can talk about the next: "I would appreciate your tying the papers in the garage in bundles about a foot high. Here is the twine." Some families make written daily or weekly checklists of things to do. They then track and reward the positive behaviors.

Being simple and clear is not a communication frill. It may be the only way of reaching someone whose sensory input mechanisms are already overloaded or on the blink. I know one schizophrenic, a very bright young man, whose mind has been so slowed by the disease that he must sound out your words with his own mouth to make sense of them. With him, I make sentences clear, short, simple.

Being understood is one problem for families. Another is being heard at all. Sometimes communication, no matter how clear and well intended, comes up against a brick wall. The schizophrenic, for instance, may not want to be in the same room with others, so no communication is possible. Or if he or she can tolerate being in the same room, it may be at a distance, with a chair pulled away from the main group. If friendly questions are asked, they may be answered with a bare "yes" or "no." Sometimes basic verbal skills are reduced to one or two responses, such as "OK" or "I don't know."

Families feel rejected when their friendly overtures are blocked, but it helps to remember that retreat from stimulation may be necessary for someone whose brain is severely disorganized. Your ill son may be protecting himself against sensory overload. In general, it seems sensible to take your clues from the person with schizophrenia. Talk if you get a positive response. Be quiet if that's what seems appropriate. Remember, as you consider what's best, that experts think the schizophrenic fares best in an environment that is quiet enough so he isn't overstimulated, but is active enough so he doesn't retreat completely into a fantasy world. Balance is what's being recommended.

It's more easily said than done, though, to let go socially, to stop trying to be everlastingly polite, especially for those of us who were brought up to include everybody in the conversation. Our family stumbled over this issue for years, especially during clan gatherings at holiday time. We and our relatives would keep on trying to include the ill one, thinking our efforts would finally "bring him out." We slowly realized that his idea of a good time was to be in the room with us, hear the laughter and conversation, smile at the jokes, but not to be talked to very much. The strain of conversation panicked him, though he seemed to be able to follow most of what people were saying. My guess is that for him, it was like being able to understand a foreign language but not being able to speak it very well. He felt clumsy when asked to try.

Now we routinely tell our guests at holiday times that our family member is happiest as a spectator and that making conversation with him is not the order of the day. Going against traditional notions of politeness has worked well for all concerned. The strain has eased for everyone, and we can have a good time, realizing that the best thing we can do for the schizophrenic we love is provide him with a roomful of people enjoying life and each other without putting any demands on him.

If you are lucky enough to have a schizophrenic relative who can and will converse with you, need I tell you to be a devout listener?

A last tip: Don't shout. Schizophrenics are not deaf. They may not understand you first time through, but it's not because their ears don't work.

The Mechanics of Everyday Life

Even people whose family members live elsewhere have to evolve a set of limits and behaviors for home visits because the mechanics of everyday life affect them, too. And families living with schizophrenics cannot survive without such guidelines, for they stabilize the chaos of severe mental illness.

To begin with, schizophrenics should have their own rooms. Someone whose peace of mind is invaded by voices and disturbing thoughts—perhaps even imaginary enemies—needs his or her own safe place. Some studies suggest that schizophrenics do better when the amount of close face-to-face contact in family life is not great. This kind of privacy is possible if there is a retreat, a room of one's own. The experience of family members would also suggest that as caretakers they will do better when they can get away from their ill family member for a while every day, even if it's just an hour's vacation in the form of a nap in the master bedroom.

As for the old problem of whose standards should prevail in the care and maintenance of the room, I vote for self-determination. The room should be the kingdom of the person who lives there. Exceptions would be health-threatening habits, like leaving month-old sandwiches around to encourage the rat population and smoking in bed. But if the health and safety issues are resolved, then anything that doesn't interfere with other members of the household may be tolerated. For instance, if your paranoid family member will only sleep well with pots and pans on the windowsill (because they will act as an alarm when the Nazis come through the window to take him away to Saturn), then let his pots and pans be.

I'm not suggesting you go along with this behavior by pretending it is reasonable. I am suggesting that you state kindly that you don't think his fears are reasonable, but if it makes him feel better to have fortified windows, you'll understand.

Another thing that continually puzzles and frustrates families is keeping to a daily routine. Most families feel that they should encourage, if not require, the maintenance of positive daily habits, if for no other reason than to keep some semblance of normalcy in everybody's lives. As one mother said, "If I didn't go in and haul him out of bed in the morning, he would spend all day in bed, do nothing, get no exercise. I push him to do simple things so he won't get completely out of touch with the real world."

There seems to be general agreement among family members that it is good to establish a schedule that includes regular and healthy meals, some exercise, the carrying out of a routine chore or responsibility, and a time to get out of the house, perhaps for a walk, a trip to the store, a session at rehab, or a class at the junior college. The preceding sentence was easy to write, but as any family member can tell you, the prescription is exceedingly difficult to execute.

Lack of motivation is a hallmark of schizophrenia. Therefore, it is difficult for the severely schizophrenic to do the basic daily things that the rest of us take for granted. Mentally ill people may vastly prefer to sit and stare all day long. Trying to engage them in activity may be like trying to move a mountain.

What can be done? Some families reduce their expectations. They are satisfied with the small victories, with getting family members out of bed by nine, with getting them to eat salads instead of packages of cookies. What may help here is setting up a simple system of rewards. Take exercise, for instance. Schizophrenics may not run three miles a day, but perhaps they will do twelve minutes on an exercise bike before dinner. I used to make the exercise bicycle a predinner ritual, like washing up before coming to the table. Dinner was the reward for the exercise.

A concern with weight is also common. Sometimes weight goes down, but more often parents mention weight gain as a problem. Medications cause some of the weight gain associated with schizophrenia, but some comes from lack of exercise and compensatory overeating. Again, you can try a variety of ways to encourage exercise to rev up the metabolism. You can also attempt to keep weight down by having foods in the house that are nonfattening. With a chowhound, you can be sure that if there is double chocolate fudge ice cream in the freezer, it will be discovered. Fresh fruits are a good snack to leave around. Nuts are not, though peanuts in the shell can be a good compromise here as the shelling slows down the eating. An unending supply of carrot and cucumber sticks is good fare, as are fresh red and green pepper strips and raw snow peas. Heaps of steamed vegetables can be served every day. Several vegetables together can tempt eaters with veggie fatigue. Broccoli and new potatoes, green beans and mushrooms with a few bits of ham, carrots and water chestnuts, peas and onions—the combinations are endless.

Another word about nutrition: Many treatment facilities and families are limiting the amount of caffeine in the daily diet of schizophrenics. They minimize the amount of coffee, tea, cocoa, chocolate, caffeinated soft drinks, and headache medications containing caffeine. While there's some debate on the issue of the mentally ill and caffeine, evidence seems to indicate that all of us would do better to limit our caffeine intake. Fruit juices and fruit-flavored mineral waters are a good substitute. Almost anybody can get healthily hooked on freshly squeezed orange juice. Many families also offer a daily multivitamin and multimineral supplement, "to be on the safe side."

Don't be discouraged if some of your nutrition efforts don't work, for they may not. A relative intent on three Big Macs and four cups of coffee will find a way to get to McDonald's, as I found out the summer I spent serving the world's most carefully researched menus. Oh, that summer! I read everything I could get my hands on about the relationship between mental health and food. Everything. And from a stack of nutrition books and charts, I made out a careful menu that included every known vitamin and mineral. What a menu! It looked like the bill of fare from a luxury ocean liner in the 1920s. Oysters on the half shell (for the zinc, of course) and on and on. What's more, I actually carried out this culinary extravaganza. My son, however, was having none of it. He was too busy going out to get "normal" food like hot dogs and fries.

I tell this story on myself to emphasize the great overriding fact about everyday life with chronic schizophrenia: No matter how hard you try, it may make no difference. If this sounds like a counsel of defeat, it isn't meant that way, for families can accomplish much to help their ill members. Nevertheless, be prepared to have things not work all the time or even half the time. Sometimes what you do and say will make a difference; sometimes it won't. Don't blame yourself or anybody else when what you try doesn't work. It's the normal state of affairs for the kind of life you're leading.

More about meals: Many of us are trained to make the family meal a time of conversation and sharing. We keep on trying to do this even when we are alone at the dinner table with a severely withdrawn schizophrenic. Be nice, I say, to both yourself and the schizophrenic. Go watch TV while you eat dinner together. A shared focus can take the edge off the most faltering social situation.

No discussion of the mechanics of daily life would be complete without considering TV, which is turned on in the average American household about seven hours a day. Some schizophrenics are so severely disorganized that watching TV is too much for them. They would rather sit alone in a quiet room. For others, TV is an electronic godsend. It amuses, teaches, and provides daily structure, a place to go, even if that place is only out of bed and onto the living-room couch. For some chronically ill viewers, the characters on TV are reliable companions, nondemanding, reassuring. They don't say, "Here, take your meds," or, "How come you never do anything?"

You may notice, after observing your family member, that someone with disorganized brain function has trouble following very long shows with complex plots. Better keep it simple. Some schizophrenics like game shows. Some love sitcoms and detective stories. On the other hand, a five-part serialization of *War and Peace* might not work.

I have only run into two kinds of negative comments from families about TV. One is not surprising: The sick person grows so accustomed to watching the tube that he or she never attempts anything else. This is a problem in many families, not just the families of the mentally ill, and each solves it differently: limiting the number of hours, agreeing on only certain shows, or using TV as a reward for more active behavior. Those are some of the solutions. Other families just go with the flow and are grateful that their relative is motivated enough to get out of bed and watch.

The other drawback of TV viewing concerns religious shows. Some schizophrenics have delusions that center on religion. They may believe they are God, the Virgin Mary, or a saint. At least a few parents feel that these delusions are encouraged by a steady diet of TV evangelism.

Another everyday issue common to most families is the handling of money. This concern has been satisfactorily worked out in a wide variety of ways. It wasn't a big problem for the families I talked with, for most had found out what to do by trial and error.

Some people with schizophrenia handle money very well, knowing what they can spend each month and staying exactly within the budget. My son is one of these. He manages his rent, food, furniture rental payments, gas, etc. with the precision of a corporate comptroller. Others are hopeless. They give away their money. They spend it foolishly. Grocery money is used for dope, coke, and booze. They hit people up for loans and sell what they don't need to get what they want. Sometimes, especially if they are after street drugs, they are ingenious about getting access to the family treasury. One young man from a wealthy New York community figured out how to use the family charge account at the local grocery store. He regularly went in and bought the finest, most expensive food (rack of lamb, filet mignon) and traded it on the street for drugs.

Appropriate family response depends entirely on the relative's skill in handling money. People with a sense of responsibility handle their own. In other cases the family handles every transaction. In still others the family takes care of the main budget items, with the ill person getting an allowance and taking on increasing responsibility as the situation warrants.

There are more issues to be worked out on a daily level, and one of them is grooming. To put it simply, there can be three problems in this area: too little grooming, too much grooming, and grooming or dressing in a way that is bizarre—bag lady couture or worse.

Take the first issue, too little grooming. That means showers are not taken, stubble isn't shaved, sanitary napkins aren't changed, and teeth aren't brushed. Sometimes these behaviors are neglected to the point of danger. A tampon not changed is unhealthy and may be related to the possibility of toxic shock. Teeth neglected can mean cavities and gum problems. So the question of too little grooming is not one of mere cosmetics.

Not surprisingly it is on the grooming issue that some parents find themselves in the uncomfortable role of caretaker-bully. They walk up to their relative with towels and soap and announce that it's bath time. Others turn into inspectors general: "Did you wash your hands today?" "Are you using the deodorant I gave you?" Still others try a reward system: "Take a bath, and we'll go out for a steak together."

The proof is in the pudding, and whenever you find something that works for you and your relative, hang on to it. If nothing works, or if the behavior is bizarre, like refusing to wear clothes at all because they are "dirty," you should ask yourself why your relative is at home and not in a facility geared to handle such extremes.

The second problem, overgrooming, may not seem like a problem at first. Is there such a thing as being too clean? Yes. An obsessive-compulsive can cause havoc in the house. One family had a son who washed his hands at least six times an hour, all the way up to his elbows, scrubbing for seven or eight minutes at a time. His hands and arms grew red, dry, and cracked. The energy bill grew large and cumbersome. Other family members had to fight to get to the bathroom. The water ran and ran. And the towels were never clean enough for the son, so he took to using paper napkins as towels. Several packages a day.

Family patience really crumbled, though, over the toilet paper incident. This young man literally used a half roll of toilet paper when he went to the bathroom. The plumbing, predictably, couldn't handle the mass of paper, so the toilet overflowed onto the carpet. Too much, the family decided, especially on a regular basis, so toilet paper rationing went into effect in that household.

The third grooming problem has to do with dressing in a strange way. This upsets families a lot, especially when expeditions are made outside the house. Some mentally ill people layer on clothes—blouse over blouse over blouse. Others want to keep on wearing clothes even when they are tattered and torn. Still others change their whole appearance. One preppy son dyed his hair carrot red, got a permanent, and took to wearing large bangles on his arms.

Again, families cope with these extremes in a variety of ways. They try reasoning: "You don't want people to treat you as though you're crazy; then don't give them ammunition." They try rewards: "How about putting just one blouse on today, and I'll make you a cheese omelet for breakfast?" They become wardrobe guerrillas, raiding the closet in secret and spiriting the offending garments away. The first two alternatives seem reasonable. The last seems certain to erode trust.

* * *

So far we've looked at the biggest decision, where to live, and considered some of the basic issues about how to live: communication, daily routines, including meals and exercise, the handling of money and problems with grooming. Let's go now to the handling of hallucinations, delusions, and odd behavior, which is the area where we are most adrift, most vulnerable and unsure—people without patterns.

Hallucinations, Delusions, and Odd Behavior

Hallucinations happen when the brain plays tricks on the person with schizophrenia. Ill people may hear, see, feel, smell, and taste things that aren't there. They may also hear, see, feel, smell, and taste things that are there, but they will perceive them in a greatly distorted way. Objects, substances, and sounds may seem "funny" to the person ill with schizophrenia. Food may taste not quite right, often the reason why ill people think they are being poisoned. Visual impressions may differ widely from what the rest of us view as "reality." More common, however, are auditory hallucinations. These are the "voices" that many of our relatives hear.

Medications often help greatly to relieve all these symptoms and, for some, can be the single most effective way to deal with them. Doctors often view hallucinations as a sign that medication should be increased.

If hallucinations are bothering your relative, please remember that these things are real for him or her. You lose ground as a trusted confidant when you tell relatives they are silly or there are no voices. One of the wisest things anyone can learn, dealing with anybody, sane or not, is that you can't agrue with perceptions. People will perceive what they will perceive. What you can say, however, in order to keep your loved one oriented to reality, is something like this: "I know you hear voices talking to you. Nobody is really in the room when that happens. It is a trick that your brain is playing on you. I guess you experience your thoughts out loud rather than quietly in your head. Anyhow, when you start talking back to your voices, it worries and scares people around you. I know you want to get along with other people, so how about trying *not* to talk back to the voices, at least not when you are out in public?"

Sometimes an appeal like this works. Sometimes it doesn't.

Voices can be a torment. For instance, one young man I know is harried by voices critical of him. They nag. They tell him he is awful. He ends up shouting at them, "Shut up!" His solution is to whistle. Whistling drowns out the voices when he is having an especially bad day. Instinctively he whistles something cheery to keep the demons away. It is not unusual to hear him whistling "Deck the Halls with Boughs of Holly" in the middle of July.

People with auditory hallucinations now have a new ally when it comes to making it through the day: the small personal stereos that come with earphones and can be tucked into shirt pockets. Some sufferers find relief with one of these, again because it drowns out the noise their own minds are making. It's worth a try, and if it doesn't work for your relative, it may work for you because it is enormously relaxing to have your favorite music flood into your head, distracting you for a while from all earthly concerns. If you think I exaggerate, try it. I recently brought a personal stereo to a friend in the hospital who was suffering from extreme post-operative pain. I lent her one tape of birdsong—nothing but birds making a glorious racket at dawn—and another of Linda Ronstadt. The tapes worked better than codeine. I myself got through the saddest parts of this book by sitting at my word processor plugged into Kenny Rogers and Beethoven.

Now what about delusions? These are thoughts that are very strange and, to the rest of us, obviously mistaken. Paranoid thoughts are often delusions—for instance, when our relatives tell us that the Gestapo is after them or that the TV set is out to get them with poison rays. Paranoid thoughts are very familiar to many of us. So is the peculiar kind of thinking that comes from an elated, overexcited state: "Let's give a big party and invite everybody, and this will promote world peace." Sometimes this grand activity is positively touching. I know one young schizophrenic woman who insisted that she could cure a boyfriend who was also a schizophrenia sufferer if only she could have a big party for him. Everyone would come, and magically, by kind attention and goodwill, the boyfriend would get better. Her shopping list for this cast of hundreds was simply this: one chocolate cake.

Well, what should a family do about delusions? Again, saying your relative is silly just hurts you and your relationship. Many families I heard from specifically stated that it's best to avoid this kind of antagonistic face-off. They've learned, instead, to play it delicately. One parent said, "Avoid confrontation. Always, for us, there is a cup of tea and an invitation to talk—which really means listen. We respond as amicably and helpfully as possible." Discussing delusions, the same parent said, "It's like having a big fish on the end of a reel. Gently play the situation to some kind of solution that is acceptable to both."

How does this advice translate into behavior? Well, if the problem for your ill son, for instance, is paranoia, you might invite him to tell you more about his fear. He may not take you up on it, mind you, thinking you are part of the conspiracy. But if he does, you could ask calmly what forms his fears take.

As the conversation develops, you might tactfully say that you don't think his fears are realistic but that you realize that he thinks they are. Your next question should be how may you help, for he does need help in dealing with such fears. If he suggests barbed wire around your suburban house, you may well say you think that is too strong an action and search for a compromise. The compromise could take many forms: a new puppy that will grow up to be a guard dog; a simple burglar alarm system; a glass vase on his windowsill, which will fall and give warning if an intruder comes through.

Mind you, you are not going along here saying that his fears are realistic. You are saying kindly that you do not agree with his assessment of danger but that you would like to make him feel comfortable and safe and are willing to come to some compromise to do this.

A compromise may work. And it may not if you are dealing with someone who is severely delusional. As stated before, medication is often more effective in dealing with hallucinations and delusions than even the most well-meant and carefully orchestrated talk.

How about odd behavior? I mean things like laughing out loud at nothing or talking to oneself, behavior that is probably caused by misperceptions of thought or feeling. What do you do, especially when you're out together in public? There was refreshing unanimity on this point. Most families simply tell their relatives to knock it off, and somehow, the relatives manage to knock it off. I don't understand how or why it happens, but I pass it along, hoping that you, too, will be successful.

Threats and Suicide

You can't take death back, so I offer sober counsel on this subject. Take every threat seriously. If someone threatens bodily harm to you or anybody else, pay attention. Do not fool yourself by pretending that you didn't hear it or that it wasn't said. Do not believe the myth that if people threaten suicide, they won't do it. They often will. They often do. They may be playing hardball, playing for keeps.

Let's first talk about threats to you or assaults on you. Remember that the mentally ill are slightly less violent than the general population. Nevertheless, it may happen that your relative threatens you or hurts you. If your relative is assaultive, call the police. I know you didn't think you'd ever have to do a thing like that, but pick up the phone and call the police.

Here's the good news. The families I heard from had nothing but raves about how the police helped them in emergencies. Many policemen are trained to deal with the mentally ill and do so effectively and sensitively. Families experienced great relief when they sought and got help from peace officers. So do it if you have to.

Also, familiarize yourself with your state law on commitment. There is a state-by-state listing of involuntary commitment laws in the Appendix of this book. I know you never thought you'd have to do that either—that is, commit your relative to an institution—but you may well have to. It may be the best thing that ever happened to him or her. Sometimes it is the only way to get the severely ill on medication that will ease their symptoms.

Suicide should be taken just as seriously as assaultive behavior toward others. You may have to resort to commitment to keep your daughter, for instance, from being successful at taking her own life, but here's the really tough part. She may still be successful at killing herself. You may have absolutely nothing to say about it.

Except good-bye.

I wish I could tell you it's easy staying behind after a suicide, but it isn't. There are some things you can do, though, to get you through. If you are the unfortunate creature who stumbles on the inert form, call your fire department or your local emergency number. Meanwhile, if you know CPR, use it. Sometimes people are comatose, not dead. Sometimes heroic measures, if applied soon enough, can get them back. Sometimes, though, families lose, and the person dies. In any event, get help. Any help, because you are not going to be thinking straight, and if your relative killed himself or herself, you are going to be lonely.

Nothing is lonelier than kneeling next to the body of someone who has decided to leave you. Under no circumstances should you endure it by yourself. You'll need to be taken care of, and there'll be all kinds of business to attend to: the emergency crew; the firemen; the hospital; the doctor; the coroner; the church; the funeral people; the relatives; the friends. Get help.

And remember that you can endure this, too. You can.

Alcohol and Drugs

Medical advice about alcohol is conflicting. Some doctors say schizophrenics should avoid it at all costs. Others say that in moderation—say, two drinks a day—alcohol is just fine. (That's assuming that the person can tolerate and handle alcohol well and is not an alcoholic.)

The case against alcohol is clear-cut, however, when it comes to a class of drugs called MAO inhibitors, which are used for depression. There is agreement that nobody on MAO inhibitors should drink red wine and certain other forms of alcohol. MAO inhibitors are not commonly used when the diagnosis is schizophrenia. Nevertheless, you should be sure you and your relative know what medication is being taken.

Street drugs are considered no-no's by physicians. They believe such drugs aggravate an already out-of-kilter biochemistry. However, many young patients, males in particular, decide to medicate themselves, particularly with marijuana and cocaine. For some, marijuana slows down speeded-up thought processes. For others, drugs provide an explanation of why they are feeling "funny" or "crazy": "I'm not going crazy . . . it's just the drugs I'm taking."

As far as biochemical misadventures go, there is something new under the sun, and it's called polysubstance abuse. It is an enormous problem for parents and professionals, to say nothing of the ill people who go this perilous route. Polysubstance abuse was an unfamiliar term to most of us. We grew up knowing what an alcoholic was, but a polysubstance abuser? Never heard of one. Now we know, for many of our relatives will put anything into their bodies that will make them feel better: wine, beer, hard liquor, marijuana, cocaine, uppers, downers—any combination of liquid, pill, or powder that changes their reality for a time. What should be remembered is that street drugs may well undermine the benefits of antipsychotic drugs.

Any family that has to deal with a polysubstance abuser needs help. Any family that wonders why professionals can't diagnose schizophrenia right away and with precision should sit in a psychiatric emergency ward on a weekend night and see the polysubstance abusers flow through.

For some, abusing drugs and alcohol is a temporary stage. These abusers may eventually scare themselves into more moderate behavior. For others it's a downward spiral to disaster. If you are unlucky enough to deal with a hell-bent polysubstance abuser, you must learn that you are not responsible for the behavior and that you have no control over it. No matter how much you wish you could change him or her, you can't.

Taking Care of Yourself

A person who takes care of someone who is ill with schizophrenia has two people to take care of. One is the schizophrenic. The other is himself or herself. But caretakers can be wonderful to others and a big flop when it comes to considering their own needs.

How come? I think it's because of something so obvious and true and part of the scene that it isn't even noted. The caretakers are mostly women, women of a certain age, say, forty on up. Look at who comes to the local meeting of the Alliance for the Mentally Ill. Women outnumber men by at least four to one. These women grew up before the self-centered me decades of the seventies and eighties. They are products of the forties and fifties, when the watchword of any good mother was *self-sacrifice*. Self-sacrifice—anything for the ones you love—was institutionalized in those days. The churches taught it. Schools taught it. (The Latin motto of my college translates roughly as "Don't let others do for you. You do for others.") We grew up thinking it was the only right and good way to be.

Here's the problem with extreme self-sacrifice: It does not work as a long-term strategy when it comes to caring for someone ill with schizophrenia. For one thing, the self-sacrificing mother is eventually going to leave this earth, and her son or daughter is then going to have to make it without the parent running interference. Better for the person with the disability to learn as much self-sufficiency as possible as early as possible.

Also, I think self-sacrificers tend to burn out early; they haven't taken care of themselves. To be effective over the long run, to keep our psychic and physical tanks full, we parents *must* take care of ourselves. One thing I noticed about the martyrs of history, the people in the paintings with all the arrows through them, is that they didn't last long. They died young. If you have chronic schizophrenia in the family, you must learn to be a long-distance runner.

How do you do that?

1. Accept what's happening. That is a huge step. If your relative has been ill for several years, despite a series of different treatment approaches and different doctors and all your best efforts, you are probably dealing with chronicity. That means you

are in it for the long haul, at least until research efforts find a prevention or cure.

There's something calming about this initial acceptance, of recognizing deep within your soul that this is it. For now there is no way out, and you stop chasing every medical rainbow. (Lord knows we chase after medical rainbows. We chase after nutritionists and allergists and psychotherapists and mainstream psychiatrists and internists that our cousin Pete told us about.) With acceptance comes a certain repose, a rest from doctor chasing, a rest from getting our hopes dashed again and again.

2. Figure out a program to care for yourself. Write it down, and do it. It may say:

- Exercise three times a week to let off steam.
- Go to monthly meetings of the Alliance for the Mentally Ill to be with people who understand you.
- Take a nap before dinner every night, no matter what.
- Get away with spouse or friend once a month, even if it is just to the next town.
- Buy or do some wonderful thing every week.

You won't believe this, or maybe you will, but I buy a big pack of sugarless bubble gum, the latest *Cosmo,* and sit in the tub, chewing shamelessly, reading, and soaking until my fingers get dents in them. This is my no-longer-secret, surefire, absolutely frivolous way of coping. I also read the funny papers every day and do my housework with a personal stereo (that again!) tucked into my back pocket, and I sing to it at the top of my lungs. My kids groan at my singing, so that makes it even more enjoyable—mother as a midlife desperado. You can figure out your own pleasurable outrage. One woman I know, a proper New England housewife, hits the roulette tables in Atlantic City whenever life gets too much on the schizophrenia front. Whatever works.

3. Keep up your social life and outside interests. This is especially important if you are a single parent. I am, and if I didn't plan and carry out a social life, I would be a basket case, and an isolated basket case at that. Friends can be good medicine.

Don't spend all your time with your friends talking about your problems. They are willing to hear a little but not a lot. Who can blame them?

4. Get involved in something bigger than you and your problems. For many families, it's church. For others, it's involvement with the Alliance for the Mentally Ill. Many are political activists for a variety of causes, chief among them being the well-being of the chronically mentally ill. Some of us get perspective and solace by watching the world's best free show every day—sunrises and sunsets.

5. Don't waste time listening to the advice and opinions of people who don't know what it means to have a schizophrenic in the family. It's like depending on the celibate clergy for realistic marriage counseling. You have better ways to spend your time. Aunt Agatha may be sure that two weeks on a ranch in Wyoming will cure your relative. Your neighbor may know a great Jungian analyst. Thank them for their concern, and move on, remembering that the most realistic advice will come from other AMI families. In a way we are like the people in Alcoholics Anonymous—our own best saviors.

6. Never forget that it's possible to be happy in the midst of adversity. I've never been so content and serene in my life. Why that's so I don't exactly know. Much of it has to do with the five points above. Much of it has to do with being involved with something that's rock-bottom significant: the battle against schizophrenia. Freedom from triviality is one great gift bestowed on those who have suffered a lot. You never again really care if the soufflé falls before the family gets to the dinner table.

7. Give up your secret search for the crucial mistake you made that "caused" your offspring's schizophrenia. Instead, read Chapter Eight, and discover the peculiar story of why and how parents became scapegoats for the disease.

CHAPTER 7

Housing, Work, Social Life, and Money

> Aftercare is a word, not a reality. The schizophrenic is left to drift like a piece of flotsam once the hospital throws him back in the world.
>
> —South Carolina father

> We thought we were doing a great thing, getting people out of mental hospitals. All we did was shift their misery from the asylum to the jail, the streets, the single-room occupancy hotels. The road to hell was paved with good intentions.
>
> —Psychiatric social worker

> What's a community mental health center? Never heard of it.
>
> —Patient recently discharged from the hospital

> Write a chapter, will you, on what happens after someone gets schizophrenia. Seems to me the biggest problem is that schizophrenics get lost. After a while nobody bothers to track them, and they just get lost. Like the old song says, lost and gone forever.
>
> —Member of AMI

Deinstitutionalization: It Seemed Like a Good Idea

I have a friend who wants each misstep of his life summed up on his tombstone with these wry words? "It seemed like a good idea at the time."

We can say the same about deinstitutionalization, a clumsy term for a good idea that turned out to be bad news. At the time deinstitutionalization began in the 1960s, it seemed like a humane and cost-effective plan: Release the institutionalized mentally ill into the community.

Hospitals then often provided very poor custodial care. Furthermore, almost everyone agreed that hospitalization resulted in a breakdown of social skills, making patients even more dependent on the institution. Deinstitutionalization, then, seemed like the right answer because, for the first time it seemed truly possible to return patients to normalcy. The advent of antipsychotic drugs provided a way to control the more florid symptoms of mental illness, and a nationwide system of community mental health centers (CMHCs) was to be put into place to provide local services to the released patients. There were to be emergency services, outpatient care, inpatient care, partial hospitalization, and consultation. At least that was the plan.

Just about everybody agreed deinstitutionalization was a good idea, both the fiscal conservatives who wanted to cut costs, and the liberals who wanted to see the disadvantaged get a fair shake. But something happened on the way to nirvana. The seriously mentally ill got lost in the shuffle.

Usurping their places in the community mental health centers were people with problems in living, people who were feeling down, perhaps, or anxious but who were not seriously mentally ill. In fact, people with schizophrenia constituted only 10 percent of the patient load of the CHMCs.

The CHMCs that were meant to serve your relative were and are now serving your neighbors.

If you find it hard to believe this huge discrepancy between what was meant to be and what is, I invite you to visit your nearest center. Pick up its brochure. Most likely it will highlight the help offered with problems of living: job-related stress, interpersonal problems, adjustment to divorce, and so forth.

Not that these services are bad, mind you. We all can use help navigating life's journey. But services for the severely mentally ill are so desperately needed, and the problems schizophrenics face so severe, that seeing the CMHCs serve the walking well is like witnessing a surgeon choosing to operate on a wart when somebody needs an artery closed.

What happened to the medical care of schizophrenics during deinstitutionalization is echoed by what happened to their housing. Both deteriorated. Since the 1960s the patient population of mental hospitals has been reduced by almost a half million. Most of the half million did not go back to live with their families. If they were lucky, they found a board and care home, a halfway house, an apartment, or a decent single-room occupancy (SRO) hotel. (Rooms in an SRO were especially difficult to find since 1 million of them, half the national total, were destroyed or converted between 1970 and 1980.)

If the recently released were not so lucky, they ended up at a flophouse, on the streets, or in jail. Jail was sometimes preferable to street living in that it was warm and three square meals a day were guaranteed. Some found the street world so harsh that they invented ways to get back into the hospital. It was: "Doc, I'm hearing things again," or "Doc, I need to go back for a while." Self-propelled reinstitutionalization.

But most of the released remained out in the world, and the legacy of deinstitutionalization is with us still: people with no decent place to live; people with no jobs; people nobody wants. The situation is made worse by the fact that thousands of the newly mentally ill who have never been institutionalized are joining the released population to compound a very large housing problem.

Media reports of the homeless now grab the headlines. Nobody knows how many there are. Estimates range from 250,000 to 2 million. Of these, perhaps one third to one half are mentally ill. Los Angeles psychiatrists Roger Farr and Kevin Flynn, who work within a two-square-mile area that has 10,000 homeless, estimate that 50 percent of its skid row population is mentally ill. The old stereotype of the drunk on skid row is being replaced by the reality of the schizophrenic on skid row: from Thunderbird to Thorazine.

Farr and Flynn also say that state mental hospitals outside California sometimes give their newly released patients bus tickets to

Los Angeles. According to the doctors, the Greyhound bus station in their district has become a psychiatric intake center for the country. The end of the road for these patients is skid row milieu treatment: homelessness, violence, and mugging.

While Los Angeles provides a vivid example of the downside of deinstitutionalization, almost any other community in the country also reflects the failure of our society to care for the mentally ill. Services that work just aren't in place. One of the tasks of the relatives of mentally ill is to forge a system that does work. What follows are examples of successful models—for instance, New York City's Fountain House, which has generated almost 100 centers for the psychiatrically disabled throughout the world.

This next section will describe the Fountain House program in some detail, to give you an idea of how it effectively addresses the needs of the mentally ill in the community.

Fountain House: House of Hope

> . . . somehow the mentally ill in the community are looked at as a great and serious problem, and I don't think this is really the case. I know the needs of the mentally ill are great, but I only want to suggest that this is the case because so little is really being done.
>
> —Ronald Peterson, Fountain House

Ronald Peterson is a member of Fountain House, where a lot is being done for the mentally ill or, rather where the mentally ill are doing a lot for themselves. Note that Fountain House has *members,* not clients or patients. It is a *club,* not a treatment facility, and its members are people who were once hospitalized for severe mental illness.

What Fountain House offers is a chance for decent housing, effective vocational training, job placement, education, friendship, and the feeling of being noticed and needed. It is a place people can go to get their lives started again, not in isolation or loneliness, but within a network put in place and kept going by other members.

If you and your relative have struggled with jobs, vocational training, housing, and education on your own, you understand what this kind of program means. As one member said, "It's like having a bottom to one's life."

Fountain House has about 1,200 members, most of whom have been diagnosed as schizophrenic. It's open every day and most evenings. About 300 people show up each day, participating in the prevocational day program, which has six units: a thrift shop, snack bar, clerical office, kitchen-dining room, administration, and education-research. This six-part program is the first level in a series of gradually stepped vocational activities. No one at Fountain House is rushed into a high-stress work situation for which he or she is unprepared. There are no miracles here, just a sensible way of building skills and shoring up confidence.

What increases member confidence is the knowledge that their help is needed. They keep the club going. Among other things, members may do office work, bus dishes, run a cash register, write a newsletter, vacuum and polish, answer phones, and run the small in-house bank.

All these activities are guided by staff people. Four to six of them help with each unit. The staff often works side by side with club members and encourages habits that are necessary for success in outside employment: being on time; dressing neatly; learning how to get along with co-workers and supervisors.

After a time spent doing prevocational work the next step for members is the transitional employment program (TEP), which begins with an idea both simple and useful: elimination of the job interview. For ex-mental patients seeking employment, the job interview is a great barrier. Ex-patients are asked where they've been the last few years. What have they done? What references do they have? These questions strike terror into the heart of someone newly released from a treatment facility and anxious to get a job.

Fountain House simply eliminates the hurdle and makes an agreement with employers to provide workers for entry-level jobs at the going rate and with the understanding that the job will always get done. The staff has learned how to do each and every job the members are hired for and is available as backup should members run into problems that keep them from work. The reward for the employer is substantial. Entry-level positions that usually have a high turnover (which, for the employer, means advertising, interviews, paper work, etc.) are kept filled by Fountain House members.

A staff person usually goes along with the newly employed member on the first day of the job for moral support. To ease the transition, one job is shared by two members, each working four hours a day. The rest of the day may well be spent back in the familiar atmosphere of the clubhouse. Average time in the TEP program is six months.

Fountain House also fills members' housing needs. As Ronald Peterson says, "It makes a difference to have your own place like others do. But you have to know that most [newly released] patients don't go out and sign leases. They don't have the money for deposits and all of those things. When you have no job, no money, and most of all, no one to live with, you don't think about having your own place. You take what you get. There is no choice."

Well, at Fountain House there is a choice, for the club provides apartments for its members. For some, the stay is a matter of weeks or months. For others, it may be longer than a year. Many of the apartments are located near the club and are shared with another member.

Services don't stop there. Members tutor one another in an educational program that tries to fill in the gaps left by schooling missed because of illness. Other services include a benign shepherding function called reachout, in which members visit dropouts from the program and people who have been rehospitalized. The point is to cultivate and encourage positive connections with the house, even among members whose personal trajectories have taken them temporarily out of the house's orbit.

To round out the program, two more services are available: a farm project in New Jersey which supplies the club dining room with some of its meat, eggs, and produce, and a full schedule of recreational and social events.

Fountain House does have some dropouts. Twenty-five percent leave after initial intake, but staying away seems to stem from an inability to use the service rather than from a rejection of what it has to offer. Being a member of Fountain House is also no guarantee against a recurrence of symptoms or rehospitalization. What does happen, though, is that members who return to the hospital are there for a significantly shorter time than others who are intermittently ill, rehospitalized, and who have *not* had the benefit of Fountain House.

Member Ronald Peterson sums up the needs of the psychiatrically disabled for work and housing programs. Talking about Fountain House, he says, "What's missing, I think, are these kinds of places for the chronic patient. And I hope that all the parts of these places are not separated out and given to us at different addresses in the community"—an eloquent plea for centralized, comprehensive, ongoing services.

To see if a Fountain House center is in your area, consult the clubhouse list in the Appendix. Readers who want more information should write to: Fountain House, 425 West Forty-seventh Street, New York, New York 10036.

Crisis Housing: A Big Plus Vote

Another excellent model has emerged to ease the stress of mental illness for families. That's the crisis house. A crisis house is not a long-term housing solution but an alternative to hospitalization. Families that have been able to find and use crisis houses find them helpful.

Here's what California families thought of crisis houses in relation to other kinds of help available for their mentally ill relative. If you look in the left-hand column of the following table, you'll see what kinds of aid families actually sought for their relatives and what percentage of the families sought each kind. For instance, the first line in the left-hand column tells us that 88 percent of families sought help from a private psychiatrist. On the right-hand side you will find a ranking of what things actually turned out to be helpful for those families. At the top of this list is the source rated most helpful, the crisis house.

The table should be mulled over for its many implications. For instance, since the clergy were rated as being the least helpful (No. 12), it looks as if they need to learn about more effective counseling for the families of the mentally ill. Of more immediate concern here, though, is an unfortunate irony about the crisis house. What families perceived as most helpful (the crisis house) is among the least available sources of help in the country.

Here, then, is what families found to be useful (and not so useful).

*Source of Help**	*% Sought*	*Source of Help*	*Rank % Helpful*
Private psychiatrist	88	Crisis house	1
Mental health clinic	78	Skilled nursing facility	2
Board and care home	58	Socialization center	3
State hospital	54	Private hospital	4
Private hospital	53	State hospital	5
Family counselor	43	Mental health clinic	6
Clergy	40	Private psychiatrist	7
Vocational rehabilitation	30	Halfway house	8
Socialization center	29	Family counselor	9
Halfway house	28	Board and care	10
Skilled nursing facility	22	Vocational rehabilitation	11
Crisis house	19	Clergy	12

* This table was compiled from a California AMI questionnaire by Pat and Bill Williams and Robert Sommer, 1983.

What are crisis houses that families rate them so highly? They are usually intimate residences, sheltering perhaps a half dozen clients, each undergoing a psychiatric emergency. Clients live in a homelike atmosphere with a staff that is there twenty-four hours a day. Staff and client ratios are excellent. For each resident there might be one or more staff members, including consulting medical personnel who visit and supervise medical care. There is probably a program director, perhaps an assistant.

Clients tend to be people who have begun acute psychotic episodes and are now on medication. The stay may be for two or three weeks, sometimes longer. Paraprofessional staff members, usually at least two, are available to provide comfort, conversation, and practical counseling about next steps for the client who will be leaving after the psychiatric crisis.

Staff and clients together carry out the daily tasks of living. As much as possible they share shopping, cooking, cleaning, and outings. Obviously the emphasis here is on normalization, on avoiding the stigma of hospitalization and the loss of self-esteem that may be part of "going to the hospital."

A crisis house can be a blessing for both client and family. The sick relative has a safe and caring place for his crisis. The family has respite. Those who have weathered someone else's acute psychosis know how desperately the family needs rest and recharging at such a time.

And if you think you're a sissy, needing a break, consider the fact that the staff in a crisis house often works just two days a week because 48 hours of crisis are all any reasonable person would expect a body to endure. I put it to you that you may have been doing a marathon stretch of 168 hours a week.

If we got overtime, we'd be rich.

Question: What makes a crisis house even better?

Answer: When it's part of an entire community care continuum, like the one in Yolo County, California. Yolo County has Safe Harbor Crisis House, but it's not an isolated module of help. It's part of a community care spectrum that offers many integrated services. There's Sihaya, a group house for young adults who need a supervised, supportive situation. For more independent clients, satellite housing is available. A long-term residence, The Farmhouse, is geared to promoting greater self-reliance. Social programs are carried out at three different sites. To complete the spectrum, a vocational program provides work skills and training.

Safe Harbor Crisis House has links with the professionals in the area, with private therapists and physicians, and with county psychiatrists and social workers. It also works with the staff from mental health services, the mobile crisis team, suicide prevention, the family service agency, and Yolo General Hospital.

Crisis houses now in existence are often the result of special funding situations or of particular grants. They are still in the model-program phase of development and are not widely available as a service. How come? Why aren't there more?

Because insurance companies won't pay for medical care in nonhospital settings. Until this funding situation is remedied, there is unlikely to be a major shift toward acute care for the mentally ill in a crisis house.

Family groups can unify and begin to work on this problem. They have a mighty argument on their side: money. According to one report, in the Washington, D.C., area it costs about $500 a day to be hospitalized in a private facility. It costs $175 a day to be hospitalized in a public facility. It costs $85 a day to be in a crisis house.

Economics and what families want and need are perfectly aligned. What needs to change are the insurance companies.

Your Situation

If housing of any kind has been a problem for you, get in touch with the people in your local AMI group. They often know the area's good facilities. They themselves may even have started a residence. Members should be able to give you information about board and care homes, skilled nursing homes, and hospitals. They know where reasonable apartments are clustered and which facilities and areas to avoid. They may give you nitty-gritty information: which board and care home stints on the meals; what the patients at X Hospital have to say about the night shift staff; what areas are high-crime and should be avoided; what private psychiatric hospital is being run for the profit of the referring physician who manages to keep patients for a length of time exactly equal to the limits of their insurance coverage. If your area has no AMI group, you can try a community mental health center or your doctor.

In the best of all possible worlds, each town would have housing accommodations available on a computer, including information about where the facility is; who is eligible to get in; how many clients there are; what it costs; what the services are; if the stay is short-term, long-term, or indefinite; if it's near transportation, medical services, shopping centers, schools, social centers, recreation; if there are any openings; how long the waiting list is; who needs and wants a roommate; whom to call for more information. Computer hackers among AMI relatives might take this on as a project for their own towns and send monthly updates to referring agencies.

If you are dissatisfied with the housing available locally, consider joining others to start your own place. Many parent groups have done this and have become experts on zoning, licensing, community relations, funding sources, grant writing, bulk purchasing, remodeling, interior design, and all the other concerns good works are heir to. There is a wide spectrum of such facilities. Some are minifarms that produce everything from wonderful herbs to fabulous raspberries. Others are beautiful houses set in posh residential areas. Still others are more modest places in the ordinary sections of a town.

For information about how to start a residence, send $1 and a request for the *Half-Way House Handbook* to George Louzensky, 1624 Trollman Avenue, San Mateo, California 94401. Mr. Louzensky, along with parents from the local AMI chapter, started two residences, Dexter Lodge and Mateo House. The handbook is a brief distillation of what they learned about getting started, doing a population and resource survey, finding funding, becoming incorporated, selecting residents, directors, and counselors, and keeping up program quality.

Rehabilitation: What It Is

Families mention, again and again, two great needs: housing and rehabilitation. Most of us already know at least something about housing. After all, having to find a home is a common experience. But many people have no clear idea of what rehab is, especially of what good rehab is.

One of the most down-to-earth rehabilitation experts in the United States is Bill Anthony of Boston. In his opinion, we relatives can gauge the quality of a particular vocational rehab program by looking for two things: skills training—changing the person—and environmental support—changing the environment.

When evaluating the first component, says Anthony, make sure your relatives' skills training is tied to their goals, not to what the counselor likes to teach. For instance, before training begins, there should be an assessment to find out what the client wants.

Some people have reservations about the second component of a good program: changing the work environment, which, for example, might mean splitting one job between two people or providing a sheltered workshop. Parents evidently worry that creating a special environment fosters dependency. Anthony downplays this worry, saying that nobody tells the physically disabled, "You're getting entirely too dependent on that wheelchair." He has a good point. Psychiatrically disabled people can use the same kind of special help extended to the physically disabled.

As far as figuring out who is, and isn't, going to do well after vocational training, Anthony says the best predictor is someone's skills, not someone's symptoms. What this means to families is that we shouldn't despair of our relatives' keeping jobs just because they hear voices, as long as they have some skills.

When looking at what is actually being taught in a rehab program, a family should make sure its relative is getting skills training in three different areas. First, the family member should be learning skills that get the basic job done: clerking, typing, assembling, programming, waitressing, whatever. Second, the program should focus on skills that make him or her a dependable worker: showing up on time, not taking long coffee breaks, and so forth. Third, getting-along skills should be emphasized. Your relative must mesh with co-workers and supervisors and should be learning basic business manners and minimal standards of grooming.

People with schizophrenia need, it seems to me, special training in how to get along in the work world. For instance, schizophrenics might work on symptom control: not laughing out loud when others aren't laughing; not talking back to hallucinated voices on the job; using eye contact when talking with others; sitting with the group at meetings rather than off in a corner.

Right now many rehab workers do not know how to do this kind of work with the mentally ill. Until recently, in fact, the psychiatrically disabled have not been part of regular rehabilitation programs. Things are changing, and rehab counselors are learning about the mentally ill—for instance, that they have a different set of limitations than does a paraplegic. One lesson rehab workers have to learn is the same one we families stumble over: that the lack of motivation found in schizophrenia is a symptom to be worked with, not a defect to be judged.

Eden Express: Rehab That Tastes Good

To call Eden Express another rehab project is to call Paris another town, Picasso another artist, and Dietrich just another pretty face. Eden Express has it, *it* being the palpable aura given off in the presence of excellence.

Unless you're told, when you first walk into Eden Express, you don't know it's a rehab project. There's not a hint of make-work, not a touch of tentativeness. What you see instead is a very pleasant restaurant-coffeehouse on the main street of Hayward, California, near San Francisco Bay. What you are presented with is an intriguing menu. What you get is excellent food, cheerful service, and good wine. When diners read the small print on the menu, they find that Eden Express is a project "for recovering mentally disabled adults to learn employable skills and to become contributing members of the community."

Is that just social work rhetoric? Bet your quiche, no, for 82 percent of Eden Express's "graduates" got jobs last year. They got restaurant jobs they were trained for at Eden Express: cashier, hostess, waiter or waitress, beverage bar, food preparation, janitorial, busing, and dishwashing.

What makes the project work? Two things for starters: an abiding belief in the possibilities of the mentally ill and plain old business sense. Director Barbara Lawson lays out the convictions of the people at Eden Express: "We think the mentally disabled have a place, deserve a place. They deserve more than sitting on the side of a bed all day. We make a place for them here. Then they help themselves. And they do help themselves, though many believe they can't. We believe that they can, and they do."

Belief, though, is just a beginning, for good intentions aren't enough to make a project succeed. Results are what count in the real world, and for a restaurant, results mean putting out consistently good food and paying attention to profit margins. Eden Express is presently 62 percent self-sustaining, the rest of funds coming from government sources. Expansion plans call for a catering and banquet service that will make the program completely self-supporting. No fund raising, no grants, no reaching out the hand to government agencies. That's the goal.

Business sense at Eden Express spills over into its marketing program. Community outreach is what it's called in the nonprofit world, but it's marketing—marketing of the best kind, with everybody getting something. For instance, community leaders have been recognized and taken into the fold. One by one they've been invited to do well-publicized stints as lunchtime celebrity chefs. Lunch crowds grew so large, in fact, that the guest chef program had to be moved to the afternoon. In the early P.M. it's now desserts (recipes provided by the featured chef) and music. The afternoon programs keep the trainees busy and off-hour income higher.

Director Lawson has harnessed people's natural desire to do "something" for the mentally disabled. People want to help, she notes, but they want to do it in a safe place. Eden Express certainly feels like a safe place, safe for the trainees, who have structure, support, and a staff that cares, and safe for the customers, who get their stereotypes of the mentally ill deflated by the pleasant, competent trainees.

Eden Express is accredited by the Commission on the Accreditation of Rehabilitation Facilities. Readers who want to learn more can visit Eden Express and have lunch at the restaurant with a personal tour of the facility for $10. People who want to replicate the program can order a detailed manual, *Restaurant Training for the Mentally Disabled.* It is a how-to book, similar to the manuals used in restaurant franchise operations. The manual costs $48.50 and may be obtained from Eden Express, 799 B Street, Hayward, California 94541. The phone number of Eden Express is (415)886-8765. Staff members are available as consultants.

Fairweather Lodges: A Built-in Buddy System

No one does well in a vacuum. We need the support of others. Never is this more true than when we are in distress. Misery not only loves company but *needs* company—to help endure the bad times; to beg, borrow, or steal the good. Well, the mentally ill need company and support, too, and some get these essentials from a residential and work program started by George Fairweather.

Fairweather worked as a psychologist in a Veterans Administration Hospital. He noticed that many patients were treated, got better, were discharged, and then showed up for readmission. Why the relapse? One reason, he thought, was inadequate community support; it's hard for any individual to succeed in isolation. So Fairweather and his colleagues established an effective buddy system, within which the ex-patient, along with his teammates, could find housing, friends, and meaningful work.

The buddy system began in the VA hospital, where patients were formed into groups that worked together, depended on each other, and learned to solve problems with each other's help. At the time of discharge the men left in a group and set up residence in what are now known as Fairweather Lodges. There they lived as a team and worked as a team, running janitorial services that they owned and operated. Essentially they provided for their own housing, social, and vocational needs in a sheltered subsociety, though they could get help from a coordinator who was available to assist them.

Follow-up studies show that Fairweather Lodge people have a much better record of remaining in the community than other ex-mental patients getting traditional aftercare. The lodges are not considered halfway houses or temporary residences. Members can and do stay, though many move on to even more independent living.

Making Friends

Not all ex-patients are lucky enough to be Fountain-Housed or Fairweather-Lodged. Some are left to seek friendship and social stimulation where they can find it.

Some don't seek it at all. In fact, many schizophrenics avoid social situations. For instance, California's Richard Lamb found that 25 percent of the residents in a board and care home would not venture even one block to a nearby socialization center. Another 25 percent who did make the trip dropped out after initial contact.

But sometimes people who have been severely mentally ill do want some social life, and they can find it at any of a group of friendship houses, drop-in centers, and clubs throughout the country. Some clubs are associated with hospitals and mental health centers. Some are projects sponsored by churches. They may offer a space to play table games, talk, watch TV, eat, play volleyball, read papers and magazines, even take a course in nutrition or budget management.

Typically these centers are staffed by volunteers who should be trained, at least minimally, to deal with the special problems of the mentally ill. Dr. Lamb, an expert in the treatment of the long-term mentally ill, suggests that at a minimum volunteers learn the limits of their responsibilities—for instance, that it's not their fault when someone runs away from the socialization center. Trained this way to deal with the realities of mental illness, volunteers are not as likely to drop out because they feel inadequate to the task.

(It's ironic that experts recommend training for volunteers who deal with the mentally ill 4 hours a week, but that so few professionals have come forth with programs to teach the *major* caretakers, families, how to deal with their full-time responsibilities. In my opinion, every town should have an educational program that tells families how to work with their mentally ill relatives. It could be at the junior college, a medical center, the mental health association, but *it should exist.* AMI chapters may well consider constructing a basic core curriculum for the families of the mentally ill. It seems sensible that people who care for the mentally ill 168 hours a week receive at least as much education as those who are on the job for 4.)

Whatever the issues about training priorities, the fact remains that for some mentally ill people, the socialization centers serve a useful function. For many, they don't. It would be helpful to find out why people reject such centers in the first place and then why they drop out after initial contact with the program. Some, of course, find social stimulation stressful and take care of themselves by avoiding excess input. If you've had a relative who has trouble getting thoughts and words together, you will be sympathetic with his or her people avoiding. The back and forth of conversation is just too much.

My hunch, though, is that there are other reasons why schizophrenics resist socialization activities. Could it be, for instance, that some dropouts are looking for peer groups they can "relate" to but can't find within present-day social centers? For instance, a young man just out of high school and into acid rock and motorcycles is not likely to buddy up to the sixty-year-old lady at the friendship club who's spent most of her life in an institution. Age and different life experiences are a barrier. And although we pretend to be a classless democracy, we aren't. People whose daddies went to Groton often are not comfortable with people whose daddies skipped town when mom got pregnant at fifteen. And vice versa.

We tend to lump the mentally ill together as one amorphous blob, classless, ageless, sexless, culturally bland. That's defective perception—a trick of an untutored eye, one that's likely to see all Orientals as the same and all men as just little boys at heart.

In fact, the schizophrenic are as stratified and specialized as the rest of us. There are the youth groups and the seniors, the Anglos, Hispanics, Asians, blacks, men, women, rich, poor, and middle class. And we dump all these together in friendship centers and expect mental illness to be their common ground.

I have wondered if the early Fairweather Lodges succeeded because the lodge members could establish bonds with each other. They were the same sex and had had the same life experiences: service in the U.S. armed forces; stays in VA hospitals; carefully fostered group experience in the hospital before they were discharged; and the same professional experience once they were out—owning and running janitorial services. Part of Fountain House's success in New York City may be that the club is so large—1,200 members—everybody can find somebody there to relate to. Perhaps it's time we rethought our assumptions about mass market socialization centers and began recognizing that mental illness does not wipe out differences in sex, age, and culture.

We could start by acknowledging these differences and by looking at "market segments" when delivering mental health services. We might, for instance, have clinics, residences, and clubs with an accent on youth: rock video on the club's TV set instead of Lawrence Welk; Brooke Shields's movies instead of Lauren Bacall's; counselors who know a "toke" from a "line" from a "lude" and who have a special interest in youth.

We might also offer culturally focused clubs if it suited the needs and interests of ethnic groups to align themselves that way. People who speak Spanish, for instance, might be more at home with a social worker who spoke the same language and might want to watch the soaps on a Spanish-language channel, instead of looking at the English-speaking game shows that monopolize a club's TV set.

I think if I were mentally ill, I would like a chance to meet with other women who were having the same experience. We might have much to say to each other. On the wards I've visited, I've noticed definite sex differences. The women in the dayroom tend to cluster in sociable unisex groups. The men, on the other hand, are more likely to be loners, stalking around the room, sitting by themselves.

Do these groups, men and women, want and need different approaches? Though one skates on thin ice these days by referring to the sexual differentiation of any human activity, I would like to suggest that women may be more interested in some activities than men are, and, of course, vice versa, and that groups could be started that reflect those interests.

If a female patient wanted to join the male Monday night football group, more power to her. And if a teenager wanted to play checkers with grandpa, fine. I'm not suggesting little segregated jails of interest but a flexible self-clustering of groups that will meet the needs we all have to be with real peers, instead of with sham buddies shoved at us by the system.

To test this idea in a low-risk way, special programs could be offered within already existing clubs: a youth night with pizza, Pepsi, and Michael Jackson; seniors' night; ladies' day; popcorn parties with TV football as the main course; and so forth.

Money Now: SSI

Money, for the many schizophrenics who do not work, means Supplemental Security Income (SSI). (Occasionally a schizophrenic has worked enough time to qualify for Social Security Disability Insurance [SSDI], which provides a higher income.) People now on SSI often refer to themselves as "being on Social Security." They get that idea because the SSI program is run by the Social Security Administration.

If your relative needs SSI, he or she may need help navigating the system. Social workers can be a godsend here, for they know the ropes and can save time and trouble. Being coached by a social worker about SSI forms and procedures is like having a bilingual guide along in a foreign country where you don't know the language.

In brief, though, your relative needs to go to the local Social Security office and begin the process by filling out some forms. Look in the phone book to see where the office is. He or she should bring proof of age and take along papers like bank books and insurance policies that would show his or her assets. The applicant is allowed a maximum of $1,500 in assets, excluding a car, home, and personal and household effects. Also bring along car registration and any paycheck receipts or proof of income.

Old hands say that even if you have a little income and wouldn't get much from SSI, you should establish eligibility for the program anyhow, because being eligible for SSI means you may be eligible for extensive benefits like housing programs, Medicaid, vocational rehabilitation, and food stamps.

If you are denied SSI, either initially or later, you may appeal. In fact, you may appeal to four higher levels. And don't get discouraged if your first appeal at the local level doesn't work because second-level appeals, heard before a judge in the U.S. Department of Health and Human Services, work in more than half the cases. Again, get guidance from a sympathetic social worker.

If your relative is on SSI and also in a transitional employment or rehab program, he or she should still be eligible for SSI, as long as the work is done without being paid or as therapy or training. If you run into trouble on this one, call the national office of the Alliance for the Mentally Ill, (202)833-3530. It is tracking the problem and can help.

Some agencies have responded beautifully to the dilemma of helping people navigate life on SSI. In San Diego the California Department of Mental Health, in conjunction with the AMI group there, published a fine booklet, *How to Survive on SSI: A Manual for Independent Living*. It tells, in a brief and simple way, how to make it on SSI, how to save money, what to cook, how to get help from agencies, where to have fun, how to use your Medi-Cal card, and so forth. It's good, and much of it is general information, applicable no matter where you live. Better still, though, would be to take the booklet as a model and, with the permission of the copyright holders, adapt it specifically to your own town. Order from the San Diego AMI chapter, 5820 Yorkshire Avenue, La Mesa, California 92041. Phone is (619)463-3672. Price: $2. For patients and families, it's $1.50.

No discussion of SSI should end without saying that the grants are not enough. The best case is California, where recipients who live alone get, at the time this book was written, $477 a month. In other states, people on SSI may get much less.

Richard Lamb, M.D., writes:

To a large extent we already know what kind of community programs are needed to raise the level of functioning of these patients and to enhance the quality of their lives. But we cannot even accomplish the first step of providing an adequate supportive living situation if our funding is only at the level of an SSI grant plus a small amount of mental health funds. We have only to compare the SSI grant on a per diem basis with that of hospitals or even the Medicaid rate for skilled nursing facilities to see the impossibility of doing what is needed with the amount of money made available to us. In my opinion there is no more pressing issue in mental health today than the need for greatly increased funding for more and better living arrangements and treatment and rehabilitation programs for the chronically mentally ill.

When You're Not Around: The PACT Program

In the survey I sent to families I asked what they thought was likely to happen to their mentally ill relatives when they, the parents, were no longer around. Here's what the parents said:

"This is every parent's nightmare. My feelings are that this is my most important work—to insure his future as best I can while I am here."

"Only God knows. It haunts me every day of my life. We are fifty-eight and sixty-two."

"At best, hospitalization. At worst, street life or suicide."

"Unless we have saved enough money for him, he will be out on the streets."

"He may become a skid row bum."

"[With these problems], all parents of the mentally ill should be rich and immortal."

We should, but we're not and so we must make provision as best we can for the time we're not around. There are several ways to do this. Earlier in the book I talked about establishing habits of self-sufficient living. With the severely disabled, however, that strategy can go just so far. Some can't master independent living.

Another long-term alternative is to count on the involvement of brothers and sisters, but sibling interest varies from family to family and, indeed, within each family.

On this issue families who have a son or daughter requiring continuous hospitalization are almost envied by other families whose relatives are out in the world. The feeling is that at least the hospitalized ones will be fed, warm, and protected from street violence whatever happens to the parents.

There is another alternative, though, and it has emerged in Chicago in the form of a program called PACT. PACT is a private, not-for-profit organization that offers information and a wide range of services to the families of the mentally disabled. When families ask how they can best help provide for their offspring, PACT is there to help get them answers. It gives direction about the complex legal issues connected with disability. For instance, it consults with families on such matters as how to get maximum benefits from government sources, special tax considerations, and the issue of legal guardianship. It especially emphasizes developing a will or trust that will meet the relative's specific needs.

PACT also offers consultation services about *current* needs, such as housing, care for your relative while you are out of town, rehab programs, and so forth. Several kinds of memberships are available in the program. They range from assessment advisory services to actual guardianship, with PACT acting as the family's surrogate. PACT also publishes a quarterly journal for its members. For information, write PACT, 6 North Michigan Avenue, Suite 1700, Chicago, Illinois 60602. Phone is (312)853-0226.

Families of the mentally ill can learn much from the parents of the retarded. They are ahead of us in their thinking about wills and trusts. In fact, your local association for the retarded may well be able to steer you to an attorney familiar with estate and tax law as it relates to the mentally disabled.

The National Alliance for the Mentally Ill offers several books on guardianships and trusts. Write NAMI at 1200 Fifteenth Street NW, Suite 400, Washington, D.C. 20005.

CHAPTER

8

Parents as Psychovermin: Why You Are Being Blamed

> I think parents should read this chapter the way blacks should read about the slave trade. You need the history to understand the cruelty.
>
> —Parent of a schizophrenic son

The Schizophrenia-Blame Connection

The history of schizophrenia is a history of blame. Over the years the schizophrenia-blame connection fueled the peculiar human activity called persecution. In the Middle Ages it was the schizophrenic who was persecuted for having the devil in him. The poor souls were imprisoned, chained, and beaten for their madness.

In twentieth-century America it was the turn of the parents. In an unprecedented spree of scapegoating, parents of schizophrenics were blamed, mistreated, and maligned. The charges leveled by psychiatrist judges were severe: Parents caused schizophrenia in their children.

Before we look at these serious charges and the men who made them, let's see why blame has been so closely tied to schizophrenia and what effect blame has had on families and patient care.

In my judgment, the genesis of blame is frustration. When people are frustrated, they look for a scapegoat. One of the greatest persecutions of all time—the gassing and burning of millions of

Jews—was propelled by the domestic frustration of Germany, where inflation ruined the lives of many. As fire needs oxygen to burn, so blame needs frustration, and what schizophrenia offers freely to all comers is frustration.

For example, is it a coincidence that the twentieth-century blamers of parents have been led by psychiatrists, who, until the advent of antipsychotic drugs, were cruelly frustrated in the treatment of their clients? On them had fallen the responsibility of cure without a certain means of bringing that cure about. For medical people of any time or place, the double bind must have hurt. "Go forth and cure" was the command, but there was no sure remedy—no immunization for schizophrenia; no reliable surgery; no way of "making it better" in a clear way that people could use and trust in the way they use and trust, for instance, vitamin C as the cure for scurvy.

We can measure the degree of medical frustration by the desperate parade of cures over the centuries. Every one of the following treatments has been tried: immersion in water, purgatives, bleeding, prayer, restraints, elixirs, excision of a reputed "fool's stone" in the forehead, distillation (in which the head is steamed), cautery, exorcism, music, dance, country air, psychotherapy, vitamins, insulin shock, electric shock, psychosurgery, and acupuncture.

Since the mid-1950s doctors have had something more effective to offer the schizophrenic patient: antipsychotic drugs. They brought relief to the doctors as well as to the patients. Doctors at last had a method that helped some of the people some of the time. What may be significant here is that since the drugs came into widespread use, no new blaming schools of thought have emerged from the psychiatric quarter. My reading is that reduced frustration levels lowered the need to blame.

Nevertheless, many mental health professionals are still suspicious of family involvement in the treatment of schizophrenic sons and daughters. Like a burr, the verdict sticks to the family: Bad makes mad—that is, bad families produce schizophrenic children. And the results are destructive.

Parents as Psychovermin

Families are still discouraged from visiting their sick sons and daughters, for fear the offspring will be contaminated by the "serious pathology" of the parents. To understand the effect of parent-causation theories on a gut level, one only needs to be a parent hearing a reproachful social worker suggest that "it would be better for all" if the family didn't visit the hospitalized schizophrenic. The mistreatment of relatives is cruel but usual punishment in the world of schizophrenia, but what makes the blaming behavior doubly, even triply wrong, is that others besides the family suffer—specifically, the professional and the patient.

Professionals lose the family as a treatment ally, which makes their job more difficult than it already is. Patients lose the chance of truly comprehensive treatment. Their recovery may be seriously retarded by the exclusion of the families, whose participation and support as care givers can be important in keeping the patient out of the hospital, out of jail, and off the streets. What happens, instead, is that families who stand accused become uncooperative and resistant to mental health professionals out of anger and outrage.

One very important thing needs to be said here. If mental health professionals think that the families of the mentally ill are upset, they may be right, especially when a psychotic episode is taking place in the home, *but the disturbance is likely to be the result, not the cause, of the illness*. Crazy behavior is upsetting to everybody.

Then, too, the families are troubled because someone they love is sick with an illness that has no known cause and no cure. They are troubled the way the parents of the retarded are troubled, or the parents of a child with cancer, but what really outrages them, makes them "difficult" to deal with, tilts them over the endurance line is the persistent professional view that they are the cause of schizophrenia.

Every parent I have talked to—every single one—has been shot at by professionals. Sometimes it's subtle—when the social worker excludes the parents from all meetings and refuses to talk for more than a minute on the phone. Sometimes it's a little more direct. One mother had a schizophrenic daughter living with her. The daughter had been ill for ten years. The mother was never invited to participate in any way in the treatment or in any discussion of it, though she had been the primary care giver for ten years. (Early on this mother had gotten the message from the outpatient unit of the hospital: "You are not welcome here. This is between your daughter and us.")

Once, only once, during a severe symptom setback, did she accompany the daughter to a meeting with her social worker. The daughter had specifically asked the mother to come because she was feeling terrified and overwhelmed by the symptoms. The mother, of course, went. She was curtly told by the social worker that her presence would not again be welcome. No thanks for handling the hard times. No recognition for valor under hallucinatory fire. Just "don't come again."

Sometimes parent blaming is more than direct. It's blatant, say, when the staff member at the halfway house tells a parent not to visit at all. Imagine such behavior being tolerated by parents in any other illness. Imagine a nurse telling a parent not to visit a son or daughter in the hospital after an auto accident. Such interference would not be endured. But if the son or daughter has an accident with schizophrenia, the message might be: "Don't come. You make it worse." It's time that parents stopped tolerating the blame barrier and began expecting to be treated like the parents of any offspring with any other illness.

There is a light at the end of this tunnel. There are intelligent, informed mental health professionals who don't need scapegoats to feel secure. They are to be treasured because they relieve the burden of families rather than magnify it. They are to be encouraged since they provide positive peer influence to others in the mental health field.

Some, like William Appleton, M.D., of the Harvard Medical School, have begun to chide their peers for parent blaming. Dr. Appleton says that the mistreatment of families "amounts to cruelty." He recommends humility to professionals who glibly state that parents are the culprits. He urges professionals to remember that "we have no evidence that the mothers of schizophrenics have caused their children's illness." What's being wasted in the blame barrage, says Appleton, are the strengths of parents, who can be used, not only as allies in treatment but as allies in the movement to understand and defeat schizophrenia. Parents can be effective "volunteers, fund-raisers, teachers." (We'll see later some examples of how this kind of fruitful cooperation is now working.)

So far we have looked at the history of the schizophrenia-blame connection, considered why the connection exists, shown how parent blaming can hurt professionals and patients as well as the parents, and seen how parents have been scorned as the psycho-vermin of mental health. Next, we will look at three men who led the parent-causation movement. Here are stories that nobody wants to believe. Some have never before been told.

Stories No One Wants to Believe

How and where did the parent blaming start? Why did it take hold with almost religious ferocity? To answer those questions, we can look at three men: Theodore Lidz, Gregory Bateson, and Loren Mosher.

This is no mere historical exercise. The theories of these men concerning the families of schizophrenics influence how you and your mentally ill relative are being treated today by old-fashioned psychiatrists, nurses, social workers, even neighbors and friends.

You should know why you're the target.

You should know if you're guilty as charged.

Lidz: Deficient Parents

It wasn't until after World War II that parent-causation theories became chic among psychotherapists. It was the time of a strong postwar emphasis on family and togetherness. Not surprisingly, psychiatric thought was influenced by the prevailing values of the Eisenhower era. Good family life was the common ideal of the fifties. The perfect scenario for the time would have had Doris Day as the mommy, Rock Hudson as the daddy, Robert Young as the scout master, an assortment of freckled faces as the offspring, and Lassie as the family dog. Such was the tenor of the times.

In this milieu worked one of the most influential of the family investigators, Theodore Lidz of Yale. Here is how Lidz summarized his twelve-year study of the families of schizophrenics: ". . . schizophrenic patients virtually always grow up in seriously disturbed families—as is now apparent to any careful observer." His study concluded: "The history of these [schizophrenic] patients impresses forcefully that one patient after another was subjected to a piling up of interfamilial forces that were major forces in molding the misshapen personality." Lidz minced no words; he minced parents. He stated that schizophrenia was a deficiency disease—a deficiency of the parents.

How did Lidz arrive at his pronouncements? Through "research" that proceeded without the benefit of even the most rudimentary methods of scientific investigation. His sample was very small, seventeen families. There were no controls, which means that it was impossible to seek out cause and effect with any precision. For instance, Lidz had no nonschizophrenic families to provide base line data.

All the interviews were after the fact, after the offspring had become ill, so information about the families was seen in the distorting light that scientists call retrospective interpretation; looking at past events and seeing them in a way that may suit any bias the investigator might have.

Last, the work suffered from ethical anemia. It was deliberately done without the consent of the subjects. According to the social worker on the project, the decision not to inform the families was made after a pilot test on family reactions to being told they were subjects in a research project. Four test families were selected. Two families were told the truth about the research, and two were not. The families told about the study became, according to one of the investigators, "uncooperative and suspicious, fearing that they and their patient were being exploited." The families not told were, in the words of the same person, "much more inclined to participate in a helpful way."

Because the project would not have been possible without the cooperation of the families, a decision was made: *Do not tell the families that they were being researched.* (It should be noted that the group did decide to inform the families if they asked about research. How often the families thought to ask whether they were the objects of research is not recorded.)

Working without consent led to another problem: confidentiality. How does an investigating group publicize its results without violating the confidentiality of the subjects, without tearing apart the traditional contract of privacy between doctor and patient? The answer in this case was to ignore the basic patient and therapist contract. Confidentiality was violated repeatedly as the seventeen family histories were discussed in articles and speeches over the years.

Alice Cornelison, one of Lidz's investigators, stated in a professional journal that "even if we could make the families unrecognizable to their friends, it would be next to impossible to disguise them from themselves. A father who has confided in us his extramarital affairs would not like to have his wife read his case history. . . . Since our families are relatively sophisticated, we cannot be sure that they will never pick up a book or article signed by people they know, coming from the hospital where they have had a patient." Not being sure, however, did not deter the group from revealing the most intimate facts about these families, including highly specific identifying details of their lives.

Critics of the Lidz studies did emerge. The critics asked a telling question. How is it that other children in these families turned out just fine? Lidz answered, in my opinion weakly, that "as many siblings were psychotic as reasonably well-integrated" and that those who did turn out to be healthy must have been treated differently by the parents.

Lidz's theories continued to exert an influence, although they had not been proved. Nevertheless, an entire generation of mental health professionals was educated to believe that families cause schizophrenia. Some of them are still treating our sons and daughters.

And still mistreating us.

Let us now turn to Gregory Bateson, another man whose influence presses upon us even in the eighties.

Bateson: The Double Bind Is Dead

Mention Gregory Bateson, and a few people recognize the name. But mention a double bind, and everybody registers. It's being damned if you do and damned if you don't. Well, it was Gregory Bateson who put the double bind on the map. He thought double binds might cause schizophrenia. Rather, he thought parents might cause schizophrenia by putting their children into double bind situations. The child was theoretically overwhelmed with conflicting messages from which he or she could not escape. This pattern of "relating" supposedly resulted in a massive distortion of communication known as schizophrenia.

A typical double bind situation could run like this: A hypothetical mother might say, "You must go to Grandma's for the summer or you must go to camp. If you go to Grandma's, you will be sorry because you will be lonesome. If you go to camp, you will be sorry because you will be lonesome. You make the choice. If you make the wrong choice, you will be sorry." So this hypothetical parent hypothetically repeats a series of no-win scenarios to a child and *voilà!* schizophrenia.

That, anyway, was the theory back in 1956. How was it arrived at? Bateson and his multidisciplinary group invented the double bind after looking at and listening to reports of psychotherapists (number, contents, conditions not specified), interviewing and taping the parents of schizophrenics (number, content, conditions not specified), and conducting the psychotherapy of two mothers and one father (numbers specified without evident embarrassment). On the basis of such "evidence," the theory of the double bind was born. The rest is history.

Though the evidence for the idea was almost nonexistent, the theory was clear and understandable, which is more than could be said for the intellectual ragbag that makes up much of the literature on schizophrenia. The double bind neatly filled the great information gap about the cause of schizophrenia, so a whole generation grew up believing that double binds caused schizophrenia.

It took a decade for researchers, among them E. Ringuette and T. Kennedy, to begin to set up effective tests of Bateson's theory. No one generated evidence for the double bind. Instead, Ringuette and Kennedy found that experts, including Bateson himself, had difficulty in test situations telling what was and wasn't a double bind. The same experts, again including Bateson himself, could not tell the difference between the communications of parents with normal children and the communications of parents with schizophrenic children.

Another researcher showed that difficulties in parent to schizophrenic communication lay with the sick child rather than with the parent, for when the parents of schizophrenic children communicated with normal children, they were as effective and clear as parents of normal children.

From a scholarly point of view the double bind was dead. Unfortunately not being true doesn't make an idea disappear, even in science. As long as an idea fills a human need, it stays in a belief system, true or not.

Some people still believe in the double bind theory the way people believed they were the center of the universe or the way, not very long ago, they believed that masturbation caused insanity. It simply suits their notion of how the world should work. The ghost of Bateson still haunts the ramparts of psychiatry; the idea of the double bind still walks, though the basis for it never existed.

Mark Twain had it right: "The trouble with humans is that they know so many things that ain't so."

Isn't it time we gave the double bind the decent burial it so richly deserves?

Mosher: Parent Blaming at the Top

If you believe, as did psychiatrist Loren Mosher, that certain negative family traits are associated with the development of schizophrenia, then one clear strategy open to you as a therapist is to remove the schizophrenic from the deficient family home and place him or her with a foster family. It was with such a parentectomy in mind that Loren Mosher, along with Alma Menn, established a residence for schizophrenics, Soteria. It was to be a medication-free alternative to hospitalization. One of its main therapeutic aims was to get young adult schizophrenics out of their homes, away from parental influence.

Describing their program and its goals, Mosher and Menn said, "We now know that certain aspects of family life are associated with psychosis. At Soteria House, we attempt to provide an environment within which an individual's needs can be responded to differently from the way the family was willing or able to respond."

Mosher and Menn then listed the "defects" of families with schizophrenic offspring in Table 10.2 of their 1978 report. Table 10.2 is officially titled "Characteristic Processes in Families with Psychotic Relatives, and Treatment Techniques Used at Soteria to Offset These Processes." Table 10.2 should go down in psychiatric history. It is a one-page catalog of parent blaming.

Here are a few of the family characteristics as seen by Mosher and Menn: "weak dependent offspring used to fill parental needs," "contradictory expectations," "emotional divorce," "lack of empathy," "covert rejection," "vague meanings," "irrationality," "stereotyped roles," "helplessness," "inability to share a focus of attention," "criticism," and "inconsistency."

Families who disagree with the Mosher and Menn assessment of their family traits will be interested to know that until recently Loren Mosher headed the one agency of the U.S. government devoted solely to the study of schizophrenia. Part of the National Institute of Mental Health, it is called the Center for Studies of Schizophrenia. Since the Center dispenses more than 90 percent of the money that goes into schizophrenia research, it is influential. It publishes the *Schizophrenia Bulletin,* a journal that professionals look to for the latest about causes, treatment, community care, and, of course, research on families.

In view of Dr. Mosher's attitude toward families and the position he held in the world of government, public information, and grant making, is it any wonder that parent blaming in the United States has taken so long to die? It has been institutionalized, supported by the tax money of the 4 million American parents that are the targets of the barrage.

My point in detailing the past is not to fight fire with fire and blame with blame. Cooperation, not war, is what is needed between professionals and families. My aim is to bring to light the details of the past so that professionals and parents can know why parent-causation theories have taken such a hold in American psychiatry despite the fact they are based on evidence so frail that the superstructure of blame cracks, totters, and falls even now. By the end of the 1980s these theories will be sad history, something future generations will wonder at, the way we wonder how ages past could have blamed the devil for schizophrenia.

Even the last rumbles of the theory, such as the expressed emotion ideas in Britain, will be stilled. The expressed emotion theories say that there is a connection between a high level of face-to-face hostility and criticism in a family and the relapse of a schizophrenic relative living in such a family environment. The implication here is that families somehow trip off the relapse by their behavior. Once again, in my opinion, researchers have it backward. A relative who is about to be hospitalized for psychosis provokes much disturbance in a family.

As for those professionals whose attitudes have already hardened into a blame habit—many of whom were educated before anybody heard of a neurotransmitter—they might well take to heart Robert Frost's definition of tragedy: "Something terrible happens and nobody is to blame." Parents who are still being drop-kicked by professionals may well want to show this chapter to the people who mistreat them.

Missing the Mark: Why?

Before we leave the subject of parent-blaming research, it may be useful to review why the investigations were so far off the mark and to add three new suggestions for the phenomenon. We've said (1) that the methods these investigators used were extremely faulty (small samples, often no controls, after-the-fact interviews, researcher bias in full bloom, etc.); (2) that their need to relieve their own frustrations with the disease made scapegoating attractive; and (3) that it was easier for them to fill the cause void with some theory, no matter how destructive, than to live and work with no theoretical basis for treatment. We've also said they may have mistaken the natural emotional fallout from the disease as a pathological cause.

There's another element that may have contributed to their missteps, an element so obvious that it's been overlooked. None of the researchers, to my knowledge, had long-term live-in experience with a schizophrenic, watching a human proceed from apparent normalcy to evident illness over a period of a quarter of a century. They were called in after the whistle had been blown, the symptoms present and labeled. They were, in fact, left to guess about the disease process. The result? Conclusions that were little more than wild guesses.

Furthermore, I think the investigators were off base on their ideas about proper family roles because they were male researchers who did not know in a practical way what it means to bring up a child. The one prominent female parent blamer, Frieda Fromm-Reichmann, inventor of the "schizophrenigenic mother," did not have children. As a parent of four I can only say that I wish I had the influence on my children that these researchers imagine. It's almost comic that they view parents as so powerful. One wonders if they ever asked a teenager to clean up his room.

Another reason so many investigators missed the mark is their narrow view of the family. They concentrated only on pathology and conveniently ignored the fact that parents of schizophrenics have reared millions of healthy children, the brothers and sisters of the mentally ill. What they might have investigated, instead, was the marvelous adaptive power of humans that can persevere and flourish under the adverse conditions of chronic mental illness.

Can It Happen Again? Guidelines for Research

The question now is: Could family studies be done as clumsily and as unethically as in the past? Could present studies be carried out without consent, with blatant violations of confidentiality?

It would be more difficult. Research is more closely monitored by government bodies, which issue standards for human research, and by universities, which have their own human research committees. Additional safeguards exist. The threat of litigation has become a great deterrent. A parent bringing a malpractice suit because of breach of confidentiality or on the issue of informed consent is not something that cheers a psychiatrist's heart. Additionally, some states have issued various forms of protective legislation. Nevertheless, parents would do well to develop a discriminating eye when it comes to research, for parent groups are approached by investigators.

Also, there is the matter of old wine in new bottles. Some contemporary parent blamers are serving up old recriminations in some of the "psychosocial" research now being done. They've toned down the accusations, but the point is still the same. The families are inadequate, providing the wrong kind of "learning environments" for the growing-up schizophrenic-to-be. Parents often don't realize that they are still targets, and as long as the cooperation of families is needed to do research and get grants, these researchers are not going to be motivated to reveal their actual points of view.

Here are seven guidelines to use when deciding whether or not to cooperate on research projects:

1. Find out what question the researcher is asking.

If he or she can't tell you this clearly and right off the bat, the project is probably not well thought out. (Or it's an antiparent project, and you are not supposed to know it.) When you get the answer, look at it carefully. Does the question to be researched reveal a strong bias on the part of the investigator?

For instance, consider this quote from a $409,881 National Institute of Mental Health grant to Lyman Wynne at the University of Rochester: "The objective is to identify early indicators of psychiatric illness among high-risk children and relate their attributes to characteristics of their parents." Note that the researcher has already made up his mind that psychiatric illness in children is related to characteristics of the parents. He is not asking whether or not the connection exists. He assumes it does and has walked off with more than $400,000 of parents' tax money to reinforce his stereotype. That money could have funded work on neurotransmitters, or viruses, or epidemiology, or on much-needed general education about schizophrenia.

2. Ask what risk there is.

Not a silly question. Some brain-imaging techniques use radiation. You have to decide, just the way you do with X rays, whether the possible benefits justify the risk.

3. What are the safeguards for confidentiality?

Who will have access to information about you and yours? Is the information in a computer file available to anybody who knows the file name? Does the researcher plan to discuss your life in great detail at professional meetings or in books or papers?

4. What are the experience and reputation of the investigator? Is he or she well respected in his field? Ask around. Are you dealing with someone who is doing research that is genuinely trying to test an important question, or are you dealing with an uninspired graduate student going through the motions for a master's thesis?

5. Who is sponsoring the work? Is it any group you've ever heard of?

6. What is the discomfort to you? Will it take a lot of your time? Much travel to clinics? Will you be reimbursed for your costs? For your time? Do you want to be? Will you be kept waiting in the clinic until it is convenient for the researcher to see you? Will anything be required from your sick family member? If so, what? How does he or she feel about it?

7. Can you see the results? (You should be able to.) When and where can you see them?

* * *

Now, after all these cautions, it is well to remember the positive side. Research has come a long way since midcentury. Studies are designed with greater sophistication. Technology has made undreamed-of things possible. NMR, genetic mapping and engineering are providing important clues to mental illness. In fact, psychiatric research has gone far beyond psychiatry to include a host of other disciplines: biochemistry, genetics, and epidemiology, to name a few. In many cases, it makes sense for parents to cooperate with these efforts, for in our lifetimes the focus of research is switching from blame to biology. The new generation of biopsychiatrists has jettisoned the notion of parents causing schizophrenia, of parents as psychovermin. They practice science, not slander. The big task now is for old attitudes and behavior to catch up with them.

So Are Parents Perfect?

You know the answer. The parents of schizophrenics are far from perfect, making them just like everyone else. In fact, according to a favorite writer of mine, Henri Amiel, we are all what he calls "one-legged ducks." He said (and I carry the words in my wallet): "We are as flawed and vulnerable as one-legged ducks, but the wonder is, we can do so much with the little that we are."

Relatives do much, a tremendous amount, no doubt about it. Living on the brink of an emotional San Andreas fault, waiting for the next quake, relatives of the mentally ill still carry on, and from this common experience certain patterns have emerged.

Mothers of schizophrenics probably are more concerned and protective than mothers of normal children, at least as far as the disabled child goes. That's understandable. (Mothers often get it in the ear for this concern, being accused of being overprotective. At the same time people like Loren Mosher accuse them of lacking empathy and being emotionally divorced. Speaking of double binds! If double binds caused schizophrenia, mental health professionals would have driven a generation of mothers to join their children in the asylums.)

Some researchers say that parents of schizophrenics show more marital disharmony than parents of normal children. Other researchers disagree. Probably marital discord would depend on a couple's ability to handle a high-stress life with skill and insight. Whether or not a family suffers more discord because of schizophrenia might depend heavily on whether or not the offspring lived with them. However, having the schizophrenic offspring in the house twenty-four hours a day is not a variable that has received much attention. It should. Most parents would tell you that it is a highly significant factor, one that contributes mightily to stress levels.

What other patterns are there in the families of schizophrenics? One debated point is whether parents of schizophrenics are more "disturbed" than the parents of normal offspring. Some say they are; some say they're not. If they are, it might be that they've just had the police cart their son off in a toga to the county psych ward. If they're not, they're lucky. As noted before, the early researchers who so easily labeled parents "psychotic" might have been picking up on the emotional distress caused by life on the schizophrenia front. If you've been there, I don't have to say more. If you haven't, be humble and gentle in your judgments about the mentally ill and their families.

No-Fault Schizophrenia: A New Concept

Our maturation as a species has been marked by the abandonment of certain profitless ideas. In a kind of Darwinian falling by the wayside, we have jettisoned many foolish notions. One of our wisest moves has been to toss overboard those ideas that have to do with fault and blame. After years of learning we came up with the idea of no-fault insurance. After decades of blaming someone—anyone—for the breakup of a marriage, we discovered no-fault divorce. How sweet not having to take sides, not having to fix blame. It was civilized, sensible. Why hadn't we thought of it sooner?

Is it not time now to extend the concept of no-fault to the field of schizophrenia? No-fault schizophrenia. Think of it. If we put the idea of no-fault schizophrenia into practice, it would mean that no one would have to be blamed, not the devil, not mothers, not fathers, not the doctors, not society, and certainly not the patients.

Though we have focused on family blame in this chapter, all these other groups have, at one time or another, been accused of being at fault. If the hospital and doctors had only been better, the patient would be well. If the patient had only really wanted to get well, he or she would be. If we really cared about our mentally ill, we would change our horrible society. The litany of blame goes on and on.

No-fault schizophrenia is an essential first step in breaking this cycle. With blame set to rest, peace might break out on the psychiatric front. Stranger things have happened. Energies that went into blaming and carping might be harnessed so people could work together to find the cause and cure for schizophrenia. That is, after all, everybody's goal, but an observer from Mars, watching how we spend our time, might be hard pressed to guess that finding causes and cures was high on our list. We have too many cannons and hand grenades in the way, too many minefields for us to be able to move toward the goal. Someone has to raise the first white flag to stop the war. Then we can substitute positive action for blame. Then we can remember that the enemy is schizophrenia—not those who have it, not the families of those who have it, and not those whose profession it is to try and conquer it.

CHAPTER 9

Organizing for Change

> Right now, the only sure cure for chronic schizophrenia is death. We can do better than that. We must do better than that.
>
> —A California mother

Closed Hearts, Closed Minds

America has rallied around its diseases. We support health care and research for cancer, heart disease, birth defects, multiple sclerosis, blindness, arthritis, and mental retardation. There's hardly a health cause that doesn't reach out to us in ways that are touching, often inventive. Think of the methods we have devised to help the sick. We rally around at pancake breakfasts, car washes, and benefit films. We respond to telethons, walkathons, and runathons. We brandish posters, ads, buttons, lapel pins, company quotas, and pledge cards. So organized are we, and so accepted and entrenched is charitable giving, that we can donate with the mere flash of a credit card.

Now ask this: What do we do for schizophrenia? Although it occupies more hospital beds than cancer, heart disease, diabetes, and arthritis combined, the answer is: almost nothing. The public's heart is closed to schizophrenia. The man, woman, or child afflicted with it is without every form of helping hand that we normally offer to people who are ill. Look hard for the schizophrenic poster child, a national fund-raising campaign, the celebrity sponsor, or the holiday telethon. You won't find them. Not yet anyway. It will be a mark of our progress when we attract a public figure who says in front of a national television audience, "Help the schizophrenic."

Underlying this neglect is a cavernous omission in funding for research. It's a measure of public apathy that only 3 percent of the funds for mental health research comes from the private sector. We leave it to government to take care of schizophrenia, to find its cause and cure, but since government allocations closely reflect the attitudes of the private sector, government support is thin, if not anorexic. As a point of reference, consider that we spend $203 in research money for each cancer patient, $88 in research money for each heart patient, and an unbelievable $7.35 in research money for each patient who is mentally ill. When we look at what schizophrenia costs us versus what we are willing to spend to eradicate it, we have to question our common sense.

The continued neglect of schizophrenia is very, very expensive to our society. For instance, would you have guessed that the costs of schizophrenia are equal to 2 percent of the gross national product? To look at these economic factors in concrete terms, think of Chicago. Imagine how many goods and services that major American city produces in a year. Imagine all the businesses, all the money changing hands on the shore of Lake Michigan, and imagine totaling up the billions of dollars of activity at the end of the year. That total is about equal to the economic burdens of schizophrenia.

Ask not for whom the bell tolls; it tolls for the taxpayer, who supports public assistance programs, hospitals, mental health centers, doctors, nurses, counselors, and rehabilitation workers. It also tolls for the schizophrenic, who endures dire loss of earning power. Only 15 to 40 percent of schizophrenic patients discharged from the hospital go on to work. Those who do often must take low-paying jobs. Families are also hard hit in the pocketbook; some lose all their assets, seeking a cure. One family spent $150,000 last year on private care for their son, with no change in his condition.

In the strange economic democracy of schizophrenia, everyone suffers.

Our neglect has had other consequences besides economic costs and minimally supported research efforts. One of the most striking is the lack of facilities giving comprehensive, effective help to the schizophrenic. For instance, every town in America should have a Fountain House. It doesn't. Donors give their money to animal shelters instead. Moreover, we who care have to digest this additional fact, as discouraging as it is: The mentally disabled are supposed to get along on SSI payments of under $500 a month.

The question is: How come? Why has the most serious disease in the country been ignored, its victims left to suffer without a cure—neglected, lonely, abandoned to the uncertain mercies of the closed hearts around them?

For an answer, look to stigma, the invisible tar and feathers of public opinion.

Stigma: The Great Compassion Killer

A stigma is a mark of disgrace or dishonor. Each person with schizophrenia walks through life with this invisible mark placed upon him or her. If you doubt the existence of a universal negative response to the disease, ask a recovering mental patient how he or she is treated if the truth about schizophrenia is told. Or spend some time in public with a man or woman who has schizophrenia and whose symptoms are not controlled by medication. Watch the watchers watching you. There are no smiles of encouragement, no helpful behavior. Startled looks, averted eyes, and moving away are the three most common behaviors, in just that sequence.

One study established a hierarchy of disability groups in terms of their acceptability to the public. Disabilities were divided into twenty-one groups. The most acceptable were people with obvious physical disabilities. In the middle were people with sensory handicaps—the blind, the deaf. The least acceptable were the ex-convict, the retarded, the alcoholic, and the mentally ill, with the mentally ill being the least preferred of all the groups. *People prefer a person with a criminal record to one with a mental illness.*

Where repugnance lives, compassion dies, for the first kills the last. And where compassion is dead, gone, too, are acts of kindness, generous funding, and a commitment to defeating schizophrenia. That the public is schizophobic is clear. What can and should be done to change the situation is one of the questions we families now face.

Families as Agents of Change

There are millions of people who are vitally concerned with schizophrenia—someone they love has it—but these families are isolated. Since they maintain secrecy, they do not know there are millions like them. Unaware of their numbers and, therefore, unaware of their power, they have not yet cohered into a force that can change things. They will, for if ever there was a sleeping giant on the world health scene, it is this huge body of families.

Already some are waking up and focusing on positive action. They are beginning to form groups. They are starting to push for research funds, to lobby, to monitor legislation and regulations that affect the mentally ill. In the United States perhaps 30,000 parents out of a pool of 4 million are presently organized for action through the National Alliance for the Mentally Ill. The rest—3,970,000—don't yet know their strength. They have much to do when they begin to flex their collective muscle. One of the first tasks will be to decide how to bring about change.

Making the Case

To get broad public support for our major goals, we must make a case. We *have* the case, the most severe health problem in America, but we haven't *made* the case, for making the case means making it clear that schizophrenia is a good cause, something to go to bat for. Right now people find it easy to ignore schizophrenia.

We need to present the issue in ways that are clear, emotionally compelling, financially convincing, and irresistible. How? We can focus on nine basic points about schizophrenia, hammering them home in brochures, articles, speeches, radio and TV spots. In brief, what we should telegraph is this:

- The immensity of the problem: 2 million Americans, 40 million worldwide, more hospital beds than any other disease.
- The nature of the illness: a biologically based brain disorder that affects many of the main functions of the brain—perception, thinking, feeling, and behavior.
- The severity of the illness: only one fifth to one third recover fully.
- The ignorance: no known prevention, cause, or cure.
- The destructiveness of the myths: Schizophrenia is a split personality; schizophrenics are all violent; bad families cause the disease.
- The financial costs: 2 percent of the gross national product.
- The emotional costs: severe emotional and financial burden on the mentally disabled and their families.
- The outrageous neglect: $7.35 in research money for each patient who is mentally ill versus $203.00 in research money for each cancer patient. *We spend about as much studying tooth decay as we do studying schizophrenia.*
- How others can help: Don't stigmatize the mentally ill and their families. Do give financial aid and moral support.

If we get across these nine points, we've told the basic story.

There are many opportunities to use these points to create public understanding and support. Here are a few ways we can do it:

- Enlist the aid of the Advertising Council in New York to develop a national media campaign about schizophrenia. The council is a highly professional nonprofit group of people in the ad business. They help worthy causes by producing sophisticated print ads and radio and TV spots. The broadcast spots, public service announcements (PSAs), are run for free by radio and TV stations across the country.

• Cooperate with state and county mental health departments to produce educational materials about the major mental illnesses. Help distribute these materials, so they're not left on the shelf.

• Publish a source document to end the secrecy. It can contain personal accounts of what schizophrenia feels like, what it means to get schizophrenia, and how the illness affects all family members.

The National Schizophrenia Fellowship in England published several books of people's personal experiences. To read one is to never again turn your back on schizophrenia. A similarly powerful anthology would be a valuable way of ending the secrecy in the United States.

Whether you are a family member, a mental health professional, or someone with schizophrenia, if you are interested in contributing to such an anthology, please send your story to me, Maryellen Walsh, P.O. Box 620435, Woodside, California 94062. Make it as long or as short as you want. Use any of the personal experiences and observations that you wish to share or that you think might benefit others. If you want to end your own personal secrecy and use your name, give me your explicit written permission to do so. If you want to remain anonymous, of course, your decision will be honored, just as it was for the families in this book. Let me know what you prefer.

I am especially interested in hearing from all members of the family, including the children, spouses, and siblings of schizophrenics. Also of great interest is the issue of women and schizophrenia, for women bear the burden of care. Their lives, more than any other healthy family members, are forced out of orbit by the presence of schizophrenia.

Besides producing an anthology of personal stories, other actions can be taken to make the case for schizophrenia:

• Produce a television documentary on schizophrenia for network TV or PBS.

• Start a speakers' bureau. If your affiliate has just one or two people who can talk, you can begin getting dates with local organizations and clubs, which are hungry for program material.

- Invite the press in for your best AMI programs.
- Give benefit events to which the public is invited.
- Nudge your state and county health departments to begin information campaigns and courses.

Organizing Effectively

I am talking about goal-directed change in this chapter. There are efficient and effective ways of traveling toward goals, and there are frustrating and ineffective ways. Let's spend a little time discussing effectiveness.

One of the most effective ways to change things is to join with others who have similar goals. There is power in numbers. Numbers are what count when you lobby to change things on a federal, state, and local level. You can join the National Alliance for the Mentally Ill. The address is 1200 Fifteenth Street, NW, Suite 400, Washington, D.C. 20005. Phone: (202)833-3530. Ask if your state also has an AMI group that lobbies in its capital. Some do; some don't.

You can also join your local chapter of AMI. Look in the telephone directory or in the back of this book for the chapter closest to you. AMI's purposes are educational, political—and emotional. We'll look at the last purpose, emotional support, see how it is achieved, and learn how to avoid having that function get tangled up with the educational and political purposes of the organization.

What do I mean by emotional support? My own story is typical. I belong to a family group, in fact, the first one in the country formed solely as advocates for the mentally ill. It's called the Alliance for the Mentally Ill of San Mateo County, and when I walked into my first meeting, I saw a roomful of people, all of whom had relatives that were severely mentally ill. I breathed a large sigh of relief. At last, here were people that I didn't have to explain myself to. They knew what my life was like without my saying a word. There was silent communication, the kind of osmotic understanding that old married couples have.

It's a wonderful feeling. So is being able to vent your feelings freely to others who are in the same boat. Venting and bonding with others, talking and escaping isolation—these are the emotional purposes of the family groups.

The other purpose is effective action in the outside world on behalf of the cause of schizophrenia. Sometimes these two purposes come into conflict, the venting activities tripping up the focus on effective action. These cross-purposes can be avoided. What it takes are awareness and appropriate scheduling of times to be political and times to be emotional. Here's how the trip-ups happen and how to avoid them.

A family group meets. An agenda is set. Time limits almost always exist. Then some pained soul gets up to talk, to tell about his or her latest problem with the medical system, or a son, or a drug, or a mean board and care operator, or how awful he or she feels. The rest of us in the room are quiet because we know what this person has probably endured, and we are respectful of it and the need to talk. And depending on how often this happens, the meetings are derailed and important work gets shoved aside.

I am not suggesting that we give up venting in order to be more effective. No. Never. We need desperately to talk about our lives. I am suggesting that we schedule unhurried time in which to meet our emotional needs. Some affiliates already do this. They have a Woe Night when everybody talks, listens, and learns. That's the only agenda. Or they set aside a half hour social time before their regular meeting for talking, advice seeking, advice giving. I went to a state meeting at which one woman organized a breakfast for people whose mentally ill children had committed suicide. Its sole purpose was mutual comfort. Good. It's the way to organize effectively, keeping the emotions separate from business.

Another way to maximize effectiveness is to become more informed. Suggested readings in the Appendix will give you some leads. You might consider the *Schizophrenia Bulletin* from the National Institute of Mental Health, a quarterly of scholarly articles. It is $21 a year and can be ordered from Superintendent of Documents, Washington, D.C. 20402.

If you join the National Alliance for the Mentally Ill, you will get an informative quarterly newsletter. Your local AMI probably also publishes one.

Some county health departments are beginning to offer educational programs for families with mentally ill relatives. For instance, Santa Clara County in California offers a seven-week course on symptoms, causes, treatments, medications, legal issues, community resources, and coping. For more information, contact Vicki Powell, LCSW, Central Mental Health, 2221 Enborg Lane, San Jose, California 95128.

Organized and informed, then, in ways we've been discussing, we can tackle the big tasks ahead. Here are a few of them:

Reduce the stigma of schizophrenia
Explode the myths about the disorder
Make the case for broad public support
Stimulate research efforts by lobbying and fund-raising
Lobby for increased SSI payments
Increase housing opportunities for the mentally ill
Support comprehensive rehabilitation programs
Lobby against legislation inimical to the interests of our families.

That's a big agenda. Can we do it? Do we have enough in common to unite and get on with it? After all, we come from many regions and states. Our economic situations are varied. Politically we are diverse. Some of us are Republicans, some Democrats, some nothing at all. Some of us are religious; some not.

Do we have enough in common with each other?

Yes, yes, and yes again.

There is a bond, forged from the searing reality of life with schizophrenia. This bond, invisible, unbreakable, unites families all over the world. Think of it. You would have more to say to a foreign family with a schizophrenic relative than you would to most of the people you know, for a family struggling with mental illness understands you and yours better than most of your neighbors.

What, then, should we be doing with these other families who understand us so well?

With the old ideas of family causation shipwrecked on the hard rocks of science, families will have lost their reason to hide, to isolate themselves. Concealment will have become counterproductive. The new biological model calls for us to rethink our ideas about schizophrenia, to find parts to play other than victim or fugitive.

What parts? If not in the closet, then where should we direct ourselves?

Everywhere we can be effective:

The voting booth—to elect people who will support research and programs for better rehabilitation and housing

The legislator's office—to get commitments on specific legislation

The podium—to educate and gain understanding

The kitchen table—to write letters to elected representatives

AMI meetings—for information and fellowship

The conference table—for working with mental health professionals on common goals.

We must take actions leading us to the two great goals:

- For now, making the very best of the fact of schizophrenia in human life
- For later and forever, seeing that we are the last generation to have to make the best of it.

As I asked my grandmother what diphtheria was, as my children ask me what polio was, I want my grandchildren to ask their parents, "And what was schizophrenia anyhow?"

Appendixes

State Involuntary Commitment Laws

These statutes were gathered by Edward Beis and appeared in *Mental Health and the Law*, published by Aspen Systems, copyright © 1983. They are reprinted with the permission of Aspen Systems Corporation. These statutes also appeared in the July/August 1983 issue of *The Mental Disability Law Reporter*, published by the American Bar Association.

State laws do change. Check for changes with your AMI group, mental health department, or mental health professional.

Alabama

Criteria

Mentally ill and as a consequence poses a real and present threat of substantial harm to himself or others as evidenced by a recent overt act.

Maximum Length of Disposition

None.

Alaska

Criteria

Mentally ill and likely to injure himself or others or in need of immediate care or treatment, and because of illness lacks sufficient insight or capacity to make responsible decisions concerning hospitalization.

Maximum Length of Disposition

Indeterminate.

Arizona

Criteria

Mental disorder and as a result poses a danger to himself or others or is gravely disabled.

Maximum Length of Disposition

Variable: 60 days to one year.

Arkansas

Criteria

Person has a mental illness, disease or disorder and as a result is homicidal, suicidal or gravely disabled.

Homicidal means the person poses a significant risk of physical harm to others as manifested by recent overt behavior evidencing homicidal or other assaultive tendencies toward others.

Suicidal means the person "poses a substantial risk of physical harms to himself as manifested by evidence of threats of, or attempt at suicide or serious self-inflicted bodily harm, or by evidence of other behavior or thoughts that create a grave and imminent risk to his physical condition.

Gravely disabled "refers to a person who is likely to injure himself or others if allowed to remain at liberty or is unable to provide for his own food, clothes, or other shelter by reason of mental illness or disorder.

Maximum Length of Disposition

Initial 45 days. With additional 120 days.

California

Criteria

Mental disorder and as a result attempted, inflicted or made a substantial threat of physical harm upon the person of another, or himself or is gravely disabled ("a condition in which a person, as a result of mental disorder, is unable to provide for his basic personal needs for food, clothing or shelter").

Maximum Length of Disposition

194 days for persons dangerous to others; 28 days for suicidal persons; and no limit for gravely disabled except dissolution of conservatorship.

Colorado

Criteria

Mentally ill and as a result person is dangerous to others, himself or is gravely disabled.

"Mentally ill person" means a person who is of such mental condition that he is in need of medical supervision, treatment, care, or restraint.

"Gravely disabled" means a condition in which a person, as a result of mental illness, is unable to take care of his basic personal needs or is making irrational or grossly irresponsible decisions concerning his person and lacks the capacity to understand this is so.

Maximum Length of Disposition

12 months.

Connecticut

Criteria

Mentally ill and dangerous to himself or others or gravely disabled.

"Mentally ill person" means any person who has a mental or emotional condition which has substantial adverse effects on his or her ability to function and who requires care and treatment excluding drug dependence and alcoholism.

"Dangerous to self or others" means there is a substantial risk that physical harm will be inflicted by an individual upon his or her own person or upon another person.

"Gravely disabled" means that a person, as a result of mental or emotional impairment, is in danger of serious harm as a result of an inability or failure to provide for his or her own basic human needs such as essential food, clothing, shelter or safety and that hospital care is necessary and available and that such person is mentally incapable of determining whether or not to accept such treatment because his judgment is impaired by his mental illness.

Maximum Length of Disposition

Duration of mental illness.

Delaware

Criteria

Mental disease and poses a real and present threat to himself or others, or to property. Threat must be based upon manifest indication that person is likely to commit or suffer serious harm to himself or others or property if immediate care and treatment is not given.

"Mentally ill person" means a person suffering from a mental disease or condition which requires such person to be observed and treated at a mental hospital for his own welfare and which either (1) renders such person unable to make responsible decisions with respect to his hospitalization, or (2) poses a real and present threat, based upon manifest indications that such person is likely to commit or suffer serious harm to himself or others or to property if not given immediate hospital care and treatment.

Maximum Length of Disposition
6 months to indefinite.

District of Columbia

Criteria
Mental illness and likely to injure himself or others. "Mental illness" means a psychosis or other disease which substantially impairs the mental health of a person.

Maximum Length of Disposition
Indeterminate.

Florida

Criteria
Suffers from an apparent or manifest mental illness; has refused voluntary placement, is unable to determine for himself whether placement is necessary; is "manifestly incapable of surviving alone or with the help of willing and responsible family or friends, or alternative services, and without treatment is likely to suffer from neglect or refuse to care for himself and such neglect or refusal poses a real and present threat of substantial harm to his well being or it is more likely than not that in the near future he will inflict serious harm on another person, as evidenced by behavior causing, attempting, or threatening such harm, including at least one incident thereof within 20 days prior to initiation of proceedings."

"Mental illness" means an impairment of the emotional process, of the ability to exercise conscious control of one's actions, or of the ability to perceive reality or to understand, which impairment substantially interferes with a person's ability to meet the ordinary demands of living, regardless of etiology, excluding developmental disabilities, simple alcoholism or conditions manifested only be antisocial behavior or drug addiction.

Maximum Length of Disposition
Initial 6 month period with additional six month periods.

Georgia

Criteria

Mental illness and a substantial risk of imminent harm to self or others (as manifested by either recent overt acts or recent expressed threats of violence which present a probability of physical injury to himself or others) or is unable to care for his own physical health and safety as to create an imminently life threatening crisis.

Mental illness means having a disorder or thought mold which significantly impairs judgment, behavior, capacity to recognize reality or ability to cope with the ordinary demands of life.

Maximum Length of Disposition

Up to 20 months.

Hawaii

Criteria

Mental illness or substance abuse and dangerous to himself or others or to property and in need of care and treatment. Must also be least restrictive alternative.

"Mentally ill person" means a person having psychiatric disorder or other disease which substantially impairs his mental health and necessitates treatment or supervision.

"Dangerous to other" means likely to do substantial physical or emotional injury on another, as evidenced by a recent act, attempt or threat.

"Dangerous to self" means likely to do substantial physical injury to one's self, as evidenced by a recent act, attempt or threat to injure one's self physically or by neglect or refusal to take necessary care for one's own physical health and safety together with incompetence to determine whether treatment for mental illness or substance abuse is appropriate.

"Dangerous to property" means inflicting, attempting or threatening imminently to inflict damage to any property in a manner which constitutes a crime, as evidenced by a recent act, attempt or threat.

Maximum Length of Disposition

90 days.

Idaho

Criteria

Mentally ill and either likely to injure himself or others or is gravely disabled.

"Likely to injure self or others" means:

(1) A substantial risk that physical harm will be inflicted by the proposed patient upon his own person, as evidenced by threats or attempts to commit suicide or inflict physical harm upon himself; or

(2) A substantial risk that physical harm will be inflicted by the proposed patient upon another as evidenced by behavior which has caused such harm or which places another person or persons in reasonable fear of sustaining such harm.

"Mentally ill" shall mean a person who as a result of a substantial disorder of thought, mood, perception, orientation, or memory, which grossly impairs judgment, behavior, capacity to recognize and adapt to reality, requires care and treatment at a facility.

Gravely disabled shall mean a person who, as a result of mental illness, is in danger of serious physical harm due to the person's inability to provide for his essential needs.

Maximum Length of Disposition

3 years.

Illinois

Criteria

Mental illness and as a result the person is reasonably expected to inflict serious physical harm on himself or another in the near future, or is unable to provide for his basic physical needs.

Maximum Length of Disposition

180 days.

Indiana

Criteria

Mentally ill and gravely disabled or dangerous and in need of custody, care or treatment.

"Mental illness" means a psychiatric disorder which substantially disturbs a person's thinking, feeling, or behavior and impairs the person's ability to function. It includes mental retardation, epilepsy, alcoholism or addiction to narcotics or dangerous drugs.

"Gravely disabled" means a condition in which a person as a result of a mental illness is in danger of coming to harm because of his inability to provide for his food, clothing, shelter or other essential needs.

"Dangerousness" means a condition in which a person as a result of mental illness presents a substantial risk that he will harm himself or others.

Maximum Length of Disposition

Indeterminate.

Iowa

Criteria

Seriously mentally impaired and is likely to injure himself or herself or other persons if allowed to remain at liberty.

"Seriously mentally impaired" means a mental illness (every type of mental disease or disorder except mental retardation) and because of illness lacks sufficient judgment to make responsible decisions with respect to his or her hospitalization or treatment, and who:

(a) is likely to physically injure himself or herself or others if allowed to remain at liberty without treatment; or

(b) is likely to inflict serious emotional injury on members of his or her family or others who lack reasonable opportunity to avoid contact with the afflicted person if the afflicted person is allowed to remain at liberty.

Serious emotional injury is an injury which does not necessarily exhibit any physical characteristics but which can be recognized and diagnosed by a licensed physician or other qualified mental health professional and which can be causally connected with the act or omission of a person who is, or is alleged to be, mentally ill.

Maximum Length of Disposition

Indeterminate.

Kansas

Criteria

Mentally ill person who is dangerous to himself or others or who is unable to meet his or her own basic physical needs.

(1) "Mentally ill person" means any person who is mentally impaired to the extent that such person is in need of treatment and who is dangerous to himself or herself and others, and

(a) who lacks sufficient understanding or capacity to make responsible decisions with respect to his or her need for treatment, or

(b) who refuses to seek treatment. Proof of a person's failure to meet his or her basic physical needs, to the extent that such failure threatens such person's life, shall be deemed as proof that such person is dangerous to himself or herself, except that no person who is being treated by prayer in the practice of the religion of any church which teaches reliance on spiritual means alone through prayer for healing shall be determined to be a mentally ill person unless substantial evidence is produced upon which the district court finds that the proposed patient is dangerous to himself or herself or others.

Maximum Length of Disposition
90 days.

Kentucky

Criteria
Mentally ill person who presents a danger or threat of danger to self, family, or others and can reasonably benefit from treatment.

"Mentally ill person" means a person with substantially impaired capacity to use self control, judgment or discretion in the conduct of his affairs and social relations, associated with maladaptive behavior or recognized emotional symptoms where impaired capacity, maladaptive behavior or emotional symptoms can be related to physiological, psychological or social factors.

"Danger" or "threat of danger to family or others" means substantial physical harm or threat of substantial physical harm upon self, family or other, including actions which deprive self, family or others of the basic means of survival including provision for reasonable shelter, food or clothing.

Maximum Length of Disposition
360 days.

Louisiana

Criteria
Mental illness or substance abuse which causes a person to be dangerous to self or others or gravely disabled.

"Mentally ill" person "means any person with a psychiatric disorder which has substantial adverse effects on his ability to function and who requires care and treatment. It does not include persons suffering from mental retardation, epilepsy, alcoholism or drug abuse.

"Dangerous to others" means the condition of a person whose behavior or significant threats support a reasonable expectation that there is a substantial risk that he will inflict physical harm upon another person in the near future.

"Dangerous to self" means the condition of a person whose behavior, significant threats or inaction supports a reasonable expectation that there is a substantial risk that he will inflict physical or severe emotional harm upon his own person.

Maximum Length of Disposition
Indeterminate. Alcoholism 45 days (initial) and up to two 60-day periods thereafter.

Maine

Criteria

Mental illness and poses a likelihood of serious harm and inpatient hospitalization is best available means of treatment.

"Mentally ill individual" means an individual having a psychiatric or other disease which substantially impairs his mental health. Does not include mentally retarded or sociopathic individuals. Does include persons suffering from drugs, narcotics, hallucinogens or intoxicants, including alcohol.

"Likelihood of serious harm" means:

A substantial risk of physical harm to the person himself as manifested by evidence of recent threats of, or attempts at, suicide or serious bodily harm to himself, and, after consideration of less restrictive treatment settings and modalities, a determination that community resources for his care and treatment are unavailable; or

A substantial risk of physical harm to other persons as manifested by recent evidence of homicidal or other violent behavior or recent evidence that others are placed in reasonable fear of violent behavior and serious physical harm to them and, after consideration of less restrictive treatment settings and modalities, a determination that community resources for his care and treatment are unavailable; or

A reasonable certainty that severe physical or mental impairment or injury will result to the person alleged to be mentally ill as manifested by recent evidence of his actions or behavior which demonstrate his inability to avoid or protect himself from such impairment or injury, and, after consideration of less restrictive treatment settings and modalities, a determination that suitable community resources for his care are available.

Maximum Length of Disposition

1 year.

Maryland

Criteria

A person who has a mental disorder and needs inpatient care or treatment for the protection of self or others. Individual presents a danger to the life or safety of the individual or others.

Maximum Length of Disposition

Not available.

Massachusetts

Criteria

Person is mentally ill and discharge would create a likelihood of serious harm.

"Likelihood of serious harm" means:

(1) a substantial risk of physical harm to the person himself as manifested by evidence of threats of, or attempts at, suicide or serious bodily harm; (2) a substantial risk of physical harm to other persons, as manifested by evidence of homicidal or other violent behavior or evidence that others are placed in reasonable fear of violent behavior and serious physical harm to them; or (3) a very substantial risk of physical impairment or injury to the person himself as manifested by evidence that such person's judgment is so affected that he is unable to protect himself in the community and that reasonable provision for his protection is not available in the community.

Maximum Length of Disposition

1 year.

Michigan

Criteria

Mentally ill person who can reasonably be expected within the near future to intentionally or unintentionally seriously physically injure himself or another and who has engaged in an act or acts or made significant threats that are substantially supportive of the expectation or is unable to attend to basic physical needs, such as food, clothing, or shelter that must be attended to in order for him to avoid serious harm in the near future, and who has demonstrated that inability by failing to attend to those basic physical needs.

"Mental illness" means a substantial disorder of thought or mood which significantly impairs judgment, behavior, capacity to recognize reality, or ability to cope with the ordinary demands of life.

A mentally ill person is one whose judgment is so impaired that he is unable to understand his need for treatment and whose continued behavior is the result of mental illness that can reasonably be expected on the basis of competent medical opinion to result in significant physical harm to himself or others.

Maximum Length of Disposition

Indeterminate, following commitment periods of 60, then 90, days.

Minnesota

Criteria

Mentally ill, mentally retarded or chemically dependent person.

Mentally ill person means a substantial psychiatric disorder of mood, perception, orientation or memory which grossly impairs judgment, behavior, capacity to recognize reality, or to reason or understand, which:

(a) is manifested by instances of grossly disturbed behavior or faulty perceptions;

(b) poses a substantial likelihood of physical harm to self or others as demonstrated by:

i. a recent attempt or threat to physically harm himself or others; or

ii. a failure to provide necessary food, clothing, shelter or medical care for himself, as a result of the impairment.

This impairment excludes (a) epilepsy, (b) mental retardation, (c) brief periods of intoxication caused by alcohol or drugs, or (d) dependence upon or addiction to any alcohol or drugs.

"Chemically dependent person" means any person (a) determined as being incapable of managing himself or his affairs by reason of the habitual and excessive use of alcohol or drugs; and (b) whose recent conduct as a result of habitual and excessive use of alcohol or drugs poses a substantial likelihood of physical harm to himself or others as demonstrated by (i) a recent attempt or threat to physically harm himself or others, (ii) evidence of recent serious physical problems, or (iii) a failure to provide necessary food, clothing, shelter, or medical care for himself.

Maximum Length of Disposition

6 months.

Mississippi

Criteria

Person afflicted with mental illness if reasonably expected at the time determination is made or within reasonable time thereafter to intentionally or unintentionally physically injure himself or others or is unable to care for himself so as to guard himself from physical injury or to provide for his own physical needs. It does not include mental retardation.

Maximum Length of Disposition

Indeterminate.

Missouri

Criteria

Mental disorder which causes the likelihood of serious physical harm to himself or others.

Maximum Length of Disposition

1 year, 3 months.

Montana

Criteria

Seriously mentally ill which means suffering from a mental disorder which has resulted in self-inflicted injury to self or others or the imminent threat thereof or which has deprived the person afflicted of the ability to protect his life or health. For this purpose, injury means physical injury. No person may be involuntarily committed because he is epileptic, mentally deficient, mentally retarded, senile or suffering from a mental disorder unless the condition causes him to be seriously mentally ill.

Maximum Length of Disposition

One year. Thereafter, commitment proceedings must be initiated again.

Nebraska

Criteria

Mentally ill dangerous person who poses a substantial risk of serious harm to himself or others.

Mentally ill dangerous person shall mean any mentally ill person or alcoholic person who presents:

(1) a substantial risk of serious harm to another person or persons in the near future, as manifested by evidence of recent violent acts or threats of violence by placing others in reasonable fear of harm, or

(2) a substantial risk of serious harm to himself within the near future, as manifested by evidence of recent attempts at or threats of, suicide or serious bodily harm, or evidence of inability to provide for his basic human needs, including food, clothing, shelter, essential medical care or personal safety.

Maximum Length of Disposition

Indeterminate.

Nevada

Criteria

A person who is mentally ill and who exhibits observable behavior that he is likely to harm himself or others if allowed to remain at liberty, or that he is gravely disabled.

Maximum Length of Disposition

6 months.

New Hampshire

Criteria

Person in such mental condition as a result of illness as to create a potentially serious likelihood of danger to himself or others.

"Mental illness" means a substantial impairment of emotional processes or of the ability to exercise conscious control of one's actions, or of the ability to perceive reality or to reason, which impairment is manifested by instances of extremely abnormal behavior extremely faulty perceptions. It does not include impairment primarily caused by: (a) epilepsy; (b) mental retardation; (c) continuous or noncontinuous periods of intoxication caused by substances such as alcohol or drugs; dependence upon or addiction to any substance such as alcohol or drugs.

Maximum Length of Disposition

2 years.

New Jersey

Criteria

Person so afflicted with mental disease that he requires care and treatment for his own welfare or the welfare of others or of the community.

Maximum Length of Disposition

Indeterminate.

New Mexico

Criteria

Client with mental disorder that presents a likelihood of serious harm to himself or others, the client needs and is likely to benefit from proposed treatment consistent with least restrictive alternative.

"Mental disorder" means a substantial disorder of the person's emotional processes, thought or cognition which grossly impairs judgment, behavior or capacity to recognize reality.

Likelihood of serious harm to oneself means that it is more likely than not that in the near future the person will attempt to commit suicide or will cause serious bodily harm to himself by violent or other self-destructive means including but not limited to grave passive neglect as evidenced by behavior causing, attempting or threatening the infliction of serious bodily harm to himself.

Likelihood of serious harm to others means the person will inflict serious, unjustified bodily harm on another person or commit a criminal sexual offense as evidenced by behavior causing, attempting or threatening such harm, which behavior gives rise to a reasonable fear of such harm from said person.

Maximum Length of Disposition

One year.

New York

Criteria

Person who has a mental illness for which care and treatment as a patient in a hospital is essential to such person's welfare and whose judgment is so impaired that he is unable to understand the need for such care and treatment.

Mental illness for which immediate inpatient care and treatment in a hospital is appropriate and which is likely to result in serious harm to himself or others; "likelihood of serious harm" shall mean:

(1) substantial risk of physical harm to himself as manifested by threats of or attempts at suicide or serious bodily harm or other conduct demonstrating that he is dangerous to himself; or

(2) a substantial risk of physical harm to other persons as manifested by homicidal or other violent behavior by which others are placed in reasonable fear of serious physical harm.

Maximum Length of Disposition

2 years.

North Carolina

Criteria

Mentally ill, mentally retarded or inebriate person who because of an accompanying behavior disorder is dangerous to himself or others, or is mentally retarded and because of accompanying behavioral disorder, is dangerous to others.

a. "Dangerous to himself" shall mean that within the recent past:

1. The person has acted in such manner as to evidence:

I. That he would be unable without care, supervision, and the continued assistance of others not otherwise available to exercise self control, judgment, and discretion in the conduct of his daily responsibilities and social relations, or to satisfy his need for nourishment, personal or medical care, shelter, or self-protection and safety; and

II. That there is a reasonable probability of serious physical debilitation to him within the near future unless adequate treatment is afforded. A showing of behavior that is grossly irrational or of actions which the person is unable to control or of behavior that is grossly inappropriate to the situation or other evidence of severely impaired insight and judgment shall create a *prima facie* inference that the person is unable to care for himself; or

2. The person has attempted suicide and that there is reasonable probability of suicide unless adequate treatment is afforded under this Article; or

3. The person has mutilated himself or attempted to mutilate himself and that there is a reasonable probability of serious self-mutilation unless adequate treatment is afforded under this Article.

b. "Dangerous to others" shall mean that within the recent past, the person has inflicted or threatened to inflict serious bodily harm on another or has acted in such a manner as to create a substantial risk of serious bodily harm to another and that there is a reasonable probability that such conduct will be repeated.

Maximum Length of Disposition

90 days.

North Dakota

Criteria

Mentally ill person requiring treatment.

"Mentally ill person" means an individual with an organic, mental, or emotional disorder which substantially impairs the capacity to use self-control, judgment, and discretion in the conduct of personal affairs and social relations. Does not include mentally retarded.

"Person requiring treatment" means either:

a. A person who is mentally ill, an alcoholic or a drug addict and who as a result of such condition can reasonably be expected within the near future to intentionally or unintentionally seriously physically harm himself or another person and who has engaged in an act or acts or made significant threats that are substantially supportive of this expectation; or

b. A person who is mentally ill, an alcoholic or a drug addict and who as a result of such condition is unable to attend to his basic physical needs, such as food, clothing or shelter that must be attended to for him to avoid serious harm in the near future, and who has demonstrated that inability by failing to meet those basic physical needs.

Maximum Length of Disposition
90 days.

Ohio

Criteria
Mentally ill person who creates a substantial risk of physical harm to himself or others, or who would benefit from treatment.

(A) "Mental illness" means a substantial disorder of thought, mood, perception, orientation, or memory that grossly impairs judgment, behavior, capacity to recognize reality, or ability to meet the ordinary demands of life.

(B) "Mentally ill person subject to hospitalization by court order" means a mentally ill person who, because of his illness:

(1) Represents a substantial risk of physical harm to himself as manifested by evidence of threats of, or attempts at, suicide or serious self-inflicted bodily harm;

(2) Represents a substantial risk of physical harm to others as manifested by evidence of recent homicidal or other behavior, evidence of recent threats that place another in reasonable fear of violent behavior and serious physical harm, or other evidence of present dangerousness;

(3) Represents a substantial and immediate risk of serious physical impairment or injury to himself as manifested by evidence that he is unable to provide for and is not providing for his basic physical needs because of his mental illness and that appropriate provision for such needs cannot be made immediately available in the community; or

(4) Would benefit from treatment in a hospital for his mental illness and is in need of such treatment as manifested by evidence of behavior that creates a grave and imminent risk to substantial rights of others or himself.

Maximum Length of Disposition
Two years.

Oklahoma

Criteria
A person who has a mental illness and in the near future can be expected to intentionally or unintentionally harm himself or others or is unable to care for his basic physical needs.

(c) "Mentally ill person" means any person afflicted with a substantial disorder of thought, mood, perception, psychological orientation or memory that significantly impairs judgment, behavior, capacity to recognize reality or ability to meet the ordinary demands of life;

(o) "Person requiring treatment" means either:

(1) A person who has a demonstrable mental illness and who as a result of that mental illness can be expected within the near future to intentionally or unintentionally seriously and physically injure himself or another person and who has engaged in one or more recent overt acts or made significant recent threats that substantially support that expectation; or

(2) A person who has a demonstrable mental illness and who as a result of that mental illness is unable to attend to those of his basic physical needs such as food, clothing or shelter that must be attended to in order for him to avoid serious harm in the near future and who has demonstrated such inability by failing to attend to those basic physical needs in the recent past; but

(3) Person requiring treatment shall not mean a person whose mental processes have simply been weakened or impaired by reason of advanced years, a mentally deficient person or a person with epilepsy unless the person also meets the criteria set forth in this paragraph. However, the person may be hospitalized under the voluntary admission provisions of this act if he is deemed clinically suitable and a fit subject for care and treatment by the person in charge of the facility.

Maximum Length of Disposition

Indeterminate.

Oregon

Criteria

Mentally ill person who is dangerous to himself or others or is unable to provide for his own basic personal needs. A mentally ill person means a person who, because of a mental disorder, is either:

(a) dangerous to himself or others; or

(b) unable to provide for his basic personal needs and is not receiving such care as is necessary for his health or safety.

Maximum Length of Disposition

180 days.

Pennsylvania

Criteria

A severely mentally disabled person who poses a clear and present danger to others or himself.

(a) Whenever a person is severely mentally disabled and in need of immediate treatment, he may be made subject to involuntary emergency examination and treatment. A person is severely mentally disabled when, as a result of mental illness, his capacity to exercise self-control, judgment and discretion in the conduct of his affairs and social relations or to care for his own personal needs is so lessened that he poses a clear and present danger of harm to others or to himself.

(1) Clear and present danger to others shall be shown by establishing that within the past 30 days the person has inflicted or attempted to inflict serious bodily harm on another and that there is a reasonable probability that such conduct will be repeated. If, however, the person has been found incompetent to be tried or has been acquitted by reason of lack of criminal responsibility on charges arising from conduct involving infliction of or attempt to inflict substantial bodily harm on another, such 30-day limitation shall not apply so long as an application for examination and treatment is filed within 30 days after the date of such determination or verdict. In such case, a clear and present danger to others may be shown by establishing that the conduct charged in the criminal proceeding did occur, and that there is a reasonable probability that such conduct will be repeated. For the purpose of this section, a clear and present danger of harm to others may be demonstrated by proof that the person has made threats of harm and has committed acts in furtherance of the threat to commit harm.

(2) Clear and present danger to himself shall be shown by establishing that within the past 30 days:

(i) the person has acted in such manner as to evidence that he would be unable, without care, supervision and the continued assistance of others, to satisfy his need for nourishment, personal or medical care, shelter, or self-protection and safety, and that there is a reasonable probability that death, serious bodily injury or serious physical debilitation would ensue within 30 days unless adequate treatment were afforded under this act; or

(ii) The person has attempted suicide and that there is a reasonable probability of suicide unless adequate treatment is afforded under this act. For the purposes of this subsection, a clear and present danger may be demonstrated by the proof that the person has made threats to commit suicide and has committed acts which are in furtherance of the threat to commit suicide; or

(iii) the person has substantially mutilated himself or attempted to mutilate himself substantially and that there is the reasonable probability of mutilation unless adequate treatment is afforded under this act. For the purposes of this subsection, a clear and present danger shall be established by proof that the person has made threats to commit mutilation and has committed acts which are in furtherance of the threat to commit mutilation.

Maximum Length of Disposition
90 days. Up to one year if criminal charges involving dangerous acts.

Rhode Island

Criteria
A person who is so insane as to be dangerous to the peace or safety of the people of the state or so as to render his restraint and treatment necessary for his own welfare.

Maximum Length of Disposition
Indeterminate.

South Carolina

Criteria
A person who is mentally ill, needs treatment and because of his condition:
(1) lacks sufficient insight or capacity to make responsible decisions with respect to his treatment; or
(2) there is a likelihood of serious harm to himself or others.

Maximum Length of Disposition
Indeterminate.

South Dakota

Criteria
Mentally ill person who lacks sufficient understanding and capacity to meet the ordinary demands of life or is dangerous to himself or others. The term "mentally ill" as used in this title includes any person whose mental condition is such that his behavior establishes one or more of the following:
(1) He lacks sufficient understanding or capacity to make responsible decisions concerning his person so as to interfere grossly with his capacity to meet the ordinary demands of life; or
(2) He is a danger to himself or others.

Maximum Length of Disposition
Indeterminate.

Tennessee

Criteria

A person is mentally ill and poses a likelihood of serious harm and is in need of care and treatment.

"Likelihood of serious harm" means:

(1) A substantial risk of physical harm to the person himself as manifested by evidence of threats of, or attempts at, suicide or serious bodily harm; or

(2) A substantial risk of physical harm to other persons as manifested by evidence of homicidal or other violent behavior or evidence that others are placed in a reasonable fear of violent behavior and serious physical harm to them; or

(3) A reasonable certainty that severe impairment or injury will result to the person alleged to be mentally ill as manifested by his inability to avoid or protect himself from such impairment or injury and suitable community resources for his care are unavailable.

Maximum Length of Disposition

Indefinite.

Texas

Criteria

A person who is mentally ill and requires hospitalization for his own welfare and protection or the welfare and protection of others.

Mentally ill person means a person whose mental health is substantially impaired.

Maximum Length of Disposition

Indefinite.

Utah

Criteria

(a) The proposed patient has a mental illness; and

(b) Because of the patient's illness the proposed patient poses an immediate danger of physical injury to others or self, which may include the inability to provide the basic necessities of life, such as food, clothing, and shelter, if allowed to remain at liberty; and

(c) The patient lacks the ability to engage in a rational decision-making process regarding the acceptance of mental treatment as demonstrated by evidence of inability to weigh the possible costs and benefits of treatment; and

(d) There is no appropriate less restrictive alternative to a court order of hospitalization.

"Mental illness" means a psychiatric disorder as defined by the current *Diagnostic and Statistical Manual of Mental Disorder* which substantially impairs a person's mental, emotional, behavioral or related functioning.

Maximum Length of Disposition

Indeterminate.

Vermont

Criteria

(17) "A person in need of treatment" means a person who is suffering from mental illness and, as a result of that mental illness, his capacity to exercise self-control, judgment, or discretion in the conduct of his affairs and social relations is so lessened that he poses a danger of harm to himself or others;

(A) A danger of harm to others may be shown by establishing that:

(i) he has inflicted or attempted to inflict bodily harm on another; or

(ii) by his threats or actions he has placed others in reasonable fear of physical harm to themselves; or

(iii) by his actions or inactions he has presented a danger to persons in his care.

(B) A danger of harm to himself may be shown by establishing that:

(i) he has threatened or attempted suicide or serious bodily harm; or

(ii) he has behaved in such a manner as to indicate that he is unable, without supervision and the assistance of others, to satisfy his need for nourishment, personal or medical care, shelter or self-protection and safety, so that it is probable that death, substantial bodily injury, serious mental deterioration or serious physical debilitation or disease will ensue unless adequate treatment is afforded.

(14) "Mental illness" means a substantial disorder of thought, mood, perception, orientation or memory, any of which grossly impairs judgment, behavior, capacity to recognize reality, or ability to meet the ordinary demands of life, but shall not include mental retardation.

Maximum Length of Disposition

Indeterminate.

Virginia

Criteria

A person who (a) presents an imminent danger to himself or others as a result of mental illness, or (b) has otherwise been proven to be so seriously mentally ill as to be substantially unable to care for himself, and (c) that there is no less restrictive alternative to institutional confinement and treatment and that the alternatives to involuntary hospitalization were investigated and were deemed not suitable.

Maximum Length of Disposition

180 days.

Washington

Criteria

A person who has threatened, attempted, or inflicted: (a) physical harm upon the person of another or himself, or substantial damage upon the property of another, and (b) as a result of mental disorder presents a likelihood of serious harm to others or himself; or

(2) Such person was taken into custody as a result of conduct in which he attempted or inflicted harm upon the persons of another or himself, and continues to present, as a result of mental disorder, a likelihood of serious harm to others or himself.

(3) Such person has been determined to be incompetent and criminal charges have been dismissed and has committed acts constituting a felony, and as a result of a mental disorder, presents a substantial likelihood of repeating similar acts. In any proceeding pursuant to this subsection it shall not be necessary to show intent, willfulness or state of mind as an element of the felony; or

(4) Such person is gravely disabled.

"Gravely disabled" means a condition in which a person, as a result of mental disorder: (a) is in danger of serious physical harm resulting from a failure to provide for his essential human needs of health or safety, or (b) manifests severe deterioration in routine functioning evidenced by repeated and escalating loss of cognitive or volitional control over his or her actions and is not receiving such care as is essential for his or her health or safety.

"Mental disorder" means any organic, mental or emotional impairment which has substantial adverse effects on an individual's cognitive or volitional functions.

"Likelihood of serious harm" means either: (a) A substantial risk that physical harm will be inflicted by an individual upon his own person, as evidenced by threats or attempts to commit suicide or inflict physical harm on one's self, (b) a substantial risk that physical harm will be inflicted by an individual upon another, as evidenced by behavior which has caused such harm or which places another person or persons in reasonable fear of sustaining such harm, or (c) a substantial risk that physical harm will be inflicted by an individual upon the property of others, as evidenced by behavior which has caused substantial loss or damage to the property of others.

Maximum Length of Disposition
180 days.

West Virginia

Criteria

Mental illness, retarded or addicted and is likely to cause serious harm to himself or to others. Mental illness means a manifestation in a person of significantly impaired capacity to maintain acceptable rules of functioning in the areas of intellect, emotion and physical well being.

"Likely to cause serious harm" refers to a person who has:

(1) A substantial tendency to physically harm himself which is manifested by threats of or attempts at suicide or serious bodily harm or other conduct, either active or passive, which demonstrates that he is dangerous to himself; or

(2) A substantial tendency to physically harm other persons which is manifested by homicidal or other violent behavior which places others in reasonable fear of serious physical harm; or

(3) A complete inability to care for himself by reason of mental retardation; or

(4) Become incapacitated.

Maximum Length of Disposition
2 years.

Wisconsin

Criteria

(1) A person who is mentally ill, drug dependent, or developmentally disabled and is a proper subject for treatment: and

(2) Is dangerous because the individual:

(a) Evidences a substantial probability of physical harm to himself or herself as manifested by evidence of recent threats of or attempts at suicide or serious bodily harm;

(b) Evidences a substantial probability of physical harm to other individuals as manifested by evidence of recent homicidal or other violent behavior, or by evidence that others are placed in reasonable fear of violent behavior and serious physical harm to them, as evidenced by a recent overt act, attempt or threat to do . . . serious physical harm;

(c) Evidences such impaired judgment, manifested by evidence of a pattern of recent acts or omissions, that there is a . . . substantial probability of physical impairment or injury to himself or herself. The probability of physical impairment or injury . . . *is not* substantial under this subparagraph if reasonable provision for the subject individual's protection is available in the community, . . . if the individual is appropriate for placement under s. 55.06 or, in the case of a minor, if the individual is appropriate for services or placement under s. 48.13(4) or (11). The subject individual's status as a minor does not automatically establish a . . . substantial probability of physical impairment or injury under this subparagraph; or

(d) Evidences behavior manifested by recent acts or omissions that, due to mental illness, he or she is unable to satisfy basic needs for nourishment, medical care, shelter or safety without prompt and adequate treatment so that a substantial probability exists that death, serious physical injury, serious physical debilitation or serious physical disease will imminently ensue unless the individual receives prompt and adequate treatment for this mental illness.

Maximum Length of Disposition

One year.

Wyoming

Criteria

A person is mentally ill based on evidence of recent overt acts, or threats. A mentally ill person means a person who presents an imminent threat of physical harm to himself or others as a result of a physical emotional, mental or behavioral disorder which grossly impairs his ability to function socially, vocationally or interpersonally and who needs treatment and who cannot comprehend the need for or purposes of treatment and with respect to whom the potential risk and benefits are such that a reasonable person would consent to treatment.

Maximum Length of Disposition

Indeterminate.

National Alliance for the Mentally Ill Affiliate List

National Organization
National Alliance for the Mentally Ill
1200 Fifteenth Street, NW, Suite 400
Washington, D.C. 20005
Phone: (202)833-3530

Alabama
Birmingham
Jefferson-Blount St. Clair
M.H./M.R. Authority (CSP)
3820 Third Avenue, South, Suite 100
Birmingham, AL 35222

Madison County
Huntsville Support Alliance for the Mentally Ill
403 Westburg Avenue
Huntsville, AL 35801

Mobile
Mobile Family Support Group
4508 Kingsway Court
Mobile, AL 36608

Alaska
Anchorage
REACH
c/o Alaska MHA
2611 Fairbanks Street
Anchorage, AK 99503

Fairbanks and North Star Borough
Families of CMI Victims
SR Box 30754
Fairbanks, AK 99701

Soldotna
Kenai AMI
PO Box 301
Soldotna, AK 99669

Arizona
State Organization
Arizona AMI
4129 East Catalina
Phoenix, AZ 85018

Phoenix
Family AMI-Maricopa County
4129 East Catalina
Phoenix, AZ 85018

Tucson
AMI of Southern Arizona
5055 East Broadway C-214
Tucson, AZ 85711

Arkansas
Little Rock
Help and Hope, Inc.
Arkansas Families & Friends of the Mentally Ill
4313 West Markham
Hendrix Hall 125
Little Rock, AR 72204

Northwest Arkansas
Help and Hope, Inc.
503 Cheri Whitlock Drive
Siloam Springs, AR 72761

California
State Organization
California AMI
5820 Yorkshire Avenue
La Mesa, CA 92041

Alameda County
American Schizophrenia Association
2401 Le Conte Avenue
Berkeley, CA 94709

Butte County
AMI of Butte County
PO Box 385
Oroville, CA 95965

Contra Costa County
Contra Costa Alliance for the Mentally Ill, Inc.
PO Box 2357
Walnut Creek, CA 94595

Fresno County
Family Support Group
MHA of Greater Fresno
1759 Fulton, Suite 146
Fresno, CA 93721

Humboldt County
Families for Mental Recovery
Alliance for the Mentally Ill
PO Box 6404
Eureka, CA 95501

Kern County
Alliance for the Mentally Ill of Kern County
3017 Pomona
Bakersfield, CA 93305

Los Angeles
Advocates for the Mentally Ill
3139 Colby Avenue
Los Angeles, CA 90066

Los Angeles and Coastal Region
Westside and Coastal Friends
P.O. Box 241576
Los Angeles, CA 90024

Marin County
Marin Parent Advocates for Mental Health
Box 1039
Ross, CA 94957

Modesto
Alliance for the Mentally Ill
PO Box 1903
Modesto, CA 95353

Monterey County
AMI of Monterey County
1012 Forest Avenue
Pacific Grove, CA 93950

Northern California
AMI of Napa State Hospital
2716 Henry Avenue
Pinole, CA 94564

North Inland San Diego County
Family Alliance for the Mentally Disabled
PO Box 27386
Escondido, CA 92027

Norwalk
AMI of Norwalk
11400 South Norwalk Boulevard
Norwalk, CA 90650

Oakland
Families of the Mentally Ill of the Mental Health Association
1801 Adeline Street, Room 203
Oakland, CA 94607

Orange County
Orange County AMI
17341 Irvine Boulevard, Suite 105
Tustin, CA 92680

Pasadena
Relatives and Friends of the Mentally Disabled
595 East Washington Boulevard, No. K
Pasadena, CA 91104

Placer County
Foothill Families and Friends for Mental Recovery
PO Box 930
Auburn, CA 95603

Riverside
Friends and Families of the Mentally Disabled
5499 Grassy Trail Drive
Riverside, CA 92504

Riverside County
Friends and Families of the Mentally Disabled
44981 Viejo Drive
Hemet, CA 92344

Sacramento
Sacramento AMI
PO Box 2154
Fair Oaks, CA 95628

San Diego
San Diego AMI
5820 Yorkshire Avenue
La Mesa, CA 92041

San Francisco
San Francisco AMI
631 Myra Way
San Francisco, CA 94127

San Francisco Schizophrenia Association
290 Seventh Avenue
San Francisco, CA 94118

San Gabriel Valley
AMI
1495 Bedford
San Marino, CA 91108

San Joaquin County
AMI San Joaquin County
Mental Health Center
1212 North California Street, Box C
Stockton, CA 95202

San Mateo County
San Mateo AMI
PO Box 3333
San Mateo, CA 94403

Santa Clara County
Parents of Adult Mentally Ill
44 South Fifth Street
San Jose, CA 95112

Santa Cruz County
Mental Health Alliance
Santa Cruz County
1515A Capitola Road
Santa Cruz, CA 95062

Sonoma County
Sonoma County AMI
415 Pythian Road
Santa Rosa, CA 95405

Tulare County
Tulare County AMI
1325 West Center Street
Visalia, CA 93291

Van Nuys
Families and Friends
6740 Kester Avenue
Van Nuys, CA 91405

Ventura County
AMI of Ventura County
PO Box AH
Ventura, CA 93002

Yolo County
AMI of Yolo County
615 J Street
Davis, CA 95616

Canada

Association of Relatives & Friends of the Mentally & Emotionally Ill
PO Box 322, Snowdon Branch
Montreal, Quebec, CD H3X3T6

Colorado
State Organization
Colorado AMI
PO Box 28008
Lakewood, CO 80228

Boulder
Boulder AMI
980 Sixth Street
Boulder, CO 80302

Colorado Springs
Pikes Peak AMI
14425 Timberedge Lane
Colorado Springs, CO 80908

Denver
Denver AMI
PO Box 31001
2022 South University Boulevard
Denver, CO 80210

Jefferson County
Friends of Jefferson Mental Health
9808 West Cedar Avenue
Lakewood, CO 80453

Lakewood
Support Inc.
11335 West Exposition Avenue
Lakewood, CO 80226

Larimer County
Friends and Families of Adult Mentally Ill
636 South College Avenue, Suite 123
Fort Collins, CO 80524

Connecticut
Greenwich
Pathways Inc.
40 Doubling Road
Greenwich, CT 06830

Hamden
Families of the MI Group
262 Battis Road
Hamden, CT 06514

Delaware
Wilmington
New Castle County AMI
2117 Largo Road
Wilmington, DE 19803

District of Columbia

Threshold D.C.
PO Box 23167
Washington, DC 20024

Florida
Brevard County
AMI of Brevard County
2718 Hillcrest Avenue
Titusville, FL 32796

Collier County
REACH
660 Ninth Street North
Naples, FL 33940

Fort Myers and Lee County
REACH
PO Box 06137
Fort Myers, FL 33906

Hernando County
Family Support Group
1131 Ponce de Leon Boulevard
Brooksville, FL 33512

Miami
Community Advocates for the Mentally Ill
c/o Fellowship House
5711 South Dixie Highway
Miami, FL 33176

Naples
REACH
660 Ninth Street North, Suite 37
Naples, FL 33940

North-Central Florida
AMI of North Central Florida
402 Southwest Forty-first Street
Gainesville, FL 32607

Northwest Florida
LOMI (Loved Ones of the Mentally Ill)
MHA of Bay County
PO Box 2245
1316 Harrison Avenue, Suite 203
Panama City, FL 32401

Palm Beach County
Alliance for the Mentally Ill of Palm Beach
666 Laconia Circle
Lake Worth, FL 33463

Tamarac
Concerned Relatives and Friends of South Florida State Hospital, Inc.
9109 Northwest Eighty-first Court
Tamarac, FL 33321

Venice
Families Together for Mental Health
1355 Cambridge Drive
Venice, FL 33595

Georgia

Athens
Northeast Georgia CMH/MR
1247 Prince Avenue
Athens, GA 30606

Atlanta
Georgia Friends of the Mentally Ill
1390 DeClair Drive
Atlanta, GA 30329

Central Georgia
Central Georgia MH/MR
Consortium Adult MH Sub-Committee Central State Hospital
PO Box 325
Milledgeville, GA 31062

Southeastern Coastal Georgia
AMI Chatham Area
30 Chatuachee Circle
Savannah, GA 31411

Hawaii
Honolulu
Hawaii Families and Friends of Schizophrenics, Inc.
PO Box 10532
Honolulu, HI 98616

Idaho
American Falls
Idaho Alliance for the Mentally Ill
321 Buchanan
American Falls, ID 83211

Illinois
Arlington Heights
Northwest Suburban AMI
PO Box 1778
Arlington Heights, IL 60006

Bloomington
REACH
612 Hilltop Court
Bloomington, IL 61701

Boone, Stephenson, and Winnebago County
Northern Illinois AMI
817 Haskell Avenue
Rockford, IL 61103

Champaign County
Supportive Families of the Mentally Ill
702 West Illinois
Urbana, IL 61801

Dyle, Lee, Whiteside, and Carroll County
Sauk Valley AMI
1038 North Eighth Street
Rochelle, IL 61068

Normal
Livingston-McLean REACH
1111 Sheridan Road
Normal, IL 61761

Northern Illinois
Illinois AMI
PO Box 1016
Evanston, IL 60204

Peoria
Tri-County AMI
1027 North Santa Fe
Chillicothe, IL 61523

Rock Island and Mercer Counties
AMI of Rock Island and Mercer County
PO Box 933
Rock Island, IL 61201

South Cook and Will County
AMI of the South Suburbs (AMISS)
PO Box 275
Olympia Fields, IL 60461

Springfield
Focus on Families
c/o MHC
710 Eighth Street
Springfield, IL 62702

Vermilion County
Vermilion MH & Development Center
605 North Logan
Danville, IL 61832

West Suburban Chicago
Schizophrenia Association of West Suburban Chicago

PO Box 237
Downers Grove, IL 60515

Indiana
Fort Wayne
Fort Wayne AMI
909 East State Boulevard
Fort Wayne, IN 46805

Marion County
Marion County TLC (Together We Learn to Cope)
555 Sunset Boulevard
Greenwood, IN 46142

San Joseph County
South Bend AMI
1140 East Ewing
South Bend, IN 46613

Iowa
Cedar Rapids
Reach for Family and Friends of Mentally Ill
c/o Mental Health Advocates of Linn County
1118 First Avenue NE
Cedar Rapids, IA 52402

Davenport
Advocates for Mental Health
2504 Telegraph Road
Davenport, IA 52804

Dubuque County
Dubuque AMI
723 Fifth Street SE
Dyersville, IA 52040

Eagle Grove
Iowa Alliance for the Mentally Ill
520 SE First Street (Box 334)
Eagle Grove, IA 50533

Johnson County
Johnson County Family Support Group
505 East College
Iowa City, IA 52240

Northern Iowa
Northern Iowa AMI
Beeds Lake
RR2
Hampton, IA 50441

Scott County
The Advocates—An Alliance for Mental Health
3611 Wakonda Drive
Bettendorf, IA 52722

Kansas
Harvey, Marion, and McPherson Counties
Prairie View Community Support Program
Box 467
Newton, KS 67114

Shawnee County
Families for Mental Health
Shawnee County
4538 NE Meriden Road
Topeka, KS 66617

Kentucky
Louisville
Schizophrenia Association of Louisville
7702 Brownwood Drive
Louisville, KY 40218

Louisiana
Greater New Orleans
Friends Alliance for the Mentally Ill

6028 Magazine Street
New Orleans, LA 70118

Lafayette
Families & Friends for Mental Health
178 Ronald Boulevard
Lafayette, LA 70503

New Orleans
Family Support Group
500 Walnut Street
New Orleans, LA 70118

Shreveport
Caddo-Bossier AMI
PO Box 2029
Shreveport, LA 71166

Westwego
Association for Research in Children's Emotional Disorders (ARCED)
PO Box 511
Westwego, LA 70094

Maine
Androscoggin County
Relatives and Friends Together for Support (RAFTS)
Star Route, Box 390
Poland, ME 04273

Bath
Brunswick SEA
348 Washington Street
Bath, ME 04530

Eastern Maine
Citizen's Interest Group, Inc.
PO Box 108
Bangor, ME 04401

Kennebec County
Alliance for Troubled Families, Inc.
RFD 1, Box 4420
Oakland, ME 04963

Northern Aroostook County
Valley Family Support Group, Inc.
97 Thirteenth Avenue
Madawaska, ME 04756

Northern Oxford and Southern Franklin Counties
AIMED (Alliance Involved with the Mentally and Emotionally Disabled)
RFD 1, Box 470
Dixfield, ME 04224

Portland
AMI of Maine
PO Box 5196, Station A
Portland, ME 04101

Maryland
State Organization
AMI of Maryland, Inc.
2323 York Road
Timonium, MD 21093

Baltimore
Mental Health Association of Metropolitan Baltimore, Inc.
323 East Twenty-fifth Street
Baltimore, MD 21218

Springfield Hospital Family Support Group
c/o Martin Gross Service Building
Springfield Hospital Center
Sykesville, MD 21784

AMI of Baltimore, Inc.
PO Box 16277
Baltimore, MD 21210

Howard County
Threshold of Howard County
PO Box 2484
Columbia, MD 21045

Montgomery County
AMI of Montgomery County
7300 Whittier Boulevard
Bethesda, MD 20817

Prince Georges County
Threshold Families & Friends of the Mentally Ill, Inc.
7509 Newberry Lane
Lanham, MD 20706

Southwestern Area Baltimore County
HOPE (Help Others Perform Equally) AMI
PO Box 21060
Catonsville, MD 21228

Massachusetts
State Organization
AMI of Massachusetts, Inc.
227 Mount Hope Road
Somerset, MA 02726

Beverly
PSALMS (People Support/Advocacy Liberating Mental Sickness)
14 Colgate Road
Beverly, MA 01915

Boston
Massachusetts Association of Social Clubs, Inc. (Former Patients' Group)
PO Box 9216
Boston, MA 02114

Brockton
Self-Help Group for Families of the Mentally Ill at Massasoit Community College
One Massasoit Boulevard
Brockton, MA 02402

Cambridge/Middlesex Counties
AMI Cambridge/Middlesex Counties
PO Box 165
Somerville, MA 02144

Cape Cod
Amicus of Cape Cod
PO Box 962
Osterville, MA 02655

Coastal Massachusetts
Coastal AMI
PO Box 149
Accord, MA 02018

Eastern Middlesex County
AMI of Eastern Middlesex County
22 Kensington Avenue
Reading, MA 01867

Fall River
Area Citizens Concerned with Ensuring Support Services (ACCESS)
PO Box 1865
Fall River, MA 02722

Middlesex County
AMI of Middlesex County, Inc.
PO Box 3009
Framingham, MA 01701

Montachusett
Families of Adult Mentally Ill
40 Laurel Street
Leominster, MA 01453

Newton-Wellesley
Alliance for the Mental Health of Newton-Wellesley
190 Hickory Road
Weston, MA 02193

Norfolk County
Medfield State Family Alliance, Inc.
35 Bicknell Street
Foxboro, MA 02035

Northeastern Massachusetts
Merrimack Valley Advocacy for Mental Health
1018 Osgood Street
North Andover, MA 01845

Northeast Essex District
Alliance for the Mentally Ill
Whitehall Road
Amesbury, MA 01913

Quincy
Citizens Organization Assisting Mental Patients, Inc.
Odan Street
North Quincy, MA 02171

South Norfolk
South Norfolk AMI
82 Pleasant Street
Medfield, MA 02052

Western Massachusetts
Western Massachusetts AMI Citizens, Inc.
PO Box 500
Agawam, MA 01001

Michigan

Dearborn
Residential Care Alternatives Family Support Group
24920 Hickory
Dearborn, MI 48124

Detroit
Neighborhood Service Organization
51 West Warren
Detroit, MI 48201

Flint
Family Support for Mental Recovery
PO Box 1320
Flint, MI 48501

Grand Rapids
Self Help Association for Relatives Enlightment (SHARE)
PO Box 1405
Grand Rapids, MI 49501

Kalamazoo
SHARE of Kalamazoo
c/o Edison Neighborhood Center
1331 Race Street
Kalamazoo, MI 49001

Midland
Citizens for Action in Mental Health, Inc. (CAMH)
1202 Corrinne Street
Midland, MI 48640

Wayne, Oakland, and Macomb Counties
AMI of Michigan
17596 Meadowood
Lothrup Village, MI 48076

Minnesota
St. Paul
Mental Health Advocates Coalition of Minnesota, Inc.
265 Fort Road (West Seventh Street)
St. Paul, MN 55102

Mississippi
Hattiesburg
Families and Friends of the Mentally Ill
PO Box 1286
Hattiesburg, MS 39401

Missouri
Greater Kansas City
Greater Kansas City Chapter AMI
PO Box 33086
Kansas City, MO 64114

St. Louis
AMI St. Louis
135 West Adams
St. Louis, MO 63122

American Schizophrenia Association of St. Louis
10426 Lackland Road
St. Louis, MO 63114

Southwest Missouri
AMI of Springfield, Missouri, Chapter, Inc.
1504 North Roberson
Springfield, MO 65803

Montana
Cascade County
Great Falls AMI
North Central Montana MHC
PO Box 3048
Great Falls, MT 59403

Kalispell
FLAME (Families Loving Allied for Mental Health)
640 Conrad Drive
Kalispell, MT 59901

Lewis and Clark County
Helena AMI
479 South Park
Helena, MT 59601

Missoula
A New Beginning for the Mentally Disordered
2405 Thirty-ninth Street
Missoula, MT 59807

Nebraska
Lincoln
AMI of Nebraska, Inc.
Lincoln Center Building
215 Centennial Mall South
Lincoln, NE 68508

Nevada
Las Vegas
Nevada AMI Support Group
4220 South Maryland Parkway, Building A 108
Las Vegas, NV 89109

New Hampshire
Nashua
Greater Nashua MHA
20 Cabot Drive
Nashua, NH 03060

Southern New Hampshire
NAMI in New Hampshire
PO Box 544
Peterborough, NH 03458

Winnipesaukee County
Winnipesaukee Advocates for the Mentally Ill
35 Ridgewood Avenue
Gilford, NH 03246

New Jersey
Atlantic City
Atlantic County MH Family Support Group
c/o CCP
1125 Pacific Avenue
Atlantic City, NJ 08401

Bergen County
Family Organization of the Mid-Bergen Community MHC
11 Park Place
Paramus, NJ 07652

MH Advocacy Group
340 Twelfth Street
Palisades Park, NJ 07650

Burlington
Focus Mental Health—Delaware House
Wood and Pearl Streets
Burlington, NJ 08016

FACE
PO Box 1322
Delran, NJ 08075

Camden County
Pioneers for Mental Health
19 East Ormond Avenue
Cherry Hill, NJ 08034

Essex County
Concerned Families for Improved Mental Health Services
424 Main Street
East Orange, NJ 07018

Middleton
Concerned Citizens for Chronic Psychiatric Adults
Box 158
Middleton, NJ 07748

Ridgewood
West Bergen MHC
74 Oak Street
Ridgewood, NJ 07450

Salem County
TLC (Together, Learning, Coping) of Salem County
RD 2, Box 346
Woodstown, NJ 08098

South Amboy
Family & Friends of the MI
200 South Feltus Street, No. 35
South Amboy, NJ 08879

New Mexico
Albuquerque
Community Alliance for Mental Health
12712 Mountain View, NE
Albuquerque, NM 87123

Santa Fe
Community Alliance for Mental Health
819 Bishops Lodge Road
Santa Fe, NM 87501

Silver City
Community Alliance for MH
PO Box 1827
Silver City, NM 88062

New York
State Organization
AMI of New York State
42 Elting Avenue
New Paltz, NY 12561

Albany
Relatives
920 Myrtle Avenue
Albany, NY 12208

Brooklyn
APRIL (Association of Parents for Rehabilitation and Independent Living)
72 Livingston Street, No. 11A
Brooklyn, NY 11201

Cortland
REACH
17 Charles Street
Cortland, NY 13045

Dutchess, Ulster, and Orange Counties
Mid-Hudson Chapter NAMI
Mill House
Marlboro, NY 12542

Erie County
REACH (MHA of Erie County)
1237 Delaware Avenue
Buffalo, NY 14209

Long Island
People Acting Together with Hope (PATH)
307 Lido Boulevard
Lido Beach, NY 11561

Manhasset
Caring Families of the Mentally Ill
11 Brook Lane
Manhasset, NY 11030

Long Island Schizophrenia Association
1691 Northern Boulevard
Manhasset, NY 11030

Mount Vernon
Families (Family Advocates of the MI Linked in Encouragement & Support)
21 North Terrace
Mount Vernon, NY 10552

Nassau County
Growth and Rehabilitation Advocates for the Mentally Ill (GRAML)
c/o Progress House
3095 Hempstead Turnpike
Levittown, NY 11756

Nassau/Suffolk Counties
Long Island Regional Council, Inc.
Federation of Parents Organization for NYS Mentally Disabled, Inc.
80-45 Winchester Boulevard
Queens Village, NY 11427

New York City
Friends and Advocates of the Mentally Ill
c/o HAI (Hospital Audience, Inc.)
220 West Forty-second Street, Thirteenth Floor
New York, NY 10036

Friends of the Psychiatric Institute
722 West 168th Street
New York, NY 10032

Friends United to Help the Mentally Ill
50 Nevins Street
Brooklyn, NY 11217

Manhattan State Citizens Group
350 East Fifty-fourth Street
New York, NY 10022

Niagara County
Niagara AMI
610 Sandlewood Drive
Lewiston, NY 14092

Northern Westchester
Alliance for Mental Health of Northern Westchester
Box 275
Katonah, NY 10536

Onondaga County
Parents & Friends of the M.I Supporting Each Other (PROMISE)
c/o Transitional Living Service
423 West Onondaga Street
Syracuse, NY 13202

Queens County
Concerned Citizens of Creedmore
PO Box 42
Queens Village, NY 11427

Federation of Organizations for the NYS Mentally Disabled
80-45 Winchester Boulevard
Queens Village, NY 11427

Rochester
Family & Friends of the MI and Emotionally Disturbed
c/o Reformation Church
111 North Chestnut Street
Rochester, NY 14605

Rockland County
The Family Support Group of Rockland County
10 Hester Street
Piermont, NY 10968

Saratoga Springs
Alliance for the Mentally Ill of Saratoga Springs (AMISS)
15 Elizabeth Lane
Saratoga Springs, NY 12866

Schenectady County
Schenectady County Relatives Group
1444 Dean Street
Schenectady, NY 12309

Suffolk County
Suffolk Relatives of NYS AMI
37 Hawthorne Street
Mount Sinai, NY 11766

Sullivan County
Friends & Advocates for Mental Health
9 Maple Street
Liberty, NY 12754

Westchester County
Advocacy League for the Mentally Ill of Westchester (ALMI)
PO Box 1138
White Plains, NY 10602

Woodmere
Peninsula Counseling Center
League for the Advancement of MH Programs (LAMP)
124 Franklin Place
Woodmere, NY 11598

North Carolina
State Organization
North Carolina Alliance for the Mentally Ill
PO Box 10557
Greensboro, NC 27404

Greensboro
Greensboro AMI
PO Box 10557
Greensboro, NC 20704

Ohio
State Organization
Ohio Family Coalition for the MI
199 South Central Avenue
Columbus, OH 43223

Cincinnati
SOS—CAMI
PO Box 37004
Cincinnati, OH 45222

Franklin County
Families in Touch
MHA of Franklin County
634 Wager Street
Columbus, OH 43206

Northeastern Ohio
Northeast Ohio AMI
PO Box 217
Chagrin Falls, OH 44022

Summit County
Kevin Coleman MHC, Inc.
PO Box 724
275 Martinal Drive
Kent, OH 44240

Oklahoma
Oklahoma County
REACH
5104 North Francis, Suite B
Oklahoma City, OK 73118

Tulsa
Families in Touch
MHA in Tulsa
5 West Twenty-second Street
Tulsa, OK 74114

Oregon
State Organization
Oregon Alliance for Advocates of the MI
PO Box 47
Thurston, OR 97482

Coos County
Family and Friends Support Group
Route 1, Box 1135
Bandon, OR 97411

Eugene
Save a Mind
2891 Willamette
Eugene, OR 97405

Florence
SOS (Save Our Sanity)
PO Box 821
Florence, OR 97439

Jackson County
Southern Oregon AMI (SOAMI)

PO Box 924
Medford, OR 97501

Linn County
Mid Valley AMI
3308 Southview Drive
Albany, OR 97321

Marion and Polk Counties
PREMED
3324 Glen Creek Road, NW
Salem, OR 97304

Portland
AMI of Multnomah County
718 West Burnside, No. 310
Portland, OR 97209

Pennsylvania

Allegheny County
Peoples Oakland
231 Oakland Avenue
Pittsburgh, PA 15213

Eastern Pennsylvania
Families Unite for Mental Health
Box 126
Oreland, PA 19075

Main Line Mental Health Group
582 Cricket Lane
Radnor, PA 19087

Lackawanna County
CRRP—Family Support and Self-Help
307 Adams Avenue
Scranton, PA 18503

Lancaster County
Threshold of Lancaster PA
840 Grandview Boulevard
Lancaster, PA 17601

Northwestern Pennsylvania
Family Support for Mental Health
721 East Grandview
Erie, PA 16504

Philadelphia
The Family and Friends Association of Norristown State Hospital
8008 State Hospital
Philadelphia, PA 19150

Pittsburgh
Families of the Adult Mentally Ill
Northern Community MH/MR Center
River Avenue and Alcor Street
Pittsburgh, PA 15212

Families of the Adult Mentally Ill—Living, Interacting & Sharing (FAMILIAS)
1623 Denniston Avenue
Pittsburgh, PA 15217

Southwest Pittsburgh
Parents of Adult Mentally Ill
2333 Los Angeles Avenue
Pittsburgh, PA 15216

University Park
Alliance for Families of the MI
Room 112
Nursing Consultation Center, Human Development East

Pennsylvania State University
University Park, PA 16802

York County
Mental Illness Needs Devoted Support (MINDS)
RD 4, Box 942
Harrisburg, PA 17112

Rhode Island
Newport
Families & Advocates for the MI of Newport County (FAMI)
PO Box 837
Newport, RI 02840

Providence
MHA Project Reach Out
89 Park Street
Providence, RI 02908

South Carolina
Charleston
Families and Friends of the Mentally Ill
PO Box 32084
Charleston, SC 29417

Columbia and Environs County
Mid-Carolina FFMI
PO Box 61075
Columbia, SC 29260

Northern South Carolina
Piedmont Family and Friends of the Mentally Ill
112 Robin Street
Clemson, SC 29631

South Dakota
Aberdeen
Northeastern MHC
Family Support Group
703 Third Avenue, SE, Box 550
Aberdeen, SD 57401

Brookings
Brookings Area MHA
2027 Third Street
Brookings, SD 57006

Tennessee
Hamilton County
Mental Health Association of Hamilton County/Families in Touch
921 East Third Street
Chattanooga, TN 37403

Memphis
AMI of Memphis
PO Box 17304
Memphis, TN 38187

Nashville
Families in Touch
c/o MHA in Nashville
250 Venture Circle, No. 204
Nashville, TN 37228

Texas
Dallas
Dallas Alliance for Mental Recovery
PO Box 816264
Dallas, TX 75381

Houston
Alliance for Mental Recovery
4415 Breakwood
Houston, TX 77096

Citizens for Human Development
2123 Oak Creek
Houston, TX 77017

Friends of Pyramid House and the Houston Lodge, Inc.
4802 Caroline
Houston, TX 77004

San Antonio
Reclamation, Inc.
(Former Patients' Group)
2502 Waterford
San Antonio, TX 78217

Utah
Salt Lake City
Utah Alliance for the Mentally Ill
Salt Lake City Chapter
PO Box 26561
Salt Lake City, UT 84126

Weber County and Ogden
AMI—Ogden
PO Box 1427
Ogden, UT 84402

Vermont
South Burlington
AMI Vermont
9 Andrews Avenue
South Burlington, VT 05401

Virgin Islands
St. Croix
St. Croix Concerned Citizens for Mental Health, Inc.
PO Box 937 Kings Hill
St. Croix, VI 00850

Virginia
Augusta County
We Care
1245 Chatham Road
Waynesboro, VA 22980

Charlottesville
Blue Ridge Family Alliance for the Mentally Ill
1602 Gordon Avenue
Charlottesville, VA 22903

Farmville
Southside Affiliate—Town House Friends
127 North Street
Farmville, VA 23901

Harrisonburg
Massanutten Family Support Group
276 West Market Street
Harrisonburg, VA 22801

Norfolk
Norfolk Community Services Board
201 Granby Mall, Suite 103
Norfolk, VA 23510

Northern Virginia
Pathways to Independence
PO Box 651
McLean, VA 22101

Northwestern Virginia
Northwestern VA Family Support Group for the Mentally Ill
Route 2A, Box 107A-7
Boyce, VA 22620

Richmond
Richmond Area Schizophrenia Foundation (RASF)
4010 West Franklin Street
Richmond, VA 23221

Virginia Beach
Schizophrenia Foundation of VA
Box 2342
Virginia Beach, VA 23450

Washington
State Organization
Washington State Coalition of Family Associations
906 East Shelby
Seattle, VA 98102

Bainbridge Island
Bainbridge Island Advocates for the MI
c/o Helpline House
282 Knechtel Way
Bainbridge Island, WA 98110

Benton/Franklin Counties
Tri-Cities Advocates for the Mentally Ill
PO Box 1135
Richland, WA 99352

Clallum County
Peninsula Advocates for the Mentally Ill (PAMI)
87 Garden Club Road
Nordland, WA 98358

Clark County
Clark AMI
PO Box 5353
Vancouver, WA 98668

Cowlitz County
Cowlitz AMI
PO Box 385
Kelso, WA 98626

Eastern Washington
Spokane AMI
PO Box 141141
Spokane, WA 99214

Fort Steilacoom
Citizens' Guild of Western State Hospital
PO Box 94999
Fort Steilacoom, WA 98494

King County
Washington Advocates for the Mentally Ill
119 North Eighty-fifth
Seattle, WA 98103

Pierce County
Family Action for the Seriously Emotionally Disturbed (FASED)
PO Box 297
Puyallup, WA 98371

Snohomish County
SnoAmi-Snohomish County
Advocates for the Mentally Ill
4526 Federal Way, PO Box 2484
Everett, WA 98203

Yakima County
Yakima Advocates for the Mentally Ill
217 North Twenty-fifth Avenue
Yakima, WA 98902

Wisconsin

State Organization
AMI of Wisconsin, Inc.
Route 8, 1997 Highway PB
Verona, WI 53593

Ashland
AMI of Chequameson Bay
Route 3, Box 237
Ashland, WI 54806

Central Wisconsin
AMI of Central Wisconsin
1120 Third Street
Port Edwards, WI 54469

Dane County
AMI of Dane County
PO Box 1502
Madison, WI 53701

Fond du Lac County
AMI of Fond du Lac
PO Box 1007
Fond du Lac, WI 54935

Green Bay
AMI of Brown County
1024 Mount Mary Drive
Green Bay, WI 54302

La Crosse County
AMI of La Crosse County
4062 Terrace Drive
La Crosse, WI 54601

Marinette
AMI of Marinette
1428 Mary Street
Marinette, WI 54143

Milwaukee County
AMI of Greater Milwaukee
4011 West Capitol Drive,
PO Box 16819
Milwaukee, WI 53216

Oshkosh
Fox Valley AMI
4995 Pickett Road
Pickett, WI 54964

Racine County
AMI of Racine County
816 Sixth Street
Racine, WI 53403

Rock County
AMI of Rock County, Inc.
Box 842
Janesville, WI 53545

Waukesha County
AMI Waukesha County
1307 Mariner Drive
Hartland, WI 53029

Fountain House Clubhouse Programs

Alaska

Rebuilders Club
1109 Burman
Jacksonville, AK 72076

(501)982-7510 or 982-7515

Arkansas

Harmony House
2920 McClellan Drive
Jonesboro, AR 72401

(501)972-4057
Joe Heard, Clubhouse Director

Springhouse
219 South Thompson
Springdale, AR 72764

(501)751-7052
Jordan Williams, Clubhouse Director

California

Arden House
417 Arden
Glendale, CA 91203

(213)244-7257
Deborah Pitts, Clubhouse Director

Portals House
269 South Mariposa
Los Angeles, CA 90004

(213)386-5393
Marvin Weinstein, Clubhouse Director

Towne House Creative Living Center
412 Monte Vista
Oakland, CA 94611

(415)658-9480
Cecile Weaver, Clubhouse Director

Connecticut

Greater Hartford Social Club, Inc.
15 Marshall Street
Hartford, CT 06105

(203)525-1261
Jenine Glatzer-Wicks, Clubhouse Director

Reliance House, Inc.
132 Broadway
Norwich, CT 06360

(203)887-7295
David Burnett

District of Columbia

Our Place
Area D CMHC
2700 Martin Luther King Avenue SE
Washington, DC 20032

(202)574-7673
Jerry Bentley, Clubhouse Director

The Green Door
1623 Sixteenth Street NW
Washington, DC 20009

(202)462-4092
Beverly J. Russau, Clubhouse Director

Florida

Fellowship House
5711 South Dixie Highway
Miami, FL 33143

(305)667-1036
Marshall Rubin, Clubhouse Director

Colonial House
1830 East Colonial Drive
Orlando, FL 32803

(305)894-4583
William Copley, Clubhouse Director

Georgia

Community Friendship Inc.
85 Renaissance Parkway
Atlanta, GA 30308

(404)875-0381
Martha Hodge, Clubhouse Director

Vistas Unlimited
4716 Roswell Road
Atlanta, GA 30342

(404)255-3024
Dennis Goodwin, Clubhouse Director

Alexander's Corner
629 Greene Street
Augusta, GA 30901

(404)828-3183
Phil Emory, Clubhouse Director

New Beginnings
1701 North Patterson Street
Valdosta, GA 31601

(912)247-4976
C. Rick Hastings, Clubhouse Director

Hawaii

Network
1700 Lanakila Avenue
Honolulu, HI 96817

(808)847-1156 or 848-6066
Roland Talbot (Vocational Director)
Isabelle Matsumoto (Prevocational Director)

Kentucky

Beacon House
207 North Walnut
Cynthia, KY 41031

(606)234-1407
Judy Rhodus, Clubhouse Director

Valley House Club
2701 Sunset Lane
Henderson, KY 42420

(502)826-1978
Dr. Janice Hunt

The Greenhouse
215 South Main
Nicholasville, KY 40356

(606)885-6315
Sally Isaacs, BSN

Partnership House Program
401 West Third Street
Owensboro, KY 42301

(502)683-0438
Anne K. Mudd, MSW

Harmony House
412 Marshall Street
Paris, KY 40361

(606)987-6803
Debra Armstrong, Clubhouse Director

Cardinal House
303 North Third Street
Richmond, KY 40403

(606)623-1328
Judy Hudson, Clubhouse Director

Louisiana

Friendship Club
6028 Magazine Street
New Orleans, LA 70118

(504)895-2891
Bea Piker, Clubhouse Director

Maine

New Vocations
7 Russ Street
Caribou, ME 04736

(207)498-2528
Delia Kenny, Clubhouse Director

Circle Club Day Center
73 Pine Street
Lewiston, ME 04240

(207)783-9141
Patricia Samara, Clubhouse Director

Maryland

Capricorn Clever Clover Club
Suite 322
9100 Franklin Square
Baltimore, MD 21237

(301)687-6500 ext. 356-359
John White, Clubhouse Director

Changing Directions
1400 East Federal Street
Baltimore, MD 21231

(301)727-2611
Ruth Hughes, Clubhouse Director

Channel Marker
114 North Washington Street
Easton, Maryland 21601

(301)822-4611
Nancy Clem, Clubhouse Director

Omni House Inc.
9 Third Avenue
Glen Burnie, MD 21061

(301)768-6777
Lois Miller, Clubhouse Director

Cornerstone
8435 Georgia Avenue
Silver Spring, MD 20910

(301)589-8303
Hugh Mann, Clubhouse Director

Massachusetts

The Center House Inc. Center Club

48 Boylston Street
Boston, MA 02116

(617)426-5285
Mary Gregorio, Clubhouse Director

The Lynn Friendship Club Inc.
74 South Common Street
Lynn, MA 01902

(617)581-2891
Rosa L. Young, Clubhouse Director

River Trading Company
1592 Blue Hill Avenue
Mattapan, MA 02126

(617)298-0430
Kenneth Dudek, Clubhouse Director

Michigan

Charter House
606 West Shiawassee
Lansing, MI 48933

(517)371-2077
Barbara Blakely, Clubhouse Director

Minnesota

Vail Place
1002 Excelsior Avenue West
Hopkins, MN 55343

(612)938-9622
Patrick Donahue

Missouri

Independence Center
4380 West Pine
St. Louis, MO 63108

(314)533-6511
Robert Harvey

Montana

New Directions Center
1015 First Avenue North
Great Falls, MT 59401

(406)761-2104
Kenneth Kleven, ACSW

Lamplighter House
146 Third Avenue West
Kalispell, MT 59901

(406)257-1336
Dan George, Clubhouse Director

River House
225 West Front Street
Missoula, MT 59802

(406)728-0239
John Lynn, M.S.

New Hampshire

Central NH Community Mental Health Services
PO Box 2032
Concord, NH 03301

(603)228-1551
Steve Caine, Clubhouse Director

New Jersey

Park Place
913 Sewall Avenue
Asbury Park, NJ 07712

(201)776-8200
Patricia Love, Clubhouse Director

Prospect House
424 Main Street
East Orange, NJ 07018

(201)964-6096
Florence Strindberg

Genesis House
118 Dunbar Avenue
Long Branch, NJ 07740

(201)222-5200 ext. 3188
Rachel Steinberg, MSW, ACSW

New York

Four Seasons Club
205 Clinton Street
Binghamton, NY 13905

(607)797-9598
Richard Rex, Clubhouse Director

Eliot House
51 Oak Street
Brewster, NY 10509

(914)279-7156
Elaine Favilla, ACSW

Restoration Society, Inc.
383 Grant Street
Buffalo, NY 14213

(716)886-3246
John Guastaferro, Executive Director

Cohoes Social Club
Laura Drive
Cohoes, NY 12047

(518)237-9054
Linda Kleinberger, Clubhouse Director

Liberty House
54 Bay Street
Glens Falls, NY 12801

Patricia Geruso, Clubhouse Director

Harmony House
205–215 North Main Street
Herkimer, NY 13350

(315)866-7630
Kathleen McLaughlin, Clubhouse Director

Partners
150-11 Hillside Avenue
Jamaica, NY 11432

(212)739-5778
Eduarda Pena, Clubhouse Director

Beacon House
110 Prince Street
Kingston, NY 12401

(914)-338-8332
Gerald Goldman, Clubhouse Director

Academy Associates
100 Academy Avenue
Middletown, NY 10940

(914)343-4549
Carol Budd, Acting Director

Cedar House
233 Cedar Street
Oneida, NY 13421

(315)363-4413
Jeannie Straussman, Clubhouse Director

Commons
1600 South Avenue
Rochester, NY 14620

(716)461-1460
Kathy Holden, Clubhouse Director

Turning Point
630 Portland Avenue
Rochester, NY 14621

(716)266-0750

Sunrise
212 Ash Street
Syracuse, NY 13208

(315)473-7542
Ed Benson, Clubhouse Director

Spring House
1423 Genesee Street
Utica, NY 13501

(315)738-1428
Margaret Batson, Clubhouse Director

Plymouth House (Bldg. 54)
Box "A"
West Brentwood, NY 11717

(516)231-9149, 231-8000 ext. 637, 177
Marion Kraskow, CRC

Adirondack House
RD 1, Box 12
Westport, NY 12993

(518)962-8231
Robert Horne, Clubhouse Director

North Carolina

Carolina Friendship House
207 North Water Street
Boone, NC 28607

(704)264-5596
Denica Joyce, Clubhouse Director

Piedmont Pioneer House
910 Roberts Drive
Gastonia, NC 28052

(704)866-8751
Grace Gordon, Clubhouse Director

River Club
PO Box 11636
New Bern, NC 28560

(919)633-4171
Peggy Farmer

Spectrum House
401 East Whitaker Mill Road
Raleigh, NC 27608

(919)755-6492
Pat Hamlin, Clubhouse Director

Riverhouse Club
PO Drawer 1199
210 Smith Church Road
Roanoke Rapids, NC 27870

(919)537-6174
Patricia Pitts, Clubhouse Director

Wishing Well Club
PO Box 4047
Rocky Mount, NC 27801

(919)977-3578
Tongia Cowon, Clubhouse Director

Unity House
PO Box 419
Smithfield, NC 27577

(919)965-6892
Gloria Lavett, Clubhouse Director

Sunshine House
201 North Bridge Street
Wilkesboro, NC 28697

(919)667-4165
Gretchen Parker, Clubhouse Director

North Dakota

Community Living Program
1407 Twenty-fourth Avenue South
Grand Forks, ND 58201

(701)746-9411
Cynthia Bates Schaefer, Clubhouse Director

Ohio

Marlowe House
1623 Marlowe
Cincinnati, OH 45224

(513)681-0326
Karen Teipel, Clubhouse Director

Progress Place
870 St. Agnes Avenue
Dayton, OH 45407

James Cheshire, Clubhouse Director

Gateways
30 South Byrne Road
Toledo, OH 43615

(419)535-9662
Jane Crowley, Clubhouse Director

Oregon

Open Gate
12385 SW Allen
Beaver, OR 97005

(503)643-7311
Betty Freedman, Clubhouse Director

Kairas House
142 SW Eighth
Corvallis, OR 97333

(503)757-6896
Tom Engle, Clubhouse Director

Lee St. House
2420 Lee Street SE
Salem, OR 97302

(503)371-7380 or (503)581-4483
Claudia Krueger, Clubhouse Director

Pennsylvania

Transitional Employment Program
Human Services Center

PO Box 310
New Castle, PA 16103

(412)658-3578
Nancy Nagle, Clubhouse Director

Hedwig House Inc.
904 DeKalb Street
Norristown, PA 19401

(215)279-4400
Lois Jahsmann, Clubhouse Director

South Carolina

Progress House
216 Richland Avenue NE
Aiken, SC 29801

(803)648-2375
Sandy Moore, Clubhouse Director

Tennessee

Hiwassee House
Bates Street
PO Box 107
Charleston, TN 37310

(615)336-2884
Jimmy Catlett, Clubhouse Director

Lowenstein House
756 Jefferson Avenue
Memphis, TN 38105

(901)525-1960
Noel Nesbitt, Clubhouse Director

Texas

Independence House
1014 North Zang Boulevard
Dallas, TX 75203

(214)941-6054
Gary Ferguson, Clubhouse Director

Pyramid House
3904 Austin
Houston, TX 77004

(713)526-8478
Kate Sexton, Clubhouse Director

Vermont

Westview House
50 South William Street
Burlington, VT 05404

(802)658-3323
Sheryl Bellman, Clubhouse Director

Evergreen House
24 Washington Street
Middlebury, VT 05753

(802)388-3468
Edward Lieberman, Clubhouse Director

Rainbow Club
78 South Main Street
Rutland, VT 05701

(802)775-2381
David Ridley, Clubhouse Director

Virginia

New Horizons
10299 Woodman Road
Glen Allen, VA 23060

(804)266-4991
Margaret Beard-Eddy, Clubhouse Director

Prince William Club
9208 Centreville Road
Manassas, VA 22110

(703)361-5250
Wendy Gradison, Clubhouse Director

Hospitality Center
3314 Debree Avenue
Norfolk, VA 23508

(804)446-5126
Lankford Blair, Clubhouse Director

Shenandoah Club
114 North Lewis Street
Staunton, VA 24482

(703)885-8867 or 885-7773
Ronald Shelton, Clubhouse Director

Beach House
2420 Virginia Beach Boulevard
Virginia Beach, VA 23452

(804)463-3120
Keith Johnson, Clubhouse Director

Community House
1010 Amherst Street
Winchester, VA 22601

(703)-665-0548, 0549
Marilyn Friga, Clubhouse Director

Washington

Blue Lake Center
1111 110th NE
Bellevue, WA 98005

(206)455-1970
Margaret Currin, Clubhouse Director

Island House
902 North Main
Coupeville, WA 98277

(206)678-5555
Kathy Hunter, Clubhouse Director

Harvest House
NE 340 Maple
Pullman, WA 99163

(509)334-1133
Carol Coyle, Clubhouse Director

Conbela
945 Elliott Avenue West
Seattle, WA 98119

(206)284-3901
Geary Britton-Simmons, Clubhouse Director

Evergreen Club
North 1420 Washington
Spokane, WA 99201

(509)458-7454
Dr. E. Patterson, Clubhouse Director

Walden Place
1014 South "K" Street
Tacoma, WA 98405

(206)756-5236
Mary Holmes OTR, Coordinator

Wisconsin

Off the Square Club
310 East Washington
Madison, WI 53703

(608)251-6901
Beth Barry/Sheldon Gross, Clubhouse Directors

Canada

Phoenix Residential Society
1146 Angus Street
Regina, Saskatchewan
Canada S4T 1Y5

(306)525-9543
David Foley, Clubhouse Director

Progress Place
4644 Yonge Street
Willowdale, Ontario
Canada M2N 5L8

(416)225-3173
Brenda Singer, Clubhouse Director

For information about new programs, write:
Fountain House
425 West Forty-seventh Street
New York, NY 10036

(212)582-0340

Family Survey

This survey was sent to all NAMI affiliates to get information for this book.

1. How long has your relative been mentally ill?
   What relation is he/she to you?
   Where is he/she now?
   Age and sex of relative:
2. When and how did it first occur to you that you had a mentally ill relative?
3. What did you think schizophrenia was before you were personally involved?
   How would you describe it now?
4. What did you do when you realized your relative was ill?
5. Did you seek treatment for the relative?
   If so, what kind(s) and how did you learn about it (them)?
6. What were the results of the treatment(s)?
7. What treatment course would you recommend to others?
   Why?
8. In selecting a good treatment facility, what would you tell others to look for?
9. Did your relative cooperate in seeking treatment?
   If no, what did he/she do instead?
10. What were the costs of treatment?
11. What's your opinion of antipsychotic drugs?
12. What's your opinion of talk therapy, either group or individual?
13. What's your opinion of vitamin therapy?
14. If you were telling someone how to select a good doctor for your relative, what would you say?
15. What are your expectations about your mentally ill relative? Recovery? Chronic illness? Recovery with occasional relapse?
    What do you think is likely to happen to your relative when you're gone?
16. What was the most difficult situation that arose with your relative?
    How did you handle it?
17. Did you ever have to have your relative committed?
    If so, how did you do it and how did it work out?
18. Did you ever have to call the police?
    If so, what happened?
19. Has your relative ever been jailed?
    How many times? For what?

20. What advice would you give other parents about surviving the traumas of such painful situations?

21. What attitudes do/did your relatives have towards you and your schizophrenic?

22. Were relatives helpful/harmful?

23. How about friends?

24. If you encountered any of the following comments, how did you handle them?

"It must be from your side of the family."

"It was a bad family situation that caused the schizophrenia."

25. How do you tell people you have a mentally ill person in the family? What do you say, or do you prefer not to tell them?

How do they react when you tell them?

26. Do you ever feel guilty? . . . If so, about what?

How do you handle guilty feelings if you have them?

How would you advise others to handle them?

27. What effect did a schizophrenic in the family have on your personal relationships? (Mate, children, close friends.)

28. How has your social life been affected?

29. How has your work been affected?

30. How has the situation affected your health, physical and mental?

31. What do you do keep your life as normal as possible?

32. How do you arrange your priorities? For instance, if you have a schizophrenic child and 2 normal ones, do you give the schizophrenic most of your attention, one-third or what?

33. Schizophrenia's a heavy burden. How do you manage to keep going? (Could you be specific about what helps you endure?)

34. If there are other children in the family, how do they feel?

How old are they?

Are they afraid it will happen to them?

Other fears, concerns?

35. How do you handle interactions with your schizophrenic? For instance, if he/she has hallucinations or tells wild stories, do you humor him or her?

What threats, if any, has your relative made?

Has your relative ever harmed anyone physically? . . . If so, under what circumstances?

How did you handle it?

Has your relative ever tried to commit suicide?

36. How do you handle the situation when he/she retreats and won't communicate?

37. How do you handle the denial (if any) of a relative? (For instance, the schizophrenic insisting that there is nothing wrong with him?)

38. If your relative begins to act peculiarly with you in public, what do you do?

39. Does your relative have his or her own money to handle or does someone else do it?

How does your system work out?

40. What do you do about holidays?

41. Did/does your relative take street drugs? (Marijuana, cocaine, uppers, downers, LSD, mescaline, etc.)

If yes, what kind(s)?

If yes, do you think there's any connection between schizophrenia and street drugs?

42. Many families have stories about the cruelty of people who take advantage of the mentally ill. Has this happened to you?

What happened and how did you handle it?

43. If and when you reach a place where you've "had it" with the situation (at least for the time being), how do you handle it?

44. What's your opinion of our mental health system?

Of the mental health professionals you've encountered?

What would be your advice to others about working productively with mental health professionals?

45. Are you involved in mental health groups? If so, how and in what capacity?

Would you advise others to get involved?

Why or why not?

46. About schizophrenia and how to survive it: what do you know NOW that you wish you knew when you started?

47. What has been your biggest problem? How do you handle it?

48. If you could give advice to a family whose son was just diagnosed as schizophrenic, what would it be?

OTHER COMMENTS:

Notes and Sources

Chapter 1
Schizophrenia: What It Means to the Family

"Roughly one third of schizophrenics": E.F. Torrey, *Surviving Schizophrenia: A Family Manual* (New York: Harper & Row, 1983).

"A tendency to schizophrenia": K. Kidd, "A Genetic Perspective on Schizophrenia," in *The Nature of Schizophrenia: New Approaches to Research and Treatment,* edited by L. Wynne, R. Cromwell, and S. Matthysse (New York: John Wiley and Son, 1978).

"It's time now for the families": These families' comments and others throughout the book are from a survey of AMI relatives I did in 1981–82. The survey is printed in the Appendix. Since the families were promised confidentiality, their names will not appear in these notes.

"Forty million families": 1 percent of the world's current estimated population of 4 billion.

"That's as many people": *The Concord Desk Encyclopedia* (New York: Concord Reference Books, 1982).

Chapter 2
What Schizophrenia Is, Who Gets It, What Their Chances Are

"it occupies more beds than": "The Mentally Ill: The Sad Facts, the New Hopes," *Ladies' Home Journal* (January 1982).

"Current thinking": telephone interview with Sam Keith, M.D., chief of the Center for Studies of Schizophrenia, November 1981.

"Diabetes is often used": I. Gottesman, "Schizophrenia and Genetics," in *The Nature of Schizophrenia: New Approaches to Research and Treatment,* edited by L. Wynne, R. Cromwell, and S. Matthysse, (New York: John Wiley and Sons, 1978).

"Most people think schizophrenia": P. O'Brien, *The Disordered Mind: What We Now Know About Schizophrenia* (Englewood Cliffs, N.J.: Prentice-Hall, 1978).

"In 1911 the psychiatrist Eugen Bleuler": E. Bleuler, *Dementia Praecox, or the Group of Schizophrenias* (New York: International Universities Press, 1950).

"Mental patients are slightly less violent": D. Lunde, *Murder and Madness* (Stanford, Calif.: Stanford Alumni Association, 1975).

"Ninety-five percent": ibid.

"Harvard psychiatrist": O'Brien, op. cit. " 'over-predict dangerousness' ": President's Commission on Mental Health, *Task Panel Report,* vol. IV (Washington, D.C.: U.S. Government Printing Office, 1978).

"diagnostic practice has differed significantly": G. Shean, *Schizophrenia: An Introduction to Research and Theory* (Cambridge, Mass.: Winthrop Publishers, 1978).

"The most widely used diagnostic guide": American Psychiatric Association Task Force on Nomenclature and Statistics, *Diagnostic and Statistical Manual of Mental Disorders,* 3d ed. (Washington, D.C.: American Psychiatric Association, 1980).

"There is hope": M. Bleuler, "The Long-Term Course of Schizophrenic Psychosis," op. cit. L. Wynne, Cromwell, and Matthysse.

"the World Health Organization sponsored": World Health Organization, *Schizophrenia: An International Follow-up Study* (New York: John Wiley and Sons, 1979).

"hits 1 person in every 100": Studies vary enormously in terms of numbers at risk for schizophrenia. The figures depend, among other things, on the country where the research was done and on the social class of the people studied. For instance, among lower social strata, rates have varied from 0.45 to 13 percent: K. Bernheim and R. Lewine, *Schizophrenia: Symptoms, Causes, Treatments* (New York: W. W. Norton, 1979). The figure of 1 percent is most generally accepted, but there seem to be wide variances within subpopulations.

"The average age at first hospital admission": ibid.

"who had been brain-damaged on either the right or the left side": T. Blakeslee, *The Right Brain: A New Understanding of the Unconscious Mind and Its Creative Power* (New York: Doubleday, 1980).

"a California survey": P. Williams, W. Williams, and R. Sommer, *CAMI Survey* (San Diego: California Alliance for the Mentally Ill, 1983).

"people with schizophrenia tended to be born in the winter and early spring": E.F. Torrey, *Surviving Schizophrenia: A Family Manual* (New York: Harper & Row, 1983).

"What is the story in Ireland?": E.F. Torrey, *Schizophrenia and Civilization* (New York: Jason Aronson, 1980).

"an alkaloid called solanine": "Solanine Poisoning," *British Medical Journal* (December 8, 1979).

"let's stick with the mundane potato": O. Smith, *Potatoes: Production, Storing, Processing* (Westport, Conn.: AVI Publishing, 1977).

"foods with high methionine": Food and Agriculture Organization of the United Nations, *Amino Acid Content of Foods and Biological Data on Proteins* (Rome: FAO, 1970).

Chapter 3
Running in the Family: Fact or Fiction?

"Detectives in Denmark": S. Kety, "Mental Illness in the Biological and Adoptive Relatives of Schizophrenic Adoptees: Findings Relevant to Genetic and Environmental Factors in Etiology," *American Journal of Psychiatry* (June 1983). Also, S. Kety, D. Rosenthal, P. Wender, F. Schulsinger, B. Jacobsen, "The Biologic and Adoptive Families of Adopted Individuals Who Became Schizophrenic: Prevalence of Mental Illness and Other Characteristics," in *The Nature of Schizophrenia: New Approaches to Research and Treatment,* edited by L. Wynne, R. Cromwell, S. Matthysse (New York: John Wiley and Sons, 1978).

"A few people have been reluctant to go along": T. Lidz, S. Blatt, B. Cooke, "Critique of the Danish-American Studies of Adopted-away Offspring of Schizophrenic Parents," *American Journal of Psychiatry,* vol. 131 (1974).

"A Lot More Than Peas": J. Shields, "Genetics," in *Schizophrenia: Towards a New Synthesis,* edited by J. Wing (New York: Grune and Stratton, 1978).

" 'strain . . . is also often mentioned' ": E. Bleuler, *Dementia Praecox, or the Group of Schizophrenias* (New York: International Universities Press, 1950).

" 'no specific type of life event' ": M. Tsuang, *Schizophrenia: The Facts* (Oxford, England: Oxford University Press, 1982).

"especially slow-acting viruses": T. Crow, "Is Schizophrenia an Infectious Disease?" *Lancet* (January 22, 1983). Also, E.F. Torrey, "Cytomegalovirus as a Possible Etiological Agent in Schizophrenia," in *Advances in Biological Psychiatry* (Basel, Switzerland: Karger, 1983).

Schizophrenia risk table: adapted from Shields, op. cit.

Chapter 4
It's Not All in the Head: Physical Clues

"It's called nuclear magnetic resonance": P. Bottomley, "Nuclear Magnetic Resonance: Beyond Physical Imaging," *IEEE Spectrum* (February 1983).

"Finding Abnormal Ventricles": D. Weinberger, E.F. Torrey, A. Neophytides, and R. J. Wyatt, "Lateral Cerebral Ventricular Enlargement in Chronic Schizophrenia," *Archives of General Psychiatry,* vol. 36 (July 1979).

"something that isn't quite right in the ocular function": P. Holzman, "Smooth Eye Movements in Psychopathology," *Schizophrenia Bulletin,* vol. 9, no. 1 (1983).

"Touchings That Don't Take": E.F. Torrey, "Neurological Abnormalities in Schizophrenia Patients," *Biological Psychiatry,* vol. 15, no. 3 (1980).

Chapter 5
Treatment: Benefits, Risks, Limits

"One survey": P. Williams, W. Williams, and R. Sommer, *CAMI Survey* (San Diego: California Alliance for the Mentally Ill, 1983). For more reading on the drug treatment of schizophrenia, try A. Mason and R. Granacher, *Clinical Handbook of Antipsychotic Drug Therapy* (New York: Brunner Mazel, 1980), or D. Klein, R. Gittleman, F. Quitkin, and A. Rifkind, *Diagnosis and Drug Treatment of Psychiatric Disorders: Adults and Children* (Baltimore: Williams & Wilkins, 1980).

"clear that ongoing maintenance medications protect patients against relapse": M. Tsuang, *Schizophrenia: The Facts* (Oxford, England: Oxford University Press, 1982). See also J. Davis, C. Schaffer, G. Killian, C. Kinard, and C. Chan, "Important Issues in the Drug Treatment of Schizophrenia," *Schizophrenia Bulletin,* vol. 6, no. 1 (1980).

"Can You Get Hooked?": E.F. Torrey, *Surviving Schizophrenia: A Family Manual* (New York: Harper & Row, 1983).

"severe cardiac effects": L. Hollister, *Clinical Pharmacology of Psychotherapeutic Drugs* (New York: Churchill Livingstone, 1978).

"Anti-psychotic drugs have side effects": See Torrey, op. cit., and Hollister, op. cit.

"damage of the eye lens or retina": Torrey, op. cit.

"sums up the situation like this": American Psychiatric Association

Task Force on Late Neurological Effects of Antipsychotic Drugs, *Tardive Dyskinesia: Report of the American Psychiatric Association Task Force on Late Neurological Effects of Antipsychotic Drugs* (Washington, D.C.: American Psychiatric Association, 1979).

"for small reasons": Hollister, op. cit.

"prevalence of persistent TD": D. Jeste and R. Wyatt, "Changing Epidemiology of Tardive Dyskinesia: An Overview," *American Journal of Psychiatry* (May 1981).

"estimate of prevalence is far greater than any in [my] experience": Hollister, op. cit.

"reviewed more than 500 patients who were on continued antipsychotic treatment": G. Gardos and J. Cole, "The Prognosis of Tardive Dyskinesia," *Journal of Clinical Psychiatry* (May 1983).

" 'Open your mouth' ": F. Ayd, "Tardive Dyskinesia, 1983," *Psychiatric Annals* (January 1984).

"one carried out by P.R.A. May": P. May, *Treatment of Schizophrenia: A Comparative Study of Five Treatment Methods* (New York: Science House, 1968).

"analogous to directing a flood": E.F. Torrey, *Surviving Schizophrenia* (New York: Harper & Row, 1983).

Chapter 6
A Family Survival Kit

This chapter is based almost entirely on the personal experience of the families, my own and about 100 others. To preserve confidentiality, no names are used.

" 'do better living somewhere other than at home' ": E.F. Torrey, *Surviving Schizophrenia: A Family Manual* (New York: Harper & Row, 1983).

Chapter 7
Housing, Work, Social Life, and Money

"only 10 percent of the patient load": E.F. Torrey, *Surviving Schizophrenia* (New York: Harper & Row, 1983).

"1 million of them": "Homeless in America," *Newsweek* (January 2, 1984).

"Los Angeles psychiatrists": Roger Farr, *The Homeless, Chronically Mentally Ill in the Los Angeles "Skid Row" Area* (Los Angeles: Los Angeles County Department of Mental Health, 1983).

"Being a member of Fountain House is also no guarantee": study conducted by Fountain House, Education Department.

"it costs about $500 a day": M. Kresky-Wolff, S. Matthews, F. Kalibat, and L. Mosher, "Crossing Place: A Residential Model for Crisis Intervention," *Hospital and Community Psychiatry,* vol. 35, no. 1 (January 1984).

"Bill Anthony of Boston": speech, National Convention of the Alliance for the Mentally Ill, 1983.

"known as Fairweather Lodges": H. Richard Lamb, *Treating the Long-Term Mentally Ill* (San Francisco: Jossey-Bass, 1982). See also P. Vine, *Families in Pain* (New York: Pantheon, 1982).

"would not venture even": Lamb, op. cit.

"He or she should bring proof of age": R. Schwartz, *The Family Handbook on Mental Health Issues and Resources* (San Diego: Parents of Adult Schizophrenics of San Diego County, 1982).

" 'no more pressing issue in mental health today' ": Lamb, op. cit.

Chapter 8
Parents as Psychovermin: Why You Are Being Blamed

"degree of medical frustration": S. Gilman, *Seeing the Insane* (New York: John Wiley and Sons, 1982).

" 'amounts to cruelty' ": W. Appleton, "Mistreatment of Patients' Families by Psychiatrists," *American Journal of Psychiatry* (June 1974).

"summarized his twelve-year study": T. Lidz, S. Fleck, and A. Cornelison, *Schizophrenia and the Family* (New York: International Universities Press, 1965).

"a deficiency disease": T. Lidz, "A Developmental Theory," in *Schizophrenia: Science and Practice,* edited by J. C. Shershow (Cambridge, Mass.: Harvard University Press, 1978).

"science ignored": Lidz, Fleck, and Cornelison, op. cit.

"deliberately done without the consent": A. Cornelison, "Casework Interviewing as a Research Technique in a Study of Families of Schizophrenic Patients," in Lidz, Fleck, and Cornelison, op. cit.

" 'uncooperative and suspicious' ": ibid.

"Do not tell the families they were being researched": ibid.

" 'we cannot be sure they will not pick up a book or article signed by people they know": ibid.

" 'as many siblings were psychotic as reasonably well-adjusted' ": T. Lidz, S. Fleck, and A. Alanen, "Schizophrenic Patients and Their Siblings," in Lidz, Fleck, and Cornelison, op. cit.

"That, anyway, was the theory back in 1956": G. Bateson, D. Haley, and J. Weakland, "Toward a Theory of Schizophrenia," *Behavioral Science,* vol. 1 (1956).

"could not tell the difference", S. Hirsch and J. Leff, *Abnormalities in Parents of Schizophrenics* (London, England: Oxford University Press, 1975).

"Haley, in 1968": ibid.

"characteristics as seen by Mosher and Menn": L. Mosher and A. Menn, "The Surrogate 'Family,' an Alternative to Hospitalization," in op. cit., edited by Shershow.

Chapter 9
Organizing for Change

"only 3 percent of the funds for mental health research": J. Gunderson and Loren Mosher, "The Cost of Schizophrenia," *American Journal of Psychiatry* (September 1975).

"we spend $203 in research money for each cancer patient": J. D. Barchas and P. Berger, "Scientific Advances in Psychobiological Treatment of Severe Mental Disorders," President's Commission on Mental Health (Washington, D.C.: U.S. Government Printing Office, 1978).

"the costs of schizophrenia are equal to": Gunderson and Mosher, op. cit.

"Only 15 to 40 percent": ibid.

"People prefer a person with a criminal record": President's Commission on Mental Health, *Task Panel Report,* vol. IV (Washington, D.C.: U.S. Government Printing Office, 1978).

"perhaps 30,000 parents": personal communication, B. Smith, National Alliance for the Mentally Ill, 1984.

Bibliography

Alpert, M., and Friedhoff, A. "An Un-Dopamine Hypothesis of Schizophrenia." *Schizophrenia Bulletin*, vol. 6, no. 3 (1980).

American Psychiatric Association Task Force on Late Neurological Effects of Antipsychotic Drugs. *Tardive Dyskinesia: Report of the American Psychiatric Association Task Force on Late Neurological Effects of Antipsychotic Drugs*. Washington, D.C.: American Psychiatric Association, 1979.

American Psychiatric Association Task Force on Nomenclature and Statistics. *Diagnostic and Statistical Manual of Mental Disorders*, 3d ed. Washington, D.C.: American Psychiatric Association, 1980.

Ammer, C., and Sidley, N. *The Common Sense Guide to Mental Health Care*. Brattleboro, Vt.: Lewis Publishing Company, 1982.

Anderson, C. "Family Intervention with Severely Disturbed Inpatients." *Archives of General Psychiatry*, vol. 34 (June 1977).

Appleton, William. "Mistreatment of Patients' Families by Psychiatrists." *American Journal of Psychiatry*, vol. 131 (June 1974).

Arieti, S. *The Interpretation of Schizophrenia*. New York: Basic Books, 1974.

———. *Understanding and Helping the Schizophrenic: A Guide for Family and Friends*. New York: Simon & Schuster, 1979.

Armstrong, B. "Society v. the Mentally Ill: Exploring the Roots of Prejudice." *Hospital and Community Psychiatry*, vol. 29, no. 9 (September 1978).

Ayd, F. "Tardive Dyskinesia, 1983." *Psychiatric Annals*, vol. 14, no. 1 (January 1984).

Bachrach, L. "Planning Services for the Young Adult Schizophrenic Outpatient." *The Schizophrenic Outpatient: A Clinical Information Service*, vol. 2, no. 1 (1983).

Bailey, D., and Dreyer, S. *Therapeutic Approaches to the Care of the Mentally Ill*. Philadelphia: F. A. Davis, 1979.

Bateson, G., Jackson, D., Haley, J., and Weakland, J. "Toward a

Theory of Schizophrenia." *Behavioral Science,* vol. 1 (1956).

Beck J. "Social Influences on the Prognosis of Schizophrenia." *Schizophrenia Bulletin,* vol. 4, no. 1 (1978).

Beis, E. "State Involuntary Commitment Statutes." *Mental Disability Law Reporter, American Bar Association* (July/August 1983).

Bennett, G. *When the Mental Patient Comes Home.* Philadelphia: Westminster Press, 1980.

Berger, P., and Rexroth, K. "Biochemistry and the Schizophrenias: Old Concepts and New Hypotheses." *The Journal of Nervous and Mental Disease,* vol. 169, no. 2 (1981).

———. "Tardive Dyskinesia: Clinical, Biological, and Pharmacological Perspectives." *Schizophrenia Bulletin,* vol. 6, no. 1 (1980).

Bernheim, K., Lewine, R., and Beale, C. *The Caring Family: Living with Chronic Mental Illness.* New York: Random House, 1982.

Bernheim, K., and Lewine, R. *Schizophrenia: Symptoms, Causes, Treatments.* New York: W. W. Norton, 1979.

Bernheim, K. "Supportive Family Counseling." *Schizophrenia Bulletin,* vol. 8, no. 1 (1982).

Blakeslee, T. *The Right Brain: A New Understanding of the Unconscious Mind and Its Creative Power.* New York: Doubleday, 1980.

Bleuler, E. *Dementia Praecox, or the Group of Schizophrenias.* New York: International Universities Press, 1950.

Bleuler, M. "The Long-Term Course of Schizophrenic Psychosis." In *The Nature of Schizophrenia: New Approaches to Research and Treatment,* edited by L. Wynne, R. Cromwell, and S. Matthysse. New York: John Wiley, 1978.

Borus, J., and Hatow, E. "The Patient and the Community." In *Schizophrenia: Science and Practice,* edited by J. C. Shershow. Cambridge, Mass.: Harvard University Press, 1978.

Bottomly, P. "Nuclear Magnetic Resonance: Beyond Physical Imaging." *IEEE Spectrum* (February 1983).

Bowers, M. B., Jr. "Biochemical Processes in Schizophrenia: An Update." *Schizophrenia Bulletin,* vol. 6, no. 3 (1980).

Brown, B. *Responsible Community Care of Former Mental Hospital Patients.* Washington, D.C.: U.S. Government Printing Office, 1977.

Brown, G., Birley, J., and Wing, J. "Influence of Family Life on the Cause of Schizophrenic Disorders: A Replication." *British Journal of Psychiatry,* vol. 121 (1972).

Castle, B. *Social Provision for Sufferers from Chronic Schizophrenia.* London: The National Schizophrenia Fellowship, 1974.

Chandler, D., and Sallychild, A. *The Use and Misuse of Psychiatric Drugs in California's Mental Health Programs.* Sacramento, Calif.: Assembly Publication Office, 1977.

Clausen, J. "Sociocultural Features in the Etiology of Schizophrenia." In *Progress in the Functional Psychosis,* edited by R. Cancro, L. Shapiro, and M. Kesselman. New York: Spectrum Publications, 1979.

———. "Stigma and Mental Disorder: Phenomena and Terminology." *Psychiatry,* vol. 44 (November 1981).

Cobb, S. "Social Support as a Moderator of Life Stress." *Psychosomatic Medicine,* vol. 38, no. 5 (1976).

Cooper, B. "Epidemiology." In *Schizophrenia: Towards a New Synthesis,* edited by J. Wing. New York: Grune and Stratton, 1978.

Cornelison, A. "Casework Interviewing as a Research Technique in a Study of Families of Schizophrenic Patients." In T. Lidz, S. Fleck, and A. Cornelison, *Schizophrenia and the Family.* New York: International Universities Press, 1965.

Creer, C., and Wing, J. *Schizophrenia at Home.* London: Institute of Psychiatry, 1974.

Creese, I., and Snyder, S. "Biochemical Investigation." In *Schizophrenia: Science and Practice,* edited by J. C. Shershow. Cambridge, Mass.: Harvard University Press, 1978.

Crow, T. "Is Schizophrenia an Infectious Disease?" *Lancet* (January 22, 1983).

Dale, P. "Prevalence of Schizophrenia in the Pacific Island Populations of Micronesia." *Journal of Psychiatric Research,* vol. 16, no. 2 (1981).

Davis, J., Schaffer, C., Killian, G., Kinard, C., and Chan, C. "Important Issues in the Drug Treatment of Schizophrenia." *Schizophrenia Bulletin,* vol. 6, no. 1 (1980).

Delman, J. "Alternatives to Hospitalization." *Advocacy Now,* vol. 2, no. 3 (1980).

Department of Health and Human Services. *Special Report: Schizophrenia 1980.* Washington, D.C.: U.S. Government Printing Office, 1980.

Donaldson, S., Gelenberg, A., and Baldessarini, R. "The Pharmacologic Treatment of Schizophrenia: A Progress Report." *Schizophrenia Bulletin,* vol. 9, no. 4 (1983).

Edell, W., and Chapman, L. "Anhedonia, Perceptual Aberration, and the Rorschach." *Journal of Consulting and Clinical Psychology,* vol. 47 (1979).

Ennis, B., and Emery, R. *The Rights of Mental Patients.* New York: Avon Books, 1978.

Food and Agriculture Organization of the United Nations. *Amino Acid Content of Foods and Biological Data on Proteins.* Rome: FAO, 1970.

Forrest, A., and Affleck, J., eds. *New Perspectives in Schizophrenia.* New York: Churchill Livingstone, 1975.

Foucault, M. *Madness and Civilization: A History of Insanity in the*

Age of Reason. New York: Random House, 1965.

Fromm-Reichmann, F. "Notes on the Development of Treatment of Schizophrenics by Psychoanalytic Psychotherapy." *Psychiatry,* vol. 11, no. 3 (1948).

———. *Psychoanalysis and Psychotherapy*. Chicago: University of Chicago Press, 1959.

Gardos, G., and Cole, J. "The Prognosis of Tardive Dyskinesia." *Journal of Clinical Psychiatry* (May 1983).

Gilman, S. *Seeing the Insane*. New York: John Wiley and Sons, 1982.

Goldberg, S. "Drug and Psychosocial Therapy in Schizophrenia: Current Status and Research Needs." *Schizophrenia Bulletin,* vol. 6, no. 1 (1980).

Goldstein, M. *New Developments in Interventions with Families of Schizophrenics*. San Francisco: Jossey-Bass, 1981.

Gunderson, J., and Mosher, L. "The Cost of Schizophrenia." *American Journal of Psychiatry,* vol. 132, no. 9 (September 1975).

Gross, M. *The Psychological Society*. New York: Random House, 1978.

Hare, E. "Schizophrenia as an Infectious Disease." *British Journal of Psychiatry,* vol. 135 (1979).

Hatfield, A "The Family as Partner in the Treatment of Mental Illness." *Hospital and Community Psychiatry,* vol. 30 (1979).

———. "Psychological Costs of Schizophrenia to the Family." *Social Work,* vol. 23 (1978).

Hirsch, S., and Leff, J. *Abnormalities in Parents of Schizophrenics*. London: Oxford University Press, 1975.

Hirsch, S., ed. *Madness Network News Reader*. San Francisco: Glide Publications, 1974.

Hoffer, A., and Osmond, H. *How to Live with Schizophrenia*. Secaucus, N.J.: Citadel Press, 1974.

Holden, D., and Lewine, R. "How Families Evaluate Mental Health Professionals, Resources, and Effects of Illness." *Schizophrenia Bulletin,* vol. 8, no. 4 (1982).

Hollister, Leo. *Clinical Pharmacology of Psychotherapeutic Drugs*. New York: Churchill Livingstone, 1978.

———. "Psychopharmocology." In *Schizophrenia: Science and Practice,* edited by J. C. Shershow. Cambridge, Mass.: Harvard University Press, 1978.

Holzman, P. "Smooth Eye Movements in Psychopathology." *Schizophrenia Bulletin,* vol. 9, no. 1 (1983).

Hyde, A. *Living with Schizophrenia*. Chicago: Contemporary Books, 1980.

Iacono, W., and Lykken, D. "The Assessment of Smooth Tracking

Dysfunction." *Schizophrenia Bulletin,* vol. 9, no. 1 (1983).

Iverson, L. "Biochemical and Pharmacological Studies: The Dopamine Hypothesis." In *Schizophrenia: Towards a New Synthesis,* edited by J. Wing. New York: Grune and Stratton, 1978.

Jacobs, S., and Myers, J. "Recent Life Events and Acute Schizophrenic Psychosis: A Controlled Study." *Journal of Nervous and Mental Disease,* vol. 162, no. 2 (1976).

Jeste, Dilip, and Wyatt, Richard. "Changing Epidemiology of Tardive Dyskinesia: An Overview." *American Journal of Psychiatry* (May 1981).

Kalman, S. "Naturally Occurring Toxic Substances in Foods." Unpublished lecture notes. Stanford University Medical Center, 1983.

Kayton, L., and Soon, K. "Hypohedonia in Schizophrenia." *Journal of Nervous and Mental Disease,* vol. 161, no. 6 (1972).

Kessler, S. "The Genetics of Schizophrenia: A Review." *Special Report: Schizophrenia.* Washington, D.C.: U.S. Government Printing Office, 1980.

Kety, S. "Heredity and Environment." In *Schizophrenia: Science and Practice,* edited by J. C. Shershow. Cambridge, Mass.: Harvard University Press. 1978.

———. "Mental Illness in the Biological and Adoptive Relatives of Schizophrenic Adoptees: Findings Relevant to Genetic and Environmental Factors in Etiology." *American Journal of Psychiatry,* vol. 140, no. 6 (June 1983).

Kint, M. "Problems for Families vs. Problem Families." *Schizophrenia Bulletin,* vol. 3, no. 3 (1977).

Klein, D. "Psychosocial Treatment of Schizophrenia or Psychosocial Help for People with Schizophrenia?" *Schizophrenia Bulletin,* vol. 6, no. 1 (1980).

Klerman, G. "The Evolution of Scientific Nosology." In *Schizophrenia: Science and Practice,* edited by J. C. Shershow. Cambridge, Mass.: Harvard University Press, 1978.

Knight, L. *Aspects of Rehabilitation: Fountain House.* London: Mindout, The Mental Health Magazine, March 1981.

Korpell, Herbert. *How You Can Help: A Guide for Families of Psychiatric Hospital Patients.* Washington, D.C.: American Psychiatric Press, 1984.

Kreisman, D., and Joy, V. "Family Response to Mental Illness of a Relative: A Review of the Literature. *Schizophrenia Bulletin,* no. 10 (Fall 1974).

Kresky-Wolff, M., Matthews, S., Kalibat, F., and Mosher, L. "Crossing Place: A Residential Model for Crisis Intervention." *Hospital and Community Psychiatry,* vol. 35, no. 1 (January 1984).

Kübler-Ross, Elisabeth. *On Death and Dying.* New York: Macmillan, 1969.

Kunin, R. *Mega-Nutrition.* New York: New American Library, 1980.

Laing, R. *The Divided Self: A Study of Sanity and Madness.* London: Tavistock Publications, 1960.

———, and Esterson, A. *Sanity, Madness, and the Family: Families of Schizophrenics.* Middlesex, England: Penguin Books, 1970.

Lamb, H. R. *Treating the Long-Term Mentally Ill.* San Francisco: Jossey-Bass, 1982.

Leff, J. "Social and Psychological Causes of the Acute Attack." In *Schizophrenia: Towards a New Synthesis,* edited by J. Wing. New York: Grune and Stratton, 1978.

Levin, S. "Smooth Pursuit Impairment on Schizophrenia—What Does It Mean?" *Schizophrenia Bulletin,* vol. 9, no. 1 (1983).

Lewine, R. "A Dialogue Among Patients, Families, and Professionals." *Schizophrenia Bulletin,* vol. 8, no. 4 (1982).

Lidz, T. "A Developmental Theory." In *Schizophrenia: Science and Practice,* edited by J. C. Shershow. Cambridge, Mass.: Harvard University Press, 1978.

———, Blatt, S., and Cooke, B. "Critique of the Danish-American Studies of Adopted-away Offspring of Schizophrenic Parents." *American Journal of Psychiatry,* vol. 131 (1974).

———, Fleck, S., and Cornelison, Alice. *Schizophrenia and the Family.* New York: International Universities Press, 1965.

Liem, J. "Family Studies of Schizophrenia: An Update and Commentary." *Schizophrenia Bulletin,* vol. 6, no. 3 (1980).

Lion, J. *The Art of Medicating Psychotic Patients.* Baltimore: Williams and Wilkins, 1978.

Lipton, R., Levy, D., Holzman, P., and Levin, S. "Eye Movement Dysfunction in Psychiatric Patients." *Schizophrenia Bulletin,* vol. 9, no. 1 (1983).

Lovejoy, M. "Expectations and the Recovery Process." *Schizophrenia Bulletin,* vol. 8, no. 4 (1982).

Lunde, Donald T. *Murder and Madness.* Stanford, Calif.: Stanford Alumni Association, 1975.

McKeever, P. "Siblings of Chronically Ill Children: A Literature Review with Implications for Research and Practice." *American Journal of Orthopsychiatry,* vol. 53, no. 2 (April 1983).

Maser, J., and Keith, S. "NIMH Activities: CT Scans and Schizophrenia—Report on a Workshop." *Schizophrenia Bulletin,* vol. 9, no. 2 (1983).

May, P., Tuma, H., and Dixon, W. "Schizophrenia: A Follow-up Study of the Results of Five Forms of Treatment." *Archives of General Psychiatry,* vol. 38 (July 1981).

May, P. *Treatment of Schizophrenia: A Comparative Study of Five Treatment Methods.* New York: Science House, 1968.

Moller, H., von Zerssen, D., Werner-Eilert, K., and Wuschner-Stockhein. "Outcome in Schizophrenic and Similar Paranoid Psychoses." *Schizophrenia Bulletin,* vol. 8, no. 1 (1982).

Mosher, Loren, and Feinsilver, D. *Special Report on Schizophrenia.* Washington, D.C.: National Institute of Mental Health, 1970.

———, and Keith, S. "Psychosocial Treatment: Individual, Group, Family, and Community Support Approaches." *Schizophrenia Bulletin,* vol. 6, no. 1 (1980).

———, and Menn, A. "The Surrogate 'Family,' an Alternative to Hospitalization." In *Schizophrenia: Science and Practice,* edited by J. C. Shershow. Cambridge, Mass.: Harvard University Press, 1978.

National Alliance for the Mentally Ill. *Anti-Stigma: Improving Public Understanding of Mental Illness.* Washington, D.C.: NAMI, 1982.

———. *Awakenings: Organizing a Support/Advocacy Group.* Washington, D.C.: NAMI, 1982.

National Schizophrenia Fellowship. *Living with Schizophrenia (by the Relatives).* Surrey, England: National Schizophrenia Fellowship, 1974.

———. *Schizophrenia at Home.* Surrey, England: National Schizophrenia Fellowship, 1974.

Norback, J. *The Mental Health Yearbook/Directory, 1979–80.* New York: Van Nostrand Reinhold, 1981.

Norwind, B. "Developing an Enforceable 'Right to Treatment' Theory for the Chronically Mentally Disabled in the Community." *Schizophrenia Bulletin,* vol. 8, no. 4 (1982).

O'Brien, Patrick. *The Disordered Mind: What We Now Know About Schizophrenia.* Englewood Cliffs, N.J.: Prentice-Hall, 1978.

Park, C., and Shapiro, L. *You Are Not Alone: Understanding and Dealing with Mental Illness.* Boston: Little, Brown and Co., 1976.

Parker, G. "Re-Searching the Schizophrenigenic Mother." *Journal of Nervous and Mental Diseases,* vol. 170, no. 8 (1982).

Peterson, D. *A Mad People's History of Madness.* Pittsburgh: University of Pittsburgh Press, 1982.

Peterson, R. "What Are the Needs of Chronic Mental Patients?" In *The Chronic Mental Patient: Problems, Solutions, and Recommendations for a Public Policy,* edited by J. Talbott. Washington, D.C.: American Psychiatric Association, 1978.

Pfeiffer, C. *Mental and Elemental Nutrients: A Physician's Guide to Nutrition and Health Care.* New Canaan, Conn.: Keats Publishing, 1975.

———. *The Schizophrenias: Yours and Mine.* New York: Harcourt Brace Jovanovich, 1977.

President's Commission on Mental Health. *Task Panel Report,* vol. IV. Washington, D.C.: U.S. Government Printing Office, 1978.

Pringle, J., and Pyke-Lees, P. "Voluntary Action by Relatives and Friends of Schizophrenia Sufferers in Britain." *Schizophrenia Bulletin,* vol. 8, no. 4 (1982).

Rabkin, J. "Public Attitudes Towards Mental Illness: A Review of the Literature." *Schizophrenia Bulletin* (Fall 1974).

Rodgers, J. "Roots of Madness." *Science* (July/August 1982).

Rutter, M. "Communication Deviance and Diagnostic Differences." In *The Nature of Schizophrenia: New Approaches to Research and Treatment,* edited by L. Wynne, R. Cromwell, and S. Matthysse. New York: John Wiley, 1978.

Savodnick, I. "The Manifest and Scientific Images." In *Schizophrenia: Science and Practice,* edited by J. C. Shershow. Cambridge, Mass.: Harvard University Press, 1978.

Schooler, C., and Spohn, H. "Social Dysfunction and Treatment Failure in Schizophrenia." *Schizophrenia Bulletin,* vol. 8, no. 1 (1982).

Schooler, N. "Neuroleptic and Psycho-Social Treatments: A Discussion." *Schizophrenia Bulletin,* vol. 6, no. 1 (1980).

Schwartz, R., and Schwartz, I. "Reducing the Stigma of Mental Illness." *Diseases of the Nervous System,* vol. 38, no. 2 (1977).

Schwartz, R. *The Family Handbook on Mental Health Issues and Resources.* San Diego: Parents of Adult Schizophrenics of San Diego County, 1982.

Seaman, M., Littman, S., Plummer, E., and Jeffries, J. *Living and Working with Schizophrenia.* Toronto: University of Toronto Press, 1982.

Shagass, C. "The Medical Model in Psychiatry." In *Hormones, Behavior, and Psychopathology,* edited by E. Sacher. New York: Raven Press, 1976.

Shean, G. *Schizophrenia: An Introduction to Research and Theory.* Cambridge, Mass.: Winthrop Publishers, 1978.

Shields, James. "Genetics." In *Schizophrenia: Towards a New Synthesis,* edited by J. Wing. New York: Grune and Stratton, 1978.

Siegler, M., and Osmond, H. *Models of Madness, Models of Medicine.* New York: Harper Colophon, 1974.

Singer, M., Wynne, L., and Toohey, M. "Communication Disorders and the Families of Schizophrenics." In *The Nature of Schizophrenia: New Approaches to Research and Treatment,* edited by L. Wynne, R. Cromwell, and S. Matthysse. New York: John Wiley, 1978.

Smith, C., and Forrest, A. "The Genetics of Schizophrenia." In *New*

Perspectives in Schizophrenia, edited by A. Forrest and J. Affleck. New York: Random House, 1965.

Smith, O. *Potatoes: Production, Storing, Processing.* Westport, Conn.: AVI Publishing, 1977.

Spohn, H., and Patterson, T. "Recent Studies of Psychophysiology in Schizophrenia." *Schizophrenia Bulletin,* vol. 5, no. 4 (1979).

———, and Larson, J. "Is Eye Tracking Dysfunction Specific to Schizophrenia?" *Schizophrenia Bulletin,* vol. 9, no. 1 (1983).

Stark, L. "Abnormal Patterns of Normal Eye Movements in Schizophrenia." *Schizophrenia Bulletin,* vol. 9, no. 1 (1983).

Stephens, J. "Long-Term Prognosis and Followup in Schizophrenia." *Schizophrenia Bulletin,* vol. 4, no. 1 (1978).

Strauss, J., and Carpenter, W. "The Prognosis of Schizophrenia: Rationale for a Multidimensional Concept." *Schizophrenia Bulletin,* vol. 4, no. 1 (1978).

———. *Schizophrenia.* New York: Plenum Medical Book Company, 1981.

Taylor, Robert. *Mind or Body: Distinguishing Psychological from Organic Disorders.* New York: McGraw-Hill, 1982.

Teschke, G. "Book Review: Die schizophrenen Geistesstorungen im Lichte langjahriger Kranken- und Familiengeschichten, by Manfred Bleuler." *Schizophrenia Bulletin,* vol. 4, no. 1 (1978).

Thurer, S. "Deinstitutionalization and Women: Where the Buck Stops." *Hospital and Community Psychiatry* (December 1983).

Torrey, E. F. "Cytomegalovirus as a Possible Etiological Agent in Schizophrenia." In *Advances in Biological Psychiatry,* edited by P. Morozov. Basel: Karger, 1983.

———. *The Death of Psychiatry.* Radnor, Pa.: Chilton Book Company, 1974.

———. "Neurological Abnormalities in Schizophrenic Patients." *Biological Psychiatry,* vol. 15, no. 3 (1980).

———. *Schizophrenia and Civilization,* New York: Jason Aronson, 1980.

———. *Surviving Schizophrenia: A Family Manual.* New York: Harper & Row, 1983.

———. "Tracking the Causes of Madness." *Psychology Today* (March 1979).

———, and Peterson, M. "The Viral Hypothesis of Schizophrenia." *Schizophrenia Bulletin,* vol. 2, no. 1 (1976).

———, Torrey, B., and Peterson, M. "Seasonality of Schizophrenic Births in the United States." *Archives of General Psychiatry,* vol. 34 (September 1977).

Tringo, J. "The Hierarchy of Preference Towards Disability Groups."

Journal of Special Education, vol. 4, no. 3 (1970).

Trotter, R. "Schizophrenia: A Cruel Chain of Events." *Science News,* vol. 111 (June 18, 1977).

Tsuang, Ming. *Schizophrenia: The Facts.* Oxford, England: Oxford University Press, 1982.

Vaillant, G. "The Distinction Between Prognosis and Diagnosis in Schizophrenia." In *The Nature of Schizophrenia: New Approaches to Research and Treatment,* edited by L. Wynne, R. Cromwell, and S. Matthysse. New York: John Wiley, 1978.

———. "Prognosis and Course of Schizophrenia." *Schizophrenia Bulletin,* vol. 4, no. 1 (1978).

Vaughn, C., and Leff, J. "The Influence of Family and Social Factors on the Course of Psychiatric Illness." *British Journal of Psychiatry,* vol. 129 (1976).

Vine, P. *Families in Pain.* New York: Pantheon, 1982.

Viscott, D. *The Making of a Psychiatrist:* Arbor House, 1972.

Vonnegut, M. "Why I Want to Bite R. D. Laing." *Harper's* (April 1974).

Wasow, M. *Coping with Schizophrenia: A Survival Manual for Parents, Relatives, and Friends.* Palo Alto, Calif.: Science and Behavior Books, 1982.

Weinberger, D., Torrey, E. F., Neophytides, A., and Wyatt, R. "Lateral Cerebral Ventricular Enlargement in Chronic Schizophrenia." *Archives of General Psychiatry,* vol. 36 (July 1979).

———, Wagner, D., and Wyatt, R. "Neuropathological Studies of Schizophrenia: A Selective Review." *Schizophrenia Bulletin,* vol. 9, no. 2 (1983).

Wender, P., and Klein, D. "The Promise of Biological Psychiatry." *Psychology Today* (February 1981).

Williams R., and Kalita, D., eds. *A Physician's Handbook on Orthomolecular Medicine.* New Canaan, Conn.: Keats Publishing, 1977.

Williams, W., Williams, P., and Sommer, R. *CAMI Families Speak: Questionnaire Results.* San Diego: California Alliance for the Mentally Ill, 1983.

Willis, M. "The Impact of Schizophrenia on Families: One Mother's Point of View." *Schizophrenia Bulletin,* vol. 8, no. 4 (1982).

Wilson, I., Garbutt, J., Lanier, C., Moylan, J., Nelson, W., and Prange, A. "Is There a Tardive Dysmentia?" *Schizophrenia Bulletin,* vol. 9, no. 2 (1983).

Wing, J., ed. *Schizophrenia from Within.* Surrey, England: National Schizophrenia Fellowship, 1975.

———, ed. *Schizophrenia: Towards a New Synthesis.* New York: Grune and Stratton, 1978.

———. "Social Influences on the Course of Schizophrenia." In *The Nature of Schizophrenia: New Approaches to Research and Treatment*, edited by L. Wynne, R. Cromwell, and S. Matthysse. New York: John Wiley, 1978.

Winokur, G. "What To Do? or What Do We Owe Our Residents?" *Biological Psychiatry*, vol. 15, no. 4 (1980).

World Health Organization. *Schizophrenia: An International Follow-up Study*. New York: John Wiley and Sons, 1979.

Wurtman, R. "The Behavioral Effects of Nutrients." *Lancet* (May 21, 1983).

Wynne, Lyman, Cromwell, Rue L., and Matthysse, Steven, eds. *The Nature of Schizophrenia: New Approaches to Research and Treatment*. New York: John Wiley, 1978.

Index